The Musical Madhouse
(Les Grotesques de la musique)

Eastman Studies in Music

Ralph P. Locke, Senior Editor
Eastman School of Music

(ISSN 1071–9989)

The Musical Madhouse

(Les Grotesques de la musique)

Hector Berlioz

Translated and Edited by Alastair Bruce
with an Introduction by Hugh Macdonald

Margaret – enjoy!

Martin Buchere. (ex-Bruce)

25.ix.12

Ⓡ University of Rochester Press

First published 2003
Soft cover edition published 2005
Transferred to digital printing 2010

University of Rochester Press
668 Mt. Hope Avenue, Rochester, NY 14620, USA
www.urpress.com
and Boydell & Brewer Limited
PO Box 9, Woodbridge, Suffolk IP12 3DF, UK
www.boydellandbrewer.com

ISSN: 1071-9989
Cloth ISBN-10: 1-58046-132-8
Cloth ISBN-13: 978-1-58046-132-0
Paperback IBSN-10: 1-58046-182-4
Paperback ISBN-13: 978-1-58046-182-5

Library of Congress Cataloging-in-Publication Data

Berlioz, Hector, 1803–1869.
   [Grotesques de la musique. English]
   The musical madhouse = Les grotesques de la musique / Hector
Berlioz ; translated and edited by Alastair Bruce ; with an introduction by
Hugh Macdonald.
      p. cm.—(Eastman studies in music, ISSN 1071-9989)
   Includes bibliographical references (p.) and index.
   ISBN 1-58046-132-8 (alk. paper)
   1. Music—Anecdotes. 2. Music—Humor. I.Title: Grotesques de la musique.
II. Bruce, Alastair, 1947– III. Title. IV. Series.

ML65.B4513 2003
780'.9–dc21   2003001049

A catalogue record for this title is available from the British Library.
This publication is printed on acid-free paper.

For Libby

Berlioz in 1862 (three years after publication of *The Musical Madhouse*). Lithograph cartoon by Étienne Carjat from *Le Boulevard*, 7 September 1862. Richard Macnutt Collection, Withyham.

Contents

Illustrations

Introduction

Hugh Macdonald

Berlioz, who believed his first obligation in life was to compose music and his second was to perform it, wrote six books. Bitterly though he resented his long years' work as a critic, he was a brilliant writer, acknowledged in his own time and ever since as the wielder of a lively pen, sharp, witty, well informed and passionate. Among the great composers of his day a number had secondary callings as writers, notably Schumann and Wagner. Berlioz's writings are much more extensive than Schumann's, much more readable than Wagner's, and much funnier than both.

The Musical Madhouse, published in 1859 as *Les Grotesques de la musique,* was Berlioz's fourth book, with a deliberate tone of levity, as reflected in its title. It was preceded by a two-volume book of autobiography (the *Voyage musical en Allemagne et en Italie* of 1844), the *Grand Traité d'instrumentation et d'orchestration modernes* of the same year, and *Les Soirées de l'orchestre* ("Evenings with the Orchestra") of 1852. Still to come were *A travers chants* in 1862 (the title is untranslatable: an early English version was entitled "Mid Realms of Song", while the most recent is simply called "The Art of Music") and the celebrated *Memoirs,* which, though compiled over many years, were not issued until 1870, after Berlioz's death. The orchestration treatise and the *Memoirs* have been widely read and translated into many languages; *Les Soirées de l'orchestre* and *A travers chants,* compiled from articles published in the Parisian press, have each been translated twice into English, while the similar compilation *Les Grotesques de la musique* has remained untranslated until now.

This oversight has no doubt come about because humorous writing is notoriously difficult to translate and because the other books appear, at least, to take on weightier concerns such as Berlioz's views on opera, on Gluck, on Beethoven, and so forth. As readers of the present volume will discover, Berlioz switches abruptly from telling teasing tales about musicians of his time to profound reflections on the nature of his art; indeed the two are entwined, since music is both an exalted expression of the spirit and an untidy element of everyday life. Amongst the grotesques and absurdities of the book there are many noble pages where Berlioz speaks passionately on behalf of music's divine power and of our obligation to treat it with the utmost seriousness. Grotesques of all kinds had been declared respectable by Victor Hugo in his preface to *Cromwell* in 1827, where he argued that our perception of beauty is conditioned by our awareness of ugliness. Abrupt contrasts between the heroic and the commonplace, so striking in Shakespeare, became a watchword of Romantic dramaturgy and occur frequently enough in Berlioz's music; in his writing we detect an instinctive sense that the grotesque serves as a butt for our jokes but also as a circuitous path to the noble, the beautiful and the sublime.

Berlioz's career as a critic began in 1833, soon after his return from Italy, when he began to make regular contributions to *Le Rénovateur* and to the *Gazette musicale*. In 1835 he became the concert critic of the *Journal des Débats*, an influential daily paper; his brief soon extended to opera and he continued to write for that newspaper for nearly thirty years, reporting on opera, concerts, new publications, visiting virtuosi, recently deceased musicians, newly invented instruments, his own travels abroad, and much else. A typical *feuilleton*, which might run to several thousand words, cost him several evenings in the theatre and long nights of agony at his desk, and it was inadequately paid. But he was glad of the modest income and had faith, at least to start with, in the power of the press to purvey his ideas on music and win readers to his cause. The Bertins, proprietors of the *Journal des Débats*, supported him strongly, but eventually he was regarded by many Parisians as a critic who tried to compose rather than as a composer of genius in their very midst. He was right to reflect that writing all those miles of prose had kept him from composing more music, and though posterity is much the poorer for that, we at least have his still lively, still pertinent writing as compensation.

During a visit to London in 1852, Berlioz conceived the plan of a book to be made up from miscellaneous articles and presented in the form of stories exchanged by members of an opera-house orchestra who are so numbed by the futility of much of the repertory they have to play that they leave the task of accompanying singers to the player of the bass drum while they chatter the evening away. The formula goes back to E. T. A. Hoffmann, perhaps to Chaucer and Boccaccio, and it was very successful as a book; it also allowed Berlioz to single out the great works which the players treat with proper respect by sticking to their duties. *Evenings with the Orchestra* appeared in December 1852 and attained its eleventh edition in 1929.

In the early 1850s Berlioz was at the height of his career as a conductor and had effectively given up composing. The haphazard genesis of *The Childhood of Christ* and its unexpected success in Paris in December 1854 brought about a striking change in his routine, for although the year 1855 was fully occupied with the first performance of the *Te Deum*, with concert tours to Weimar, Brussels and London, and with his consuming duties for the Universal Exhibition in Paris in the autumn, he was able to devote the years 1856 to 1858 almost entirely to the composition of his greatest masterpiece, *The Trojans*, with a greatly reduced concert schedule in those years. One regular invitation which he could not refuse was from Baden-Baden, the fashionable spa to which the aristocracy of all Europe flocked in the summer and where Berlioz was royally treated as an honoured guest conductor. His observations on the curious behaviour of the Baden visitors make up some of the most diverting pages of *The Musical Madhouse*, the compilation of which occupied Berlioz at the end of 1858, after *The Trojans* was completed and after three annual visits to the spa.

The Musical Madhouse was intended as a sequel to *Evenings with the Orchestra*, as we can tell from the Prologue presented in the form of a letter from the chorus of the Paris Opéra begging for a book that will while away their long periods of waiting backstage. It was dedicated to them, with Paris named as a "barbarous city" in contradistinction to the artists of "X***", a civilised city", to whom the earlier book was dedicated. The new book was not divided up in the same way, but still contained a miscellany of writings mostly drawn from *Journal des Débats* articles from the 1850s, with some important pieces from the 1840s, notably the accounts of his visits to Marseilles, Lyons and Lille in the years 1845–46. *Les Grotesques de la musique* was an attractive little volume of three hundred pages, published by A. Bourdilliat et Cie in March 1859. It remained in print until 1933 and was almost as successful as its predecessor.

Three years later Berlioz put out a third compilation of articles under the title *A travers chants*. This volume renounced the story-telling fiction and concentrated on musical and aesthetic matters much more than the biography and anecdote that had filled the earlier books. Finally, in 1865, Berlioz sent his *Memoirs* to the printers, but although a few close friends were given copies at that time, the book's existence was kept a closely guarded secret until after his death on 8 March 1869.

The Musical Madhouse is structured around four "Correspondences", in turn diplomatic, scientific, philosophic and academic, although the labels bear little relation to the content. The first is an imagined report to Queen Pomaré of Tahiti about the musical instruments at the Universal Exhibition of 1855, which have already been discussed a few pages earlier; the second describes Berlioz's visits to the summer spas; the third, scarcely philosophic, recounts the composition of *The Flight into Egypt*; and the fourth recalls Berlioz's concerts in the French provinces—not an academic topic at all. The other major essays include the "Lamentations of Jeremiah", a heartfelt cri de cœur about the critic's unhappy calling constructed in a form any musician would recognise as a rondo. "The season", along with the following essay, "Minor irritations of major concerts", gives a vivid picture of the difficulties and frustrations of giving concerts in mid-century Paris, with which Berlioz was perhaps more familiar than anyone. "The futility of glory" is a meditation on the havoc wreaked on composers' scores after their death. In an age which felt that old music ought to be brought up to date, Berlioz was a pioneer in the belief that a composer's instructions are sacrosanct, bearing an integrity that no conductor or singer has any right to trample on. There is passion, even desperation, in his plea to perform

Figure 1. *Journal des Débats*, 10 June 1854—front page, including a Berlioz *feuilleton* from which extracts appear in *The Musical Madhouse* (at the start of "Lamentations of Jeremiah", pages 54–56, and in "Dramatic Emphasis", pages 66–68). Richard Macnutt Collection, Withyham.

C'est seulement ainsi que les grandes compositions
complexes de l'art musical peuvent être sauvées et ga-
ranties de la morsure des rats qui grouillent dans les
théâtres, dans les théâtres de France, d'Angleterre,
d'Italie, d'Allemagne même, de partout. Car il ne faut
pas se faire illusion, les théâtres lyriques sont tous les
mêmes ; ce sont les mauvais lieux de la musique, et
la chaste muse qu'on y traîne ne peut y entrer qu'en
frémissant. Pourquoi cela? Oh! nous le savons trop,
on l'a trop souvent dit, il n'y a nul besoin de le re-
dire. Répétons seulement ~~ici, pour la vingtième fois~~
~~au moins, et à propos de récente reproduction de~~
~~la Vestale à l'Opéra, d'une œuvre pareille ne pourrait~~
~~être dignement exécutée, en l'absence de l'auteur, que~~
~~sous la surveillance d'un artiste dévoué parfaitement~~
~~maître de~~ toutes les questions qui se rattachent à
la musique et aux études musicales, profondément pé-
nétré de ~~tout~~ ce qu'il y a de grand et de beau dans
l'art, et qui, jouissant d'une autorité justifiée par
son caractère, ses connaissances spéciales et l'élé-
vation de ses vues, l'exerce~~rait~~ tantôt avec dou-
ceur, tantôt avec une rigidité absolue ; qui ne con-
naît~~rait~~ ni amis ni ennemis ; un Brutus l'ancien
qui, une fois ses ordres donnés et les voyant trans-
gressés, ~~serait~~ toujours prêt à dire : *I lictor, liga
ad palum !* « Va, licteur, lie au poteau le coupable ! »
— Mais c'est M. ***, c'est Mlle ***, c'est Mme ***. — *I lictor !* » Vous demandez l'établissement du despotisme
dans les théâtres ? me dira-t-on. Et je répondrai :
Oui, dans les théâtres lyriques surtout, et dans les
établissemens qui ont pour objet d'obtenir un beau
résultat musical au moyen d'un personnel nombreux
d'exécutans de divers ordres, obligés de concourir à
un seul et même but, il faut le despotisme, souverai-
nement intelligent sans doute, mais le despotisme
enfin, le despotisme militaire, le despotisme d'un gé-
néral en chef, d'un amiral en temps de guerre. Hors
de là il n'y a que résultats incomplets, contre-sens,
désordre et cacophonie.

[handwritten marginal annotation:] qu'une œuvre de la nature d'Alceste ne sera jamais dignement exécutée en l'absence de l'auteur que sous la surveillance d'un artiste dévoué qui la connaît parfaitement, ~~petite et depuis longtemps familier avec le style du maître~~ depuis longtemps familier avec le style du maître, possédant à fond

Figure 2. *Journal des Débats*, 24 October 1861—part of Berlioz's *feuilleton* marked
up with his autograph changes for its publication in *A travers chants*, 1862, indicating how he went about editing his articles for their appearance in book form. Richard Macnutt Collection, Withyham.

Gluck according to the proper tradition, and his regard for Mozart was inspired largely by the thought that he had been cold-shouldered by the French and that his music had been grievously misrepresented.

There is passion, too, in his evocation of Mme. Sontag's wonderful performance of *The Marriage of Figaro* in London in 1851, even though it is buried in a diatribe against the obscene fees paid to star singers (a theme that has not lost its force today). Berlioz was appalled by Offenbach and the disgraceful level of Second Empire taste to which his operettas seemed to pander. He fumed at artists whose greed transcended their artistic integrity. Striking yet another modern note, we find Berlioz enraged by the way daughters are treated by pushy fathers, and curious about the movement of glaciers and the rise and fall of global temperature. There is a bemused curiosity about science throughout the book, always treated humorously, with a recurrent concern for mountain ranges, distant oceans, subterranean forces and the idyllic qualities of distant lands. In the early 1850s, when his prospects in Paris seemed particularly bleak, Berlioz spoke longingly of Tahiti and the South Seas, imagining the delights of a land where the abuses and humiliations of Parisian life did not exist. By the middle of the decade, his son Louis was sailing the oceans himself at the start of a career at sea, and the dream was to some extent transferred to him. Meanwhile Berlioz found something close to heaven on earth in St.-Valery-en-Caux, a small town on the Normandy coast, where there were no aspiring singers, no virtuoso pianists, no music critics, in fact no music—a telling contrast to the city of Euphonia described in *Evenings with the Orchestra*, where everything is devoted to the service of music and everything is organised according to enlightened (i.e., Berlioz's own) designs.

In *The Musical Madhouse*, the disillusionment is sometimes painful, but it is always leavened by humour. To make sarcasm funny is a high art of which Berlioz was a master ("Dear me!" he remarks, "What naïveté, asking a Director for direction!"), and it helped him through his final years when disappointment and chronic ill-health beset him. He even describes his sickbed and its tribulations in the essay "Concerts". Another consolation was his devotion to great literature, evidence of which is sprinkled throughout the book. He quotes freely and frequently from his favourite authors, especially Virgil, Shakespeare, La Fontaine and Molière, without feeling the need to check his memory or supply a reference. Modern readers, ever curious to know what they're reading, need a little help here, supplied in the present book by the Notes, which also identify the stream of composers, singers, critics and musicians of all kinds who appear in these pages. To a reader in 1859 who followed artistic matters (as all Parisians always do) these were no doubt familiar names, but most of them have today suffered the "futility of glory" and fallen into the obscurity of dictionaries—if they were lucky.

The reader is also presumed to understand the social and artistic hierarchy of Paris's four opera houses, then still governed by regulations that circumscribed their different repertories. The Opéra (the Académie Impériale de Musique in Napoleon III's time) commanded the highest prestige and paid the highest fees. Its repertory was "grand opera", especially the works of Meyerbeer. With its large orchestra, chorus and corps de ballet and its reputation for technological innovation, it was the theatre to which all composers aspired. Verdi wrote *The Sicilian Vespers* for it in 1855, and Berlioz's *The Trojans* was composed expressly for it, even though he guessed (correctly) that little or no interest would be shown in his opera. The Opéra-Comique was a smaller company, devoted to lighter works mostly by French composers. Spoken dialogue was mandatory, and it paraded a large number of works that enjoyed only brief success. Berlioz spent innumerable evenings there listening to trivial scores and racking his brains for something to say about them.

The Théâtre-Italien was confined to Italian opera and was by 1859 past its great days when Rossini, Donizetti and Bellini were to be heard and seen there. The newest house was the Théâtre-Lyrique, driving a wedge between the two older French repertories and skilfully skirting the regulations. At the very moment that *The Musical Madhouse* was published, it mounted Gounod's *Faust,* one of the triumphs of the age, and in 1863 it was brave enough to take on *The Trojans,* even though in the end only part of the work was staged, meting out the very dismemberment against which Berlioz had railed all his life.

Berlioz adored puns, jokes and paradoxes. Like most Frenchmen, he was an ardent conversationalist and a witty raconteur. As in Shakespeare or old volumes of *Punch*, the humour of *The Musical Madhouse* is sometimes obscure, sometimes childishly obvious, sometimes right up to date. He himself described the book (in a letter of 22 January 1859 to the Princess Carolyne Sayn-Wittgenstein) as "horribly jolly", somehow embracing its unusual blend of bitterness and fun; in a later letter to her (10 March) he called it a collection of "grunts and thrusts". "Perhaps," he went on, "it's a good idea to spread a few straws and needles in the beds of idiots and imbeciles; besides, the spreader feels better for it too." These grunts and thrusts will provoke both tears and laughter, and we do Berlioz less than justice if we resist either response. Many composers have claimed that their message lies in their music, but in Berlioz's case his message was too concerned with the real world, too verbal, too contemporary and too wide in its embrace for this to be the whole truth. The message of his music is undoubtedly his strongest and greatest legacy, but his sparkling prose is precious and personal enough for us to treasure every line.

Readers of the *Berlioz Society Bulletin* have for many years enjoyed extracts from *The Musical Madhouse* in Alastair Bruce's brilliant translation. The bicentenary of Berlioz's birth is surely an appropriate moment to gather the whole book within a single cover and offer the first full English translation. He has mastered the verbal sleight-of-hand with great skill and caught to perfection the immediacy of Berlioz's prose. All those who love Berlioz the musician and Berlioz the man owe him a great debt of thanks.

Translator's Note

Is *The Musical Madhouse* the best rendering of Berlioz's title *Les Grotesques de la musique*? Alternative possibilities include *Musical Grotesques* or *Music's Absurdities* or *Oddities of Music*, or perhaps *Musical Monstrosities*. After leaning towards the latter, which seemed closer to the sense of the French title, I finally decided on *The Musical Madhouse* because of its reflection of Berlioz's comments in his Introduction on the 'singular lunacies' inspired by music.

Perhaps this dilemma over the very title of the book should have alerted me to the translational challenge of its content. It seemed such a good idea when I first started in the 1980s. Unlike Berlioz's other two published books of essays and articles drawn from his musical criticism (*Les Soirées de l'orchestre* and *A travers chants*), *Les Grotesques de la musique* had never appeared in a complete English version. As a fervent admirer of Berlioz with a good grasp of French and a penchant for translation, I thought that filling this gap would make an ideal project for me.

So in a way it has proved, although I never expected its fulfilment to take so long. An original version appeared in instalments in the Bulletin of the UK-based Berlioz Society from late 1982 to 1987. This was a rather literal and stilted effort, riding roughshod over many of the subtleties and complexities of Berlioz's text, and often inelegant if not inaccurate. It also omitted several pieces which had previously appeared in the Bulletin in translations by others.

Since then the translation has been substantially revised, completed and improved. I have tried to maintain a balance between enhancing readability for a modern audience and preserving Berlioz's own tone and style. Finding idiomatic modern equivalents for the expressions he uses in French, without being overtly anachronistic, has presented frequent challenges, not all of which I have been able to solve. Too much polishing may result in removing even those rough edges which Berlioz himself, intentionally or not, left in.

It rapidly became clear why the book had not appeared in English before. It is a challenging work to translate, not least because of Berlioz's fondness for wordplay and other literary conceits. I have sought to retain the effect of his many puns wherever possible, but some (like the atrocious one on 'corregidor' on page 79) have defeated me—others I may not even have spotted. One whole piece ("National fatuities" on pages 117–18) is based on French proverbial sayings: I have used English equivalents where they exist and invented suitably proverbial-sounding sayings where they do not.

In his letter to the Queen of Tahiti ("Diplomatic Correspondence", pages 37–39), and also in the pieces on his travels to Plombières (see pages 93–95) and Marseilles (see pages 160–63), Berlioz seeks to reproduce real or imagined local dialects or ways of speaking. I have created my own pseudo-dialects to convey the effect of these.

To maintain a sense of Berlioz's Frenchness, I have generally used terms like 'Monsieur' and 'Madame' rather than 'Sir' or 'Madam', and have kept the French names of major theatres and institutions like the Opéra and the Académie Française. However, I have found it impossible to deal consistently with the titles of musical and other works. Again, I have tried to follow the principle of making the text as straightforward as possible for an English-speaking reader by translating most such titles into English. Exceptions are when they are well known in their original language (like the *Symphonie fantastique*) or when they are hard to translate idiomatically (like *A travers chants*); *Der Freischütz* meets both these criteria. Titles in French follow the French convention of giving an initial capital only up to and including the first noun; those in English have initial capitals for all significant words.

Quotations from Shakespeare are given in the original English, even when Berlioz's versions contain minor inaccuracies. Biblical quotations are taken from the Authorised King James Version of the Bible. In most, but not quite all, cases I have retained the French currency denominations used by Berlioz (including sous and napoleons), rather than converting them all into francs and centimes; their value is explained in the notes where necessary.

Berlioz's own few footnotes appear at the bottom of the relevant pages, marked with asterisks. My own notes, intended solely to provide helpful information and clarification for the modern reader, are indicated by small superscript numbers and grouped at the end of the volume, where they may be consulted or ignored as desired. They are followed by a list of original sources of the pieces used by Berlioz in compiling the book, based on information from Professor Léon Guichard's scholarly French edition, published by Gründ in 1969 as one of a series of Berlioz's literary works to mark the centenary of his death in 1869.

In the course of translating it, I have read the complete book quite a few times. I hope at least some of the enjoyment I have derived from it will be shared by readers of this version, and that they will be encouraged to read Berlioz's other books (especially his *Memoirs* and *Evenings with the Orchestra*, the predecessor of the present work). For even greater rewards, they should get to know Berlioz's music—easier than it used to be now that fine recordings are available of almost his entire output. He produced scarcely more than a dozen major works, all of them magnificent, and all utterly different from each other. There might have been many more if he was not condemned to earn his living as a music critic, but a book containing some of the results of that necessity is hardly the place to complain!

Berlioz was unlucky in many things, but has been outstandingly fortunate in the quality of his current interpreters and promoters. Prominent among these is Hugh Macdonald, one of today's leading Berlioz scholars. It has been an enormous privilege to have his enthusiastic support and advice on all aspects of this volume, including numerous details of the translation and the notes as well as the Introduction he has provided. His contributions to the understanding of Berlioz and the availability of his works are innumerable, not least as General Editor of the *New Berlioz Edition,* which is coming tantalisingly close to completion. I cannot thank him enough for his commitment to bringing this much smaller project to a successful conclusion as well.

Numerous other people have helped me in a variety of ways, sometimes without even being aware of their contributions. They include Professor Guichard, whose French edition has been invaluable in providing a substantial part of the information I have used in the Notes, as well as all of that in the Sources; several of the illustrations I have chosen are also ones that appear in his edition. David Cairns is another of those admirers in whom Berlioz has been so lucky; both his two-volume life of the composer and his English edition of the *Memoirs* have been essential reference sources, as well as superb reads.

Richard Macnutt, another indefatigable Berlioz admirer and evangelist, has been kind enough to provide photographs for many of the illustrations, drawing on the outstanding resources of his own collection. I am grateful to the Bibliothèque Nationale de France for permission to use the photographs obtained from them. (All photos from the Bibliothèque Nationale de France are from the Department of Prints and Photographs with the exception of Figure 38, which comes from the Department of Music.)

Gilles Bragadir has helped on matters of French translation and topography, while Jonathan and Teresa Sumption contributed both advice and accommodation for my sortie to the Bibliothèque Nationale de France in Paris. Peter Naughton was a thought-provoking, as well as thorough, reader of the proofs. The team at the University of Rochester Press and the Eastman School of Music, especially Timothy Madigan, Molly Cort, Ralph Locke (whose determination to get the book published has been magnificent) and Louise Goldberg, have been marvellously enthusiastic, encouraging and efficient. Above all I owe my thanks to my wife, Libby, who has almost single-handedly, and with boundless patience, redecorated our home at least twice over the years while I have excused myself from helping on the grounds of being engaged in translating the *Madhouse.*

My final acknowledgement must go to Berlioz himself, who through his music, his writings and his life has given me immeasurable reward and enjoyment over the thirty-five years since I first discovered his music through the *Symphonie fantastique.* This translation is a way of repaying a small part of my debt to him—I hope it may lead others to find similar pleasures through getting to know the man and his music.

Alastair Bruce
December 2002

Prologue

Letter from the Chorus of the Opéra
to the Author

Cher maître,

You have dedicated a book (*Evenings with the Orchestra*) "to your good friends the artists of X***, a civilised city".[1] This city, which we understand to be in Germany, is probably no more civilised than many others, despite the mischievous intent which led you to call it that. We take leave to doubt that its artists are any better than those of Paris, and their affection for you couldn't possibly be as lively or long-standing as ours. The choruses of Paris as a whole, and of the Opéra in particular, are devoted to you body and soul: they've proved it many times and in many ways. Have they ever grumbled at the length of your rehearsals or your insistence on musical perfection, or at your violent interjections—outbursts of fury, even—when they struggle to master the *Requiem*, the *Te Deum*, *Romeo and Juliet*, *The Damnation of Faust*, *The Childhood of Christ*, etc.?[2] Never, absolutely never! On the contrary, they've always gone about their work with zeal and unfailing patience. Yet your own behaviour at those awful rehearsals is hardly gracious towards the men nor gallant towards the ladies.

When it's almost time to start, if the entire chorus isn't all present and correct—if even one person is missing—you pace around the piano like a lion in its cage at the zoo, growling through your teeth and chewing your lower lip, with glaring yellow eyes. If someone greets you, you turn your head away. Every now and again you violently bang out dissonant chords on the keyboard, revealing your inner rage and making it clear you would be quite capable of tearing latecomers and absentees limb from limb . . . if they were there.

Then you're forever reproaching us for not singing quietly enough in *piano* passages and not attacking *fortes* together; you insist that we pronounce both *s*'s in *angoisse* and the second *r* in *traître*.[3] And if even a single poorly trained wretch has strayed into our ranks and, forgetting your lecture on grammar, persists in singing *angoise* or *traite*, you take it out on everyone and heap cruel wisecracks on us all, calling us lackeys, scullery-maids and other such things! Well, we put up with that too, and we love you all the same, because we know you love us and we realise how much you adore music.

Only the French habit of giving pre-eminence to foreigners, even when it is flagrantly unfair, could have led you to dedicate your *Evenings with the Orchestra* to German musicians.

Anyway, what's done is done, we'll say no more about it.

ACADEMIE ROYALE DE MUSIQUE.

Figure 3. Opéra, Paris—interior, during a performance of Auber's *La Muette de Portici*. Engraving by Penner Sears after J. Nash, 1830. Richard Macnutt Collection, Withyham. The opulent public face of the Opéra, in contrast to the working conditions endured by the Chorus, to whom *The Musical Madhouse* is dedicated (see pages 1–6).

But why don't you write a book for *us* now in the same vein, perhaps with a little more humour and less philosophy, to exorcise the boredom which consumes us at the Opéra?

As you know, during acts or parts of acts where the chorus doesn't appear, we're prisoners backstage. It's as gloomy as a ship's lower deck, stinking of lamp oil and with uncomfortable seating. We listen to mildewed old stories badly told, and to musty, hackneyed jokes; or else we're crushed by the combination of silence and inaction until the call-boy comes to fetch us back on stage. Oh, it's no great job, believe us. Fifty-odd rehearsals to cram our heads full of almost unsingable chorus parts in new works! Learning our parts by heart for operas which run from seven o'clock to midnight! Changing costume up to six times an evening! Penned like sheep when we're not singing! In other words, not having so much as five minutes' enjoyment all through those interminable performances! For we aren't like those German musicians of yours who are happy for only half the orchestra to play during works they don't think much of.[4] All of us sing all the time. Of course, if we took a similar liberty and only piped up in pieces we liked, there wouldn't be many sore throats in the Opéra chorus. What's more, we sing standing up and are on our feet the whole time, while the orchestra plays sitting down in its pit. It's enough to drive you cuckoo!

Come on then, be a good chap, write us a volume of true stories and fables, and jokes too, like the ones you often come up with when you're in a bad mood; we'll read it when we're below deck, by the light of our oil lamps; thanks to you we'll be spared a few hours of misery, and you'll be entitled to all our gratitude.

Yours faithfully
The sopranos, contraltos, tenors
and basses of the Opéra.

Paris, 22 December 1858

———————

The Author's Reply
to the Chorus of the Opéra

Ladies and Gentlemen,

You address me as "Cher maître"; I was on the point of replying "Dear slaves", for I know how you're deprived of both leisure and liberty. Wasn't I once in a chorus myself?[5] And in what a theatre—may God preserve you from such a place!

I know very well what hard labour you undergo, the hours of misery you suffer and the even more miserable salaries you put up with. Alas! I am no more 'master', no freer, no happier than you. You work, I work, we all work just to live; and you live, I live, we all live just to work. The Saint-Simonians claimed to know about job satisfaction, but they have kept their secret well;[6] I can assure you it's as unknown to me in my work as to you. I've stopped counting my hours of misery; they fall one after another, cold and monotonous, like the regular dripping of melting snow which weighs so heavily on the gloomy silence of winter nights in Paris.

As for my salary, don't even mention it. . . .

I acknowledge the justice of your reproach concerning the dedication of *Evenings with the Orchestra*; as the book was about music and musicians I should have offered it to my musician friends in Paris. But I was on my way back from Germany when I had the notion of writing it; I was still under the influence of the warm and cordial welcome given me by the orchestra of the "civilised city", and so little did I expect to find the least regard for my *Evenings* amongst the public that I thought of the dedication more as a means of assuring them some patronage than as any sort of flattery or compliment. Your regrets on this point seem to indicate that you hold a different opinion. In your view, some people may actually want to read my stuff . . . which means I may be wrong . . . which means I may be an imbecile! I'm overjoyed at the thought.

You tease me about my lectures on grammar. Yet I don't exactly pretend to know much about French: on the contrary, I know perfectly well that everyone knows I don't. But I do know that a considerable number of regularly used terms are barbarisms, and I have a horror of hearing them. The word *angoise* is one of these: it's often used even by some of the most highly paid singers at our opera houses. A prize-winning student at the Conservatoire persisted in singing "Mortelle angoise!" despite every re-monstrance. I managed to put her right by telling her there were three *s*'s in the word, hoping she would pronounce at least two. It worked: she finally sang "Mortelle angoisse!"

You seem to envy the orchestra sitting in their pit to play, instead of remaining on their feet for long hours like the chorus. Let's be fair. I admit they're seated, although in a "pit" which is certainly no goldmine as far as their earnings are concerned; but they play the whole time, without break or respite or reprieve, no more copying the relaxed approach of my friends in the "civilised city" than you do. The conductor allows them a few bars' rest only when the composer happens to have written it in the score. They play during overtures, arias, duets, trios, quartets and ensembles, as well as accompanying your choruses; one Opéra Director even wanted to make them play in *unaccompanied* choruses, claiming he wasn't paying them to sit around with their arms folded.

And you know how little they're paid!

It's true, of course, they don't have to change costume every half-hour; but they've recently been obliged to turn out in evening dress, which is ruinous for them. Some of our poor musical colleagues at the Opéra apparently receive only about 66 francs and 65 centimes a month. With fourteen performances that amounts to less than five francs for a five-hour session, or rather less than twenty sous an hour—below the rate for a cab-driver.[7] And now they find themselves burdened with the cost of their outfit. They need at least seven white ties a month, assuming they know how to fold them cleverly to make them do for several performances. After a while the laundry bills mount up to quite a substantial sum. What does it cost to wash and iron a starched white tie (without counting the initial purchase cost)? Fifteen centimes. Let's suppose a player does without starching, for reasons of economy, and has his tie ironed only for special performances. That will reduce the cost from fifteen centimes to ten. So you can work it out, these are the expenses he'll have to enter in his account-book at the end of the month:[8]

Tie for *Les Huguenots*	3	sous
ditto for *Le Prophète*	3	"
ditto for *Robert le Diable*	3	"
ditto for *Le Cheval de bronze*	3	"
ditto for *William Tell*	3	"
ditto for *La Favorite*, when Mme. Borghi-Mamo wasn't singing	2	"
ditto for *La Juive*	3	"
ditto for *La Sylphide*	3	"
ditto for *Le Violon du Diable*	2	"
ditto for the first two acts of *Lucia*, when Roger wasn't singing	2	"
ditto for *François Villon*	2	"
ditto for *La Xacarilla*	2	"
ditto for *The Nightingale* (the tie lasted three performances)	0	"
ditto for *La Rose de Florence* (it lasted a fourth)	0	"
Total for 14 performances and seven ties	1 fr 55 c	
For a full year	18 fr 60 c	
For ten years	186 fr	

On the budget of an unfortunate violinist with a family to support, those 186 francs could force him into the appalling necessity of using his last tie to hang himself.

So the life of an orchestral musician is no more nor less a bed of roses than that of a chorus member: they have much in common.

In any case I'd be glad, I assure you, to "soothe your weariness a while", in the words of Molière's Oronte;[9] but the humour of my anecdotes is very questionable, and I wouldn't think of yielding to your friendly persuasion were it not that even the saddest things often have their funny side. You may recall the remark of the condemned man whose tearful wife had come to say her last farewells and follow him to the place of execution. He said to her in his rough voice: "You haven't brought the little 'un, then?"

"Good God! What an idea! How could I let him see his father on the scaffold?"

"Come off it, he'd've enjoyed it no end."

So this is a little book whose character is hard to describe; at all events I shall call it *The Musical Madhouse,* even though it contains an occasional lunacy that has nothing to do with music. Readers may find it makes them laugh or cry according to their disposition. I hope you may take some pleasure in reading it; as for me, I've enjoyed writing it, much as the condemned man's child would no doubt have enjoyed his father's execution.

Farewell, ladies and gentlemen. I kiss the hands of the ladies, and cordially shake the men's, and assure you of the lively and sincere affection of your devoted colleague

Hector Berlioz

Paris, 21 January 1859

To My Good Friends

The Artists of the Chorus of the Opéra
of Paris
A Barbarous City

The Musical Madhouse

Of all the arts, music undeniably gives rise to the strangest passions and the most absurd ambitions, not to speak of the most singular lunacies. Among the unfortunates locked up in mental hospitals, those who think they're Neptune or Jupiter are easily recognised as lunatics; but there are many others enjoying complete freedom, whose parents have never dreamed of resorting to psychiatric treatment for them, yet who are obviously mad. Music has thrown their minds out of gear.

I'll restrain myself from speaking of those men of letters who write, in verse or prose, about matters of musical theory of which they lack the most elementary knowledge, using words whose meaning they don't understand; who deliberately work themselves up about ancient masters of whose music they've never heard a note; who generously attribute to them melodic and expressive ideas they never had, since melody and expression didn't even exist when they were alive; who admire indiscriminately, and with the same effusiveness, two pieces signed with the same name, of which one is indeed fine, while the other is absurd; in short, who speak and write all the extraordinary nonsense which no musician can hear without laughing. It's generally accepted that music is a *universal* art, which anyone may speak and write about: it's "accessible to all".

And yet, between ourselves, that phrase may beg the question. For music is both an art and a science; to comprehend it fully requires long, hard study; to feel the emotions it can produce, you need a cultivated mind and a practised sense of hearing; and to judge the merit of musical works, you must also possess a well-stocked memory so as to be able to make comparisons—indeed you must know all sorts of things which inevitably you can get to know only by learning them. So it's plain that people who permit themselves to pontificate about music without understanding it, although they would shrink from giving their opinions on architecture or sculpture or any other art that's foreign to them, are in a state of madness. They think they're musicians, just as the lunatics I mentioned earlier think they're Neptune or Jupiter. There's not the slightest difference.

When Balzac wrote his *Gambara* and attempted a technical analysis of Rossini's *Moïse,* and when Gustave Planche ventured to write his strange critique of Beethoven's *Eroica Symphony,* they were both mad.[10] But Balzac's was a touching folly: he admired without understanding or feeling, he just felt he was in ecstasy. Planche's insanity, on the contrary, was irritating and stupid; without understanding or feeling or knowledge, he denigrated Beethoven and claimed to be able to tell him how to write a symphony.

I could name a host of other writers who harm music and torment musicians by publishing their ideas on the art, forever mistaking Piraeus for a person, like the monkey in the fable.[11] But I'll confine myself to citing a few examples of inoffensive, and on the whole amusing, lunacy from recent times.

The right to play a symphony in the wrong key

At the time when I was just beginning to glimpse the power of our great but ill-treated art, after eight or ten years of study, a student I knew was asked by the members of an amateur Philharmonic Society, recently established in the Prado building, to invite me to conduct them.[12] I had by then conducted only one musical performance, that of my first *Mass* in the church of St.-Eustache.[13] I was extremely wary of these amateurs: their orchestra was bound to be frightful, and so it proved. All the same, the idea of getting some practice directing instrumental forces by trying it out like this with very little to lose made up my mind, and I accepted.

Rehearsal day arrived, and I presented myself at the Prado, where I found about sixty players tuning up with that grating noise peculiar to amateur orchestras. What were we to play? A symphony in D by Gyrowetz.[14] I don't suppose any boilermaker or rabbit-skin dealer or Roman grocer or Neapolitan barber ever dreamed of such platitudes. But I resigned myself, and we began. I heard an appalling discord from the clarinets. I stopped the orchestra and addressed the clarinettists:

"You've obviously got your pieces mixed up, gentlemen; we're playing in D and you were in F!"

"No, Monsieur, we definitely have the correct symphony!"

"All right, let's begin again."

Again the discord, again we stop.

"That can't be right; pass me your part."

The clarinet part was handed to me.

"Ah! That explains the racket. Your part is written in F all right, but for clarinets in A, so your written F actually sounds D. You have the wrong instruments."

"But, Monsieur, we only have clarinets in C."

"Very well then, transpose down a third."

"We don't know how to transpose."

"In that case, for heaven's sake, keep quiet!"

"Not on your life! We're members of the Society, and we've as much right to play as all the others."

At these incredible words I dropped my baton and fled as if possessed by the devil, and never heard another word from those "philharmonists".

A crowned virtuoso

A certain king of Spain, believing himself a great music-lover, liked to play Boccherini quartets; but he could never keep up with the tempo.[15] One

Figure 4. *Tartarini*. Lithograph cartoon by Gustave Doré (1832–83). Bibliothèque nationale de France.

1 Having obtained the cooperation of the Philharmonic Society, Tartarini finds that only the clarinets arrive, and concudes that the inhabitants of the town have preconceived ideas and fixed views concerning the arts.

2 From the first chords, Tartarini gains an idea of the strength of this Philharmonic Society.

3 Wounded by his show of impatience, the members of the Philharmonic Society withdraw—and return only after humble entreaties by Tartarini.

4 Definite progress—only two howlers instead of sixty

"I was extremely wary of these amateurs; their orchestra was bound to be frightful, and so it proved" (page 11).

day when he'd fallen even further behind the others than usual, they, put out by the confusion produced by the royal bow being three or four bars late, made as if to stop. "Go on, go on," cried the enthusiastic monarch, "I'll catch up with you!"

A new musical instrument

A musician well known throughout Paris came to see me one morning, fifteen or twenty years ago, carrying under his arm an object carefully wrapped in paper.

"Eureka! Eureka!" he cried, like Archimedes, as he entered. "I've been on the trail of this discovery for ages—it's bound to produce a complete revolution in music. Look at this instrument, just a plain metal box with holes in it and a piece of string attached; I'll whirl it around like a sling and you'll hear something marvellous. Listen to this now: hoo-woo-hoo! How's that for an imitation of the wind? It puts the famous chromatic scales in Beethoven's *Pastoral Symphony* completely in the shade, doesn't it? It's nature taken from the life! It's beautiful, it's new! It would be in poor taste to be too modest about it. Beethoven got it wrong, you must admit, and I've got it right. My dear fellow, what a discovery! And what an article you'll write for me in the *Journal des Débats*![16] It'll bring you exceptional honour: you'll be translated into every language. How delighted I am, really, old chap! And believe me, I'm as pleased for you as for myself. However, I must insist on being the first to use my instrument; I'm saving it for an overture I've already started, entitled *The Isle of Aeolus*; you can review it for me. After that you may use my invention as you like in your own symphonies. I'm not the kind of person who'd sacrifice the whole present and future of music to their own personal interests, no sir: 'all for art', that's my motto."

The regiment of colonels

A rich landowner was kind enough to introduce me to his son, aged twenty-two, who he said could not even read music.

"Monsieur," he said to me, "I've come to ask if you'd be good enough to give this young man lessons in serious composition. He'll be a credit to you in due course, I hope. His first thought was to be a colonel, but despite the appeal of military life, the arts seemed decidedly more attractive, and he'd prefer to be a great composer."

"Oh, Monsieur, what a mistake! If you only knew the drawbacks of such a career! Great composers eat each other up; there are so many of them! Besides, I couldn't undertake to see him through to the attainment of his noble ambition. In my view he'd do better to stick to his original idea and join the regiment you mentioned."

"What regiment?"

"Well, this regiment of colonels."

"Monsieur, your facetiousness is quite uncalled for; I shall not take any more of your time. Happily you're not the only teacher, and my son can become a great composer without your help. We bid you good day."

A cantata

Shortly before the ashes of the Emperor Napoleon I were returned to Paris,[17] Messieurs Auber, Adam and Halévy were asked to write funeral marches for the procession accompanying the late Immortal to the church of the Invalides.

In 1840 I had been commissioned to compose a symphony for the removal of the remains of the victims of the July Revolution and the inauguration of the Bastille column;[18] as a result several newspapers, under the impression that this type of music was my speciality, announced that I was the composer honoured with the Minister's favour once again on this solemn occasion.

A Belgian amateur, misled like many others, sent me a packet containing a letter, some verses and some music. The letter went like this:

"Monsieur,

"I see from the papers that you've been engaged to compose a symphony for the ceremony of removing the Imperial ashes to the Panthéon. I'm sending a cantata for you to fit into your work; sung by seven or eight hundred voices it should produce quite an effect.

"You will notice a break in the poem after the verse 'Nous vous rendons votre Empereur'. I've only been able to complete the music, as I'm not much of a poet. But you'll have no trouble filling the gap: you could get Hugo or Lamartine to do it. I am married with three *populos* (children)—if the piece brings in a few francs I'd be glad if you'd pass them on to me.[19] I'll let you take all the credit."

Figure 5. Transfer of the ashes of the Emperor Napoleon I to the Invalides, 15 December 1840—the procession passing the legislature. Anonymous graphite drawing from H. Destailleur, *Collection de Dessins sur Paris*. Bibliothèque Nationale de France.

"Shortly before the ashes of the Emperor Napoleon I were returned to Paris, Messieurs Adam, Auber and Halévy were asked to write funeral marches for the procession" (page 14).

Here is the cantata:[20]

He let *me* take the credit!!!

A programme of grotesque music

In the days when the Odéon was an opera house, pieces from the old Opéra-Comique repertory at the Feydeau theatre were often performed there. I happened to attend a rehearsal for the revival of Grétry's *La Rosière de Salency.*[21] I shall never forget the sight of the orchestra on that occasion: some of the players collapsing with hilarity during the overture, others in stitches, the violins applauding ironically, the first oboe swallowing his reed, the double basses flouncing from behind their music stands and in strangled voices demanding permission to leave "while there's still time". And the conductor, Monsieur Bloc, managing with an effort of self-control to keep a straight face;[22] and me, in a high old state of indignation at this irreverent outburst, finding the suggestion of the double-bass players thoroughly improper. But it wasn't long before these poor fellows had their revenge in full for my stupid prudishness. Half an hour after the performance of this extraordinary overture, calm had been re-established, everyone was paying earnest attention again, the orchestra was quietly accompanying a singer in the third scene, when without any warning I burst out laughing right there in the pit, letting out a scream of retrospective mirth.[23] Nature was reasserting its laws—I had just been hanging fire.

Two or three years later, reflecting on pieces of this kind which can be found, let's face it, in the works of several great masters, the idea occurred to me of presenting a selection of them in a special concert, without warning the public about the nature of the musical fare to which it was invited, but confining myself to announcing a programme made up entirely of illustrious composers.

The overture to *La Rosière de Salency* figured right at the beginning, as you may imagine, followed by the celebrated English air "Arm ye brave!", a "devilish" violin sonata and the quartet from a French opera, in which this passage occurs:

I am fond enough of Dutch girls,
And Persian girls, and English girls,
Most of all, though, I love French girls,
Their wit, their grace, their gaiety.

Then came an orchestral march which was performed, to the indescribable delight of the public, at a very serious concert in Paris six or seven years ago; the first act finale of a grand opera which is no longer in the repertoire, but in which the phrase "Come, follow me to the wilderness" also gave rise to the most scandalous hilarity amongst part of the orchestra when the masterpiece was last revived; the fugue on "Kyrie Eleison" from a *Requiem*; and a psalm setting which is supposed to be in Pindaric style, set to the words

I cieli immensi narrano
Del grande iddio la gloria!

['The heavens declare the glory of God!'—*Psalm 19*]

but whose music, full of smugness and jollity, has nothing to do with the marvels of creation, but says quite simply:

Ah, what delight to drink outside
And stuff and gorge and guzzle!
Ah, what delight to drink outside
Beneath the shady branches wide,
And go on the razzle-dazzle!

Next were some variations for bassoon on the air "Au clair de la lune", which have been famous for twenty years and made their composer's fortune; and finally a very well-known symphony (in D), for which Gyrowetz is not to blame.[24]

With this mind-boggling programme agreed upon, my accomplices in the orchestra met for a preliminary rehearsal. What a session! Needless to say, the experiment was not concluded. The *La Rosière* overture produced its extraordinary effect; the "Come, follow me" finale was completed, with the performers in an orgy of merriment, but we couldn't get through the psalm "Ah, what delight to drink outside!" Players were biting their lips, falling about and overturning music stands, and the timpanist had ripped the head of one of his drums; any idea of going on had to be abandoned. In the end, those members of the orchestra who had managed to maintain some degree of composure conferred together, and a majority declared the concert impossible, insisting it would cause a terrible scandal and that despite the deservedly high reputation of all the famous composers whose works figured on the programme, the public might well fly off the handle and start pelting us with coins.

Naïve musicians! How little you understand the public's level of sophistication! You think they'd get angry? Come off it! Of the eight hundred people in the hall we had chosen for this experiment, perhaps fifty would have laughed for all they were worth, while the rest would have remained quite serious and, I fear, loud applause would have followed the performance of the psalm and the finale. The "Kyrie" would have had people saying "What profound music!", while the symphony would have been much admired.

As for the overture, the march and the English air, one or two might have been daring enough to express some doubt and ask their neighbours: "Is this a joke?" But no more than that.

There's no shortage of stories to support this view. Here's one among twenty.

Is it a joke?

I had just conducted the second performance of my "dramatic legend" *The Damnation of Faust* in the theatre in Dresden.[25] In the second act, during the scene in Auerbach's cellar, the drunken students, after singing the song of the rat killed by poison in a kitchen, shout "Amen!" in chorus.

Let's have a fugue for the Amen!

says Brander,

A fugue, a chorale!
Let's improvise a masterpiece!

And off they go, taking up the theme of the rat's song in a broader tempo, and producing a real classico-academic fugue, in which the chorus at times vocalises on "a–a–a–a" and at other times rapidly repeats the whole word, "amen, amen, amen", accompanied by tuba, ophicleide, bassoons and double basses. This fugue is written in strictest accordance with the rules of counterpoint, and despite the senseless brutality of its style and the irreverent and blasphemous contrast intentionally created between the musical expression and the significance of the word "Amen", because the use of these horrible travesties is allowed in all the conservatoires, the public is not at all shocked by it, and the harmonic effect which results from the musical texture of this scene is applauded wherever it is heard. It recalls the success of Oronte's sonnet at the first performance of Molière's *Le Misanthrope*.

After the obbligato pedal and the final cadence of the fugue, Mephistopheles steps forward and says:

By God, gentlemen, your fugue is very fine,
So much so
That hearing it one would think oneself in a holy place.
Permit me, pray, to tell you,
Its style is learned, truly religious,
One could not better express
The pious sentiments
Which the Church, at the end of its prayers,
Sums up in a single word, etc.

During the interval a music-lover came looking for me. No doubt this recitative had given him something to think about, for he accosted me with a shy smile:
"Your fugue on 'Amen' *is* meant as a joke, isn't it?"
"Yes, Monsieur, I'm afraid it is!"
He wasn't sure!

———————

The evangelist of the drum

I have often wondered whether it's because they're mad that certain people get involved with music, or whether it's actually music that has driven them mad. Impartial observation has led me to the conclusion that music is a violent passion, like love, and can undoubtedly make people in its grip seem to lose their wits. But this mental derangement is only temporary, and in no time at all they're restored to reason; it's quite possible that this so-called derangement is in reality a sublime exaltation, an exceptional flowering of intelligence and sensibility.

In the case of the genuine lunatics, clearly music is not in any way responsible for their mental disorder, and if they take it into their heads to devote themselves to musical pursuits, it's because they lack all common sense. Music isn't to blame for their insanity.

Yet God knows what harm they could do to music if they had the chance. Luckily the public has enough good sense to recognise somebody at once as a lunatic if everything he ever does is designed to prove that he's the god Jupiter!

But there are others whom it would be an understatement to describe as lacking in intelligence; they have no intelligence at all, for their heads are quite empty, or at least half empty: they are missing either the right or left lobe of their brains, if not both. The reader will have no difficulty in classifying the examples I shall give, and will know how to distinguish the madmen from those who are simply . . . simple.

. . . .

There was once a splendid musician who was an excellent drummer. Convinced of the superiority of the side drum to all other musical instruments, he wrote a *Method* for it some ten or twelve years ago, and dedicated his work to Rossini. I was invited to comment on the merit and importance of this *Method,* and wrote a letter to its author in which I contrived to compliment him greatly on his talent as a performer.

"You're the king of drummers," I said, "and before long you'll be the drummer of kings. No regiment, whether French, Italian, English, German or Swedish, has ever had a drummer with a sound like yours. Your stick-handling technique seems like magic to people who don't know you. Your *bom-bom* is so smooth, so seductive, so gentle! It's like honey! Your *rat-a-tat* cuts like a sabre. As for your roll, it's the voice of Eternity, it's thunder, it's a bolt of lightning striking an eighty-foot poplar tree and splitting it from top to bottom."

This letter made the virtuoso drunk with joy; he would have completely lost his senses, if that had been possible. He rushed around all the orchestras of Paris and the suburbs, showing his blessed letter to all his friends.

But one day he turned up at my house in indescribable fury; "Monsieur, they had the insolence yesterday at the National Guard headquarters to insinuate that your letter was a joke, and that you were (if you will forgive me) bullsh . . . I mean making fun of me. Everyone knows I never, ever bear a grudge. But the Devil take me if I don't stick my sabre through the first person who dares say that to my face!"

Poor man! His name was *Saint-Jean*—he was the Saint John the Evangelist of the drum.

The apostle of the flageolet

Another fellow, the apostle of the flageolet, was such a zealot that he couldn't be stopped from playing in the orchestra of which he was the principal ornament, even when there was no part for flageolet.[26]

He either doubled the flute or the oboe or the clarinet; he would have doubled the double bass rather than keep quiet. When one of his colleagues remarked that he found it strange he should go so far as to play in a Beethoven symphony, he replied: "You consider my instrument only in terms of its mechanical capacity, which you regard as limited. Imbeciles! If Beethoven had known me, his works would have been full of flageolet solos, and he would have made a fortune. But he didn't know me, and he died in the poorhouse."

The prophet of the trombone

Then there was the player with a passion for the trombone. In his view the trombone would sooner or later dethrone and replace all other instruments. He was the prophet Isaiah of the trombone. Saint-Jean would have played his drum in the wilderness; this fellow, to prove the immense superiority of the trombone, boasted of having actually played it in a coach, a railway train, a steamboat, and even while swimming in a lake twenty metres deep.

Apart from appropriate exercises for playing the trombone while swimming in lakes, his *Method* includes several cheerful pieces for weddings and similar festivities. Beneath one of these masterpieces there is a note which says: "When this piece is played at a wedding, a stack of plates should be dropped at the bar marked X; this produces an excellent effect."

Conductors

A famous conductor, rehearsing a new overture, was asked by the composer to play an important passage softly. "Play softly, Monsieur?" he replied. "What academic poppycock!"

. . . .

I've come across another who thought he could conduct eighty players all sitting with their backs to him.

. . . .

A third conducted with his head down and his nose touching the score, so that he had no more idea what the players were doing than if he had been conducting the Paris Opéra orchestra from London.

Once when he was "directing" a rehearsal of Beethoven's *Seventh Symphony,* the whole orchestra got lost; the ensemble collapsed and an appalling racket ensued, so the orchestra stopped. He went on regardless, waving the baton with which he thought he was marking the tempo above his head, until eventually repeated cries of "Hey, Maestro! Stop, stop, we've lost you!" brought his indefatigable arm to a halt. He looked up and asked with an air of surprise, "What is it? What's the matter?"

"We don't know where we are, the last few minutes have been chaos."

"Oh, I see."

He hadn't noticed.

This worthy fellow—and the one before, too—enjoyed the special confidence of a king, who showered him with honours. In his own country he's still thought of, among amateurs, as one of music's great ornaments. When he's so described in front of real musicians, only the sycophants among them manage to keep a straight face.

Appreciators of Beethoven

A famous critic, professor of music, wordmonger, de-composer and corrector of the masters had produced an opera with a plot taken from two dramatists and music from four composers.[27] He found me one day in the Conservatoire library studying the score of the storm in Beethoven's *Pastoral Symphony*.

"Ah yes," he said when he recognised the piece, "I put that into my opera *The Forest of Sénart*, with some added trombone parts which produced the dickens of an effect!"

"Why did you have to add them," I asked, "when they're already there?"

"No they aren't!"

"Oh? What's this then?" (showing him the two trombone staves).

"Good heavens! I didn't notice those."

. . . .

A great and learned scholar has stated in print that Beethoven "didn't know much about music".

. . . .

A Director of Fine Arts, whose loss we lament, acknowledged in my presence that this same Beethoven was "not without talent".

The Sontag version

Sontag, an admirable and much-missed soprano, invented a phrase of her own which she substituted for the original at the end of the Masks Trio in *Don Giovanni*.[28] Her example was soon followed; it was too good to miss, and every soprano in Europe adopted Mme. Sontag's modification of the role of Donna Anna.

One day, at a rehearsal in London, a conductor I know heard this daring substitution at the end of the trio. He stopped the orchestra and said to the prima donna:

"What's going on? Have you forgotten your part, Madame?"

"No, Monsieur, I'm singing the Sontag version."

"Oh, I see. But may I be so bold as to ask why you should prefer the Sontag version to the Mozart version, which is after all the one we are concerned with?"

"Because hers is better."

! ! ! ! ! ! ! ! ! ! ! ! ! . . . .

You can't dance in E

A dancer whose success in Italy had been meteoric came to make his début in Paris. He insisted that a solo which had brought him avalanches of flowers in Milan and Naples be inserted into the ballet in which he was to appear. This was done. The time of the final rehearsal arrived, but for some reason or other the music for this particular number had been copied a tone higher than in the original score.

The rehearsal began. The dancer leapt aloft, hovered for an instant, then, returning to earth, suspended his flight and asked: "What key are you playing in, gentlemen? My solo seems more tiring than usual."

"We're playing in E."

"No wonder. Please transpose the allegro down a tone, I can only dance it in D."

Kissed by Rossini

An amateur cellist had the honour of playing for Rossini.

Ten years later he related that "The great master was so enchanted by my playing that he interrupted me in the middle of a cantabile passage to come and kiss me on the forehead. And from that day to this, to preserve the glorious imprint of his kiss, I have never washed my face."

A clarinet concerto

Döhler had just announced a concert in a great German city,[29] when a man he didn't know came to call on him:

"Monsieur," he said to Döhler, "my name is W***, I'm an accomplished clarinettist, and I've come to H*** with the intention of winning recognition of my talent. But I'm not well known here and you would do me a great service by allowing me to play a solo in the concert you're organising. The impression I expect to make will bring me the favourable attention of the public, and I shall be indebted to you for giving me the chance to make my first concert a success."

"What would you want to play in my concert?" replied Döhler obligingly.

"A splendid clarinet concerto."

"Very well, Monsieur, I accept your offer; I shall include you in my programme; come to the rehearsal this evening; I'm delighted to help you out."

Evening comes, the orchestra assembles, our man appears, and the rehearsal of his concerto begins. Following the fashion among some virtuosi he doesn't bother to play his own part, confining himself to rehearsing the orchestra and indicating the tempi. The principal tutti, which was rather similar to the Peasants' March in *Der Freischütz*,[30] seemed quite outlandish to those who were there and worried Döhler. "But", he said as he left, "the solo part will make up for it; this chap is probably a fine virtuoso; one can't expect an 'accomplished clarinettist' to be a great composer as well."

The following day, at the concert, somewhat intimidated by Döhler's resounding success, the clarinettist came on stage in his turn. The orchestra played the tutti, ending on a held dominant chord before the first solo passage: "Tram, pam, pam, tira lira la re la", just like the *Freischütz* march. The orchestra reached the dominant chord and stopped; the virtuoso planted himself on his left leg, thrust his right leg forward, put his instrument to his lips, and with both elbows stuck out sideways looked all set to begin. He blew out his cheeks and huffed and puffed and went bright red; all to no avail, for not a sound came from his rebellious instrument. So he put the bell end to his right eye and looked down it as if it were a telescope. Finding nothing, he tried again, and blew furiously: not a sound. In desperation he ordered the musicians to begin the tutti again: "Tram, pam, pam, tira lira la re la", and while the orchestra got to grips with that, the virtuoso placed his clarinet, I won't say between his knees, but rather higher up, with the bell behind and the mouthpiece in front, and frantically set about unscrewing the reed and pushing a cleaning-rod down the tube.

All this took some time, and already the relentless orchestra had finished its tutti and come to rest again on the dominant chord.

"Once more! Once more! From the beginning! From the beginning!"

cries the *suffering artist* [in Balzac's phrase] to the players.[31] And they obey: "Tram, pam, pam, tira lira la re la". And after a few moments there they are again for the third time at the inexorable bar leading into the soloist's entry. But the clarinet isn't ready. "Da capo! Once more! Once more!" And the orchestra sets off merrily again: "Tram, pam, pam, tira lira la re la".

During this last repeat the virtuoso had reassembled the various pieces of his ill-fated instrument, had put it back "between his knees", and was using a penknife from his pocket to scrape frantically at the reed of the clarinet which was . . . you know where.

The whole hall rustled with laughter and whispering: the ladies averted their eyes, or hid in the back of their boxes, while the men stood up to get a better view. Gasps and stifled cries could be heard, while the scandalous virtuoso went on scraping his reed.

Finally he thought it was ready. The orchestra had reached the end of the tutti for the fourth time, so he put the clarinet to his lips, spread his elbows wide, blew, sweated, went red, screwed up his face . . . and not a sound emerged! Then, after a supreme effort, there burst forth, like a sonic lightning flash, the most strident, ear-splitting *quack* you ever heard. You would have thought a hundred pieces of satin were being ripped at once; the shrieks of a swarm of vampires or of a ghoul in labour cannot come near the violence of that frightful *quack*!

The hall resounded with exclamations of delighted horror. There was an explosion of applause, and the distracted virtuoso, advancing to the edge of the platform, stammered out: "Ladies and gentlemen, I cannot . . . an ac . . . cident . . . with my cla . . . rinet . . . but I shall have it re . . . paired . . . and I ask you please to . . . come to my musi . . . cal evening, next Monday, to . . . to . . . to hear *the rest of my concerto*."

. . . .

Musical instruments at the Universal Exhibition

I have absolutely no intention of writing a preamble on industry and Universal Exhibitions.[32] There are some matters on which one can't put forward any hypothesis without laying oneself open to serious risk; and discussing them amounts to sheer ostentation. I realise I'm far from possessing the Olympian calm needed in such circumstances, so instead of attacking systems I find shocking, my understandable despair and frustration often lead me to the other extreme of seeming to accept and approve of them in my mind, if not in what I say or write.

This reminds me of a question I once asked an amateur chemist. Perhaps this amateur, like amateur musicians and philosophers, and indeed many amateurs of every sort, believed in the absurd. Such a belief is widely held. Perhaps, after all, reality is absurd; otherwise it would be cruel of God to have put such a love of absurdity in men's hearts. Anyway, back to my question to the chemist, and his reply.

"Suppose", I said, "you could put a quantity of gunpowder, a hundred kilograms, say, or even a thousand, right at the heart of one of the world's largest mountains, one of the Himalayas, for example, or Chimborazo; if you then ignited it by one of the techniques available nowadays, what would happen? Would it explode, do you think, and would it have sufficient force to blow up such a huge mass, with its enormous density and weight?"

The amateur chemist, taken by surprise, thought for a moment, which is something amateur musicians or philosophers rarely do, then replied hesitantly: "In all probability the gunpowder would not be powerful enough; but it would ignite, of course, and instantaneously produce gases which would be prevented from blowing up by the mass of the mountain. These gases would condense into liquid form, liable at any time to revert to gas and produce a terrific explosion the instant the pressure from above was released." I don't know how correct this dilettante scientist's theory is, but the proposition I put to him may be relevant to my theme.

There are some people, including acquaintances of my own, who, as a result of having to struggle with a mountain of absurdities, experience within themselves a rage that is immeasurable, but not enough to blow up the mountain. They ignite at once but almost immediately submit without fuss, even with a smile, to the rule of unreason, their volcanic eruptions liquefied for the time being.

The liquids produced in this way are generally black and extremely bitter. But sometimes they have neither taste nor colour, or they may even be pleasant in both appearance and taste. These are the most dangerous. In any event, many "firepots", as those monster mines used at the siege of Sebastopol were called,[33] were ignited and plenty of kilograms of gunpowder liquefied during the onerous sittings of the various juries called to give, or rather lend, their advice on industrial products.

. . . .

The special jury appointed to judge musical instruments at the last Universal Exhibition consisted of seven members: composers, performers, acousticians, academics, music-lovers and manufacturers. Taking the view that they were being consulted to ascertain the musical quality of the instruments, they quickly reached agreement on the method they would use to gain the best possible appreciation of qualities of sonority and workmanship, to do justice to useful technical innovations, and to reward skilful manufacturers with the appropriate ranking. In order not to be distracted from this arduous task—more difficult than you may think, I assure you, and extremely tedious, not to say painful—they arranged for the instruments to be brought into the Conservatoire concert hall one after another.

Figure 6. The capture of Sebastopol, September 1855. Gustave Doré (1832–83). Bibliothèque Nationale de France.

The siege of Sebastopol by a combined French and British army lasted a full year from September 1854; the city's fall led to the end of the Crimean War (see page 26).

There were thousands of them, of every sort: harmonious, cacophonous, sonorous, noisy, magnificent, admirable, useless, grotesque, ridiculous, raucous, frightful, fit to charm the angels or set demons' teeth on edge, to wake the dead or send the living to sleep, to make birds sing and dogs bark.

We began by judging the pianos. The piano—at the thought of that terrible instrument my hair stands on end and I feel a tingling in my toes; just by writing the word I am entering volcanic terrain. You of course don't know about pianos, piano-dealers, piano-makers, piano-players and piano-makers' sponsors, male and female. God preserve you from ever doing so! Other instrument makers and dealers are much less fearsome. You can almost say what you think about them, without them complaining too bitterly. You can award first place to the one who most deserves it, without all the rest immediately taking it into their heads to assassinate you. You can go so far as to put the worst in last place without the least objection from the others. You can even tell the friend of a self-styled inventor: "Your friend hasn't invented anything, this isn't new at all, the Chinese have been using his so-called 'invention' for centuries"; the disappointed friend will withdraw almost without a murmur, as no doubt the illustrious Columbus would have done had he been informed that Scandinavian navigators had discovered the American continent long before him.

But the piano, ah, the piano! "My pianos, Monsieur. . . . You can't be serious—placing me second! Giving me a mere silver medal—me, the inventor of the quadruple escapement mortise-peg with screw fixing! I deserve better, Monsieur. I employ six hundred workmen, Monsieur; my firm belongs to me; I export my products not only to Batavia, to Vittoria, to Melbourne, to San Francisco, but even to New Caledonia, to the isle of Mounin-Sima, Monsieur, to Manila, to Tinian, to the Ascension Islands, to Hawaii; there are no pianos but mine at the court of King Kamehameha III,[34] the mandarins of Peking insist on my pianos, you won't hear any others at Nagasaki, Monsieur . . . nor at St.-Germain-en-Laye,[35] for that matter, Monsieur. And you talk of giving me a silver medal, when the gold medal itself would be a pretty mediocre distinction for me. You haven't even recommended me for the ribbon first-class of the Légion d'Honneur. A fine way to treat me! But you'll see, Monsieur, this won't be the end of the matter. I protest, I *shall* protest. I'll take my case to the Emperor, I'll appeal to all the courts of Europe and all the Presidencies of the New World. I'll publish a broadsheet. Hah! A silver medal indeed for the inventor of the quadruple escapement mortise-peg with screw fixing!!!"

That, as you can imagine, detonates the thousand kilograms of gunpowder in the mountain. But as it's absolutely impossible to reply in the appropriate fashion to such outbursts by blowing one's top, condensation of the gases takes place, and nothing remains at the bottom of the firepot except *still water*.

Or again: "Alas, Monsieur, so I haven't won first prize? Is it really true? Can such an iniquity have been perpetrated? The decision must be reconsidered, I demand your support, you must do something! You won't? Oh, it's unbelievable! My pianos deserve better; they are superb instruments, and can hold their own with any at all. A musician like you, Monsieur, cannot fail to recognise that. I'm ruined, Monsieur. Monsieur, I beg you, give me your support. Oh, but it's disgraceful! Monsieur, I beseech you . . . take pity on my tears . . . I've no recourse left . . . but the Seine. . . . I'm going there now. Ah, what cruelty! I'd never have believed it of you. My poor children!"

And still one cannot explode.

Rose water!

Or again: "I've just come from Germany, where they're all laughing themselves sick at your jury. So the top piano-maker didn't win? He's been placed second, has he? He deserves nothing better than that? What nonsense! Are you saying the second best is now best? Has there ever been such a thing? I hope you're going to start all over again, for your own sakes at least. I certainly don't know about this marvellous piano you've given the prize to; I've never seen or heard it; but there it is, a decision like this makes you all look silly."

Eau de Cologne!

Or again: "I'm here, Monsieur, on a minor business matter . . . yes, a business matter. It's doubtless an oversight that my firm's pianos have been ranked so low: for everyone knows my firm deserves better. Public opinion has already drawn attention to this . . . oversight, and you will no doubt wish to rejudge the pianos. Now, to prevent another blunder being made, let me take the liberty of enlightening you, gentlemen, members of the jury, on my firm's strengths. I do a great deal of important business . . . and neither my partners nor I make too much fuss about . . . sacrifices . . . which are necessary in certain . . . circumstances. I'm sure you understand my meaning." From the way the juror frowns, the businessman realises his meaning has *not* been understood, and retires.

Camphorated fire-water!

Then again: "Monsieur, I've come about . . ."

"You've come about your pianos?"

"Yes, Monsieur."

"Your firm deserves better, is that it? We should do the judging again? The first prize should go to you?"

"That's right, Monsieur!"

"Thunder and lightning!"

The juror storms out of the room, slamming the door behind him so hard that the handle falls off.

Aqua fortis! Hydrocyanic acid!

Such were the scenes inflicted upon unfortunate jurors in the past by

piano-makers, piano-players and piano-makers' sponsors, if we are to believe a discharged former juror, now consigned to the scrap-heap and no
doubt a mischief-maker, for we certainly don't see anything like it these
days.

Let me resume my story.

For this latest Exhibition there were seven jurors. Such a mysterious,
cabalistic, fatidical number! Seven Greek sages, seven sacred candlestick
branches, seven primary colours, seven notes of the scale, seven deadly
sins, seven theological virtues. . . . No, sorry, only three, or at least there
used to be three, but I'm not sure whether Hope still exists.

On my oath as a juror, then, there were seven of us: a Scotsman, an
Austrian, a Belgian and four Frenchmen: which seems to show that France
alone is richer in jurors than Scotland, Belgium and Austria put together.[36]

This tribunal constituted a "class". Following minute and careful ex-
amination of all pertinent questions, this class then had to join in discussions with five or six other classes, forming a "group". The group had to
pronounce a majority verdict on the validity of the decisions taken separately by each class. Thus the class responsible for examining silk or woollen
fabrics, and that which had considered the merits of goldsmiths, engravers
and cabinet-makers, and several other classes, all found themselves asking
us musicians whether the prizes had been fairly awarded to this maker of
fabrics or that bronze merchant, and so on. At first my colleagues in the
musical class seemed a little hesitant about answering such questions. They
found these summary judgments rather odd, although this would not have
been the case if any of them had been called on four years earlier at the
Great Exhibition in London, where this same system was already in use
and I was able to serve my apprenticeship.

It's true I had a distressing moment of anguish on the day of the first
meeting of our group in 1851, when the English jurors, seeing me hesitate,
called on me to vote on the proposed awards for surgical instrument makers. I thought at once of all the arms and legs those terrible instruments
were going to have to amputate, of the skulls they would trepan, of the
tumours they would excise, of the arteries and nerves they would be used
to clamp, of the gallstones they would grind to powder!!! I knew not the
first thing about surgery, and even less about instrument-making techniques.
Besides, even if I had been Amussat and Charrière combined,[37] I hadn't
examined any of the dangerous instruments in question; and yet I was
about to state plainly and categorically that one maker's instruments were
much better than another's, and that A rather than B deserved the first
prize! The sweat stood out on my brow and I felt a chill run down my spine
at the thought of it. God forgive me if by my vote I have caused the deaths
of hundreds of wounded Englishmen, Frenchmen, Piedmontese and even
Russians, operated on unsuccessfully in the Crimea as a result of prizes
being given to inferior surgical instruments.

Quelle aurait dû être la composition de l'orchestre dirigé par M. Berlioz dans la salle de l'Exposition universelle.

(Cham, *Charivari*, 25 novembre 1855.)

Figure 7. "The likely composition of the orchestra conducted by Monsieur Berlioz in the Hall of the Universal Exhibition." Cartoon by Cham (Amédée de Noé, 1818–79) from *Le Charivari*, 25 November 1855. Richard Macnutt Collection, Withyham. In addition to his role as a juror (see pages 25–34), Berlioz conducted concerts in the Palais de l'Industrie on 15, 16, 18 and 24 November, the first of these with an audience of 40,000 for the presentation of awards by Prince Napoleon, and with 1,250 performers.

Little by little, though, my feelings of guilt subsided: the mine had certainly been detonated, but as usual the mountain had not blown up, and the firepot now contains nothing but a small quantity of *distilled water.* Not long ago in Paris, without the least twinge of discomfort, I awarded a prize to a wrench for pulling teeth. Besides, since this group system has been adopted in both England and France without anyone complaining, it must be good, utilitarian and moral, and it reflects nothing but shame on me to confess the feeble intelligence which makes me incapable of understanding the thinking behind it.

"There's a touch of irony in this humility of yours", you may say; "I suppose your group upset the musicians by overturning some of their judgments, and you're still bitter about it?"

Not at all. The correctness of our judgments was questioned by the group in no more than two or three instances. The rest of the time our non-musical colleagues raised their right hands to agree with us with a unison worthy of a true ensemble. No, these are just antiphilosophical reflections on human institutions which I pass on for what they are worth, which is nothing.

Well then, the seven of us sat in the Director's box in the Conservatoire concert hall, and each day the stage opposite us groaned under the weight of a batch of at least ninety pianos. Three expert piano teachers each played a different piece on the same instrument, each one always playing the same piece; thus we heard each of the three pieces ninety times a day, making 270 pieces in total, from eight in the morning until four in the afternoon. We experienced periodic changes of mood. At certain times misery was replaced by a sort of somnolence, and since two of the three pieces were, when all is said and done, very beautiful, one by Pergolesi and the other by Rossini, we listened to them with enjoyment; they plunged us into a pleasant reverie. Soon afterwards human frailty took its toll: we suffered stomach cramps and actual nausea. But now is not the time to explore this physiological phenomenon.

In order not to be influenced by the identity of the manufacturers of those awful pianos, we had had the idea of judging them without knowing whom they belonged to or were made by. For this reason the maker's name was hidden by a large sheet of cardboard with a number on it. Our test pianists, before beginning to play, would shout from the stage "Number 37" or "Number 20" or whatever. Each of the jurors made his notes by reference to that number. When the 270th piece had been played, the jurors, not content with this test alone, went on stage and examined the mechanism of each instrument close up, trying out the keyboard for themselves and modifying their initial opinions accordingly, if appropriate.

On the first day we heard grand pianos, a considerable number of them. The seven jurors rapidly picked out six, in the following order:

Figure 8. Conservatoire, Paris—concert hall. Woodcut by P. S. Germain, 1843. Richard Macnutt Collection, Withyham.

"The seven of us [jurors] sat in the Director's box in the Conservatoire concert hall, and each day the stage opposite us groaned under the weight of . . . at least ninety pianos" (page 32).

No. 9 was unanimously placed first.
No. 19 was, also unanimously, placed second.
Six out of seven voted No. 5 third.
Four out of seven voted No. 11 fourth.
Six voted No. 17 fifth.
Five voted No. 22 sixth.

Thinking that the position of the pianos on the stage, and their nearness to or distance from various sound reflectors could make a difference to their tone quality, the jurors then had the idea of hearing these six instruments a second time, in a different order and in different positions. Moreover, so as not to be influenced by their first impressions, and because they knew the colour, shape and position of each instrument, they turned their backs to the stage while the pianos were being moved, so they wouldn't know where they were put. They listened like that, without turning round, and without knowing which was played first, second, and so on; and when they consulted their notes afterwards, and the numbers were collated with the new sequence in which the pianos had just been heard, it eventually emerged that the votes for each instrument were exactly the same as in the first assessment, so clear-cut were the qualities of each. It would be hard to cite a more remarkable occurrence of this kind; it also demonstrates the painstaking care with which the jury carried out its task.

After each session the result of the voting was officially recorded in writing; a member of the jury went to uncover the names hidden by the cardboard sheets and wrote them down with their corresponding numbers. His declaration was attached to the record and enclosed in an envelope sealed with the Conservatoire's official seal.

Thus throughout the long weeks devoted to the piano judging, nobody, not even the members of the jury (except one), knew the names of the award-winning makers;[38] and that is why none of the makers themselves could protest, or complain, or come and say "Monsieur, I deserve better", etc.

The same approach was followed for baby grands, square pianos and uprights. I'm pleased to say that not one juror perished as a result of this ordeal, and the majority of them are now convalescing.

A rival to Érard

The manufacture of musical instruments is occasionally taken up very successfully by amateur craftsmen. They may even produce striking innovations in the field. Yet these men, as modest as they are ingenious, wouldn't dream of sending their products to Universal Exhibitions; they seek for themselves neither patent rights nor gold medals nor even the lowest-rank ribbon of the Légion d'Honneur.

One of them paid a visit one day to his neighbour in the Provence countryside, Monsieur d'Ortigue, a well-known critic and distinguished musician.[39] As he entered the living-room, he said "Ah, I see you have a piano."

"Yes, a fine Érard."

"I have one too."

"An Érard?"

"No, it's actually a piano of my own. I made it myself, using an entirely new system. If you're interested in seeing it, I'll have it loaded on to my cart tomorrow and bring it over."

"Please do."

The following day the rustic amateur arrives with his cart; the piano is brought in and the lid opened, and Monsieur d'Ortigue is very surprised to see that the keyboard consists exclusively of white keys.

"What about the black keys?", he asks.

"The black keys? Oh, you mean for sharps and flats; all that nonsense belongs to the old-fashioned piano, I don't use them on mine."

Figure 9. Universal Exhibition, Paris, 1855—closing ceremony. Sepia lithograph by Ph. Benoist and A. Bayot. Richard Macnutt Collection, Withyham.
"Exhibition ending soon. Our friends, judges of international competition, well satisfied" (page 37).

Diplomatic Correspondence

To Her Majesty Aïmata Pomaré, Queen of Tahiti, Ehimeo, Huahine, Raiatea, Bora-Bora, Tubuia-Manu and other islands, whose products have recently won the silver medal at the Universal Exhibition[40]

Majesty, Gracious Queen,

Exhibition ending soon. Our friends, judges of international competition, well satisfied—I also.

Have suffered much, sweated much, to hear and judge musical instruments, pianos, organs, flutes, trumpets, drums, guitars and tamtams. Judges very irritated with international manufacturers of pianos, organs, flutes, trumpets, drums, guitars and tamtams.

International competitors all wanting be first, all insisting friends be last; offering us drinks of ava and presents of fruit and pigs. We judges furious, but even without fruit or pigs giving fair verdicts on best manufacturers of pianos, organs, flutes, trumpets, drums, guitars and tamtams. Then, when all fully studied, tested and heard, we proper judges having to find other judges, who not having studied, tested or heard musical instruments, and asking them if ones chosen by us really best. They replying no. So we again very irritated, upset, wanting get away from France and Exhibition.

Then becoming *tayos* (friends) again with other judges. They doing same thing in turn: after themselves fully studying and assessing *meres* (clubs), *maros* (grass skirts), *prahos* (canoes), *tapas* (mats) and crowns exhibited by people of Tahiti, asking us if they right to give prize to *Tahiti-Una* (Queen of Tahiti). We, good fellows, knowing nothing, at once replying yes. So judges deciding to award silver medal to Gracious Majesty, for crowns made of arrowroot bark sent by fair queen to poor Europeans who never seeing them before. Then everyone going *kaï-kaï* (having banquet); and during meal, international judges speaking much of gracious Tahiti-Una, asking if she speak French, if she over twenty. International judges, even *ratitas* (nobles), very ignorant; not understanding single word of Kanak language, not knowing Gracious Majesty named Aïmata, born in 1811 (I saying nothing of this), married third time to young *arii* (chieftain), favourite of your father Pomaré III, who giving him same name as mark of friendship; nor having any idea that *po* mean "night" and *maré* "cough", since once your great-grandfather Otu having bad cold and coughing much in night, and next day one of his guards saying "King po maré" (King cough

Figure 10. Queen Pomaré IV of Tahiti with three of her *arii* (chiefs): her second husband Fa'aite and two of their eight sons. Bibliothèque Nationale de France. "International judges speaking much of gracious *Tahiti-Una*, asking if she speak French, if she over twenty." Queen Pomaré, born in 1813, reigned for a full 50 years, from 1827 to 1877 (see pages 36–39).

in night), which giving His Majesty inspired idea of taking name for himself and becoming King Pomaré First.

Frenchmen knowing gracious queen having many children, and laughing much that Gracious Majesty not wearing stockings. They saying also fair Una smoking too much large cigars, drinking too much large glasses of eau-de-vie, playing too much cards alone at night with commander of French garrison which protecting islands.[41]

After meal, international judges going together to Exhibition galleries to see product of your fair hands, to which they just having given prize without knowing what it like, and at once finding it charming and agreeing Tahitian crowns, though delicate, nonetheless quite secure, more secure than much European crowns.

International judges, *arii* (chiefs) as well as *boué-ratiras* (farmers, landowners), starting to talk again on way out about fair queen and silver medal she soon able to hang around neck; and each declaring he very much liking to take medal's place for hour or two. Lucky for fair Una-Aïmata this not possible, for we international judges all very ugly.

Not one of us tattooed, not one comparing with young men of Bora-Bora, still less with great, handsome (though French) captain who commanding Protectorate three years ago and who, let us admit, such fine protector.

Farewell, Gracious Majesty, Exhibition *tititeu-teu* (staff, servants) already busy making silver medal, and pretty box to put it in, with plenty big fat cigars and two pairs fine gold-embroidered stockings. All soon on way to islands.

I wishing at first write to Una-Aïmata in Kanak, but then not daring, since I not knowing beautiful language well enough, so simply writing in French as being spoken at Tahitian court.

Our *ioreana* (salutations, greetings) and friendly wishes to French friends of Protectorate; hoping no troubles spoil your *houpa-houpas* (entertainments), and great *Oro* (god) deliver you from all Pritchards.[42] With two respectful *comas* (kisses) for delicate royal hands, I remaining, fair Aïmata, Your Majesty's humble tititeu-teu,

Hector Berlioz
One of international judges

Paris, 18 October 1855

P.S. I omitting mention to Gracious Majesty possibility of tying embroidered stockings to medal and cigars and wearing on head.

Prudence and sagacity of a provincial—Alexandre's melodium

A music-lover who had heard Alexandre's melodium organs highly praised in every quarter wanted to donate one to the church of the village where he lived.[43] "This instrument", he thought to himself, "is said to have a delightful sound quality, with a dreamy, mysterious character which makes it particularly suitable for the expression of religious sentiment; it's moderately priced too, and anyone who can more or less manage a piano keyboard can play it without difficulty. That would be just what I need. But one should never buy a pig in a poke, so why don't I go to Paris and judge for myself whether the eulogies lavished on Alexandre's instrument by the press throughout Europe, and even in America, are justified? I'll look at it, listen to it, try it out, and then decide whether to buy it."

The prudent music-lover came to Paris, obtained directions to Alexandre's shop and lost no time in going there.

To understand his extraordinary behaviour after examining the organs, you should know that Alexandre's instruments, in addition to the bellows which produce a flow of air to vibrate the copper reeds, are equipped with a system of hammers designed to strike the reeds and set them in motion just at the moment when the air flow begins to have its effect. The vibration caused by the hammer striking the reed makes the action of the bellows more immediate, and avoids the brief delay which would otherwise occur in producing the sound. The action of the hammers striking the copper reeds also produces a small, dry sound, imperceptible when the bellows are functioning, but which can be heard quite distinctly from close by when only the keys are pressed.

With this explanation, let us follow our music-lover into Alexandre's large showroom, amongst the harmonious population of instruments displayed there.

"I should like to buy an organ."

"Certainly, sir, we can arrange for you to listen to some and then you can choose."

"No, no, I don't want you to arrange for me to listen to them. The skill of your players is bound to bamboozle a listener concerning the instruments' failings, or even turn them into advantages. I insist on trying them out myself, free from any other influence or impression. Let me be left alone for a while in your shop."

"Whatever you wish, sir. We'll leave you alone. All the melodiums are open, please try them."

Thereupon Monsieur Alexandre departs; the music-lover goes to an organ, and not realising that to play it you have to work the bellows underneath the case with your feet, he runs his fingers over the keyboard as you would to try out a piano.

At first he is astonished not to hear anything, but almost at once his attention is caught by the small, dry sound of the hammer mechanism I have described: click, clack, tick, tack, ping, pong; nothing more. He attacks the keys with redoubled energy: still click, clack, tick, tack, ping, pong. "This is scarcely credible," says he, "it's ludicrous! How could such a miserable instrument make itself heard in a church, even a small one? And to think these things are praised all over the place, and Monsieur Alexandre has made a fortune manufacturing them! It just shows how far shameless advertising and irresponsible journalism have gone."

Even so, the indignant music-lover goes to another organ, then another, then a fourth, to satisfy his conscience. But since he always tries them out in the same way, the result is always the same: click, clack, tick, tack, ping, pong. He stands up at last, his mind made up, takes his hat, and is making for the door when Monsieur Alexandre, who has been watching the whole thing from a distance, comes hurrying up:

"Well, Monsieur, have you made your choice?"

"My choice! Good God, you certainly lay it on thick for us provincials, with your reviews, your advertisements, your medals, your prizes. You must think us pretty stupid if you have the nerve to offer us such ludicrous instruments. The first requirement of music is that it should be heard! Well, your so-called organs, which thank goodness I have tried out for myself, are inferior to the most pitiful spinets of the last century—they produce literally no sound at all—no, Monsieur, none at all. I'm not deaf, nor stupid either. Good day to you!"

———

The tromba marina—The saxophone—Experts in instrumentation

At each performance of *Le Bourgeois Gentilhomme* at the Théâtre-Français, the occupants of the pit commit a howler which cannot fail to make any musicians in the audience laugh heartily.[44]

In the first scene of Act II, the music master says, "You will need three voices, a treble, a high tenor and a bass, accompanied by a viola da gamba, a theorbo and a harpsichord for the basso continuo, with two violins to play the ritornelli."

Monsieur Jourdain replies: "We must have a tromba marina too. I like the tromba marina, and it harmonises well."

At the words "tromba marina" the pit unfailingly explodes with mirth. These fine fellows imagine the tromba marina, which is a very melodious instrument consisting of a single string passing over a bridge and played like a cello, to be some horrible wind instrument, a sort of triton's shell, fit to outbray a donkey. They suppose Molière was making Monsieur Jourdain utter a colossal stupidity, when in fact his remark is merely naïve. It's no more absurd than if some present-day Monsieur Jourdain were to say in similar circumstances, "We must have a guitar too. I like the guitar, and it harmonises well."

A Jupiter among critics who recently made a violent attack on Sax's admirable instruments ranked the saxophone among the most frightful and offensive to the ear.[45] The saxophone is a reed instrument with a delightful veiled tone—he had confused it with the saxhorn, a brass instrument with a mouthpiece.

This distinguished and conscientious Aristarchus had no doubt studied instrumentation from the pit of the Théâtre-Français.[46]

"Ha ha ha! The tromba marina! Bravo, pit! The dreadful saxophone! Bravo, Jupiter!"

Jaguarita—Female savages

All civilised men with a little imagination have at some time in their lives shared the same illusion regarding the female savages of the Americas, confusing them with the graceful Tahitians, who are not savages at all. They form strange fantasies about these dusky creatures and picture them possessed of formidable and wonderful charms. "Mexican (or Guyanese, or Chilean, or young Comanche) girls", they say, "are enchanting daughters of unfettered nature, with the warmth of the tropics, gazelles' eyes, humming-birds' voices, the suppleness of liana, the bravery of lionesses, the constancy of turtledoves; with the perfume of pineapple and the satiny skin of camellias; maidens worthy of an ideal love, like Chateaubriand's Atala, Marmontel's Cora or de Jouy's Amazily."[47]

Young idiots! Not-so-young idiots! You are the ones behaving like children of nature, by clinging to such illusions! You only have to have crossed the Atlantic once or twice to have been disabused of these poetic fancies. As for the tropics, you should know by now that the tropic of Cancer is no warmer than that of Capricorn; that young Comanche girls with gazelles' eyes have the intelligence of Canada geese; that their voices are grating; that their skin is either rough or greasy to the touch, and the colour of rusty iron; that their bravery extends only to cutting the throats of sleeping children; that their constancy lasts only twenty-four hours; that their perfume, not a bit like pineapple, is strong enough to kill the mosquitos which so torment Europeans.

Besides, you young poets, Chateaubriand's Atala was a white European girl, not a female savage at all; no other maiden like Marmontel's Cora has ever been seen in Peru; and de Jouy's Amazily, who called herself Marina, was a real virago according to Cortez's companions: she fully deserved the torture with which the Aztecs so often threatened her, and after living for six or seven years with the ravager of her country, otherwise known as the conqueror of Mexico, she married a plain corporal in the great man's army. It is said, in fact, that she ended up carrying brandy kegs in a Spanish regiment and died an old vivandière.[48]

Thus youth, imagination and emotional naïvety, together with a fresh sensibility and irrepressible longing for an unknown beauty, fascinate certain souls and lead them to cause cruel delusions in others. Messieurs Halévy, de Saint-Georges and Leuven, who evidently possess many of these qualities, have produced in their opera *Jaguarita* a work that I fear will prove dangerous for the civilised young men of the boulevards and the Temple district.[49]

For these enthusiasts, who seldom cross the Atlantic, have few opportunities to regain their sense of reality. So, you see, most of them have fallen prey to the wildest fantasies about savages since the first performance of *Jaguarita*.[50] Some practise archery in their attics, others try poisoning arrows by dipping them in cheap wine; this one eats his meat raw, that one goes about scalping barber's blocks; all of them would go naked in the full glare of the sun if the sun ever showed itself again; and all this just for love of the Guyanese woman whose image dominates their thoughts, inflames their hearts and makes their pulses race, for the Cora, the Amazily with the ravishing plumage and the seductive warble, whose deceptive charms have been revealed to them in *Jaguarita*.

Mme. Cabel, who plays the part, is much to blame for adding the attractions of her own civilised charms to the glamour of this poetic creation.[51] If the conjunction of art and nature, of satin and humming-bird feathers, of pearls and cashew-apples, of gold bracelets and necklaces of human teeth, succeeds in overwhelming the senses of our young opera-loving workers, Paris, until recently so active and industrious, will soon present the desolate aspect of the Carthaginian capital following Aeneas's arrival, when Dido was out of sorts; and we shall be saying like the Latin poet, "Pendent opera interrupta!"[52]

You poets, you Virgils of every age and every land, little do you suspect how many misfortunes are brought about by your *un*interrupted operas, or how many tears they cause to be shed, which you make no attempt to dry! If it were not evident that poets are superior beings, sent occasionally to earth by Providence to accomplish a mysterious mission, no doubt in accord with the great laws of the universe, it would be hard to prevent oneself from cursing their appearance, blaspheming their works and banishing the poets themselves from our republics, after decking them with flowers.

But we aren't like Plato, true philosophers though we may be. We have the advantage over that great man of possessing the light of Christianity.

We know God's designs are unfathomable, and we resign ourselves to the poets He sends us. We don't deck them with flowers, but we put up with them.

———————

The Astucio family

Monsieur Scribe, in his opera *The Court Concert,*[53] has portrayed under the name of Signor Astucio a character who aroused, and still arouses, a combination of admiration and awe among artists.

At the time of the opera's first performances it was said that Astucio was a faithful portrait of the composer Paër, hardly exaggerated at all.[54] It was going rather far in my opinion to attach the name of this Italian master to Monsieur Scribe's vignette.

Was Paër the only rascally musician of his period? Is the race of Astucios extinct? And was the composer of *Griselda* its chief member? Phooey! There always have been and there always will be Astucios; even now we are surrounded, circumvented, undermined and contaminated by them. There are prudent Astucios and foolhardy Astucios, stupid Astucios and witty Astucios, poor Astucios and rich Astucios. Look out for this last sort— they're the most dangerous of all. The witty Astucio may not be rich, but the rich Astucio is nearly always possessed of wit. The former pokes his nose into everything and grabs what he can; the latter wriggles out of even the most hopeless positions without leaving a trace: you could shut him in a bottle like a genie and he'd get out without even removing the cork. The former uses his wit to go where money can't buy admittance, as easily as entering a ruin. But where wit is commonplace and therefore worthless, the latter knows how to manipulate situations to produce fabulous results.

Most Astucios have learnt from ants the art of destroying without seeming to attack.

The white ants of India establish themselves in a beam and little by little eat away its interior; then they move on to another beam, and to all the other supports of the house in turn. The inhabitants of the doomed dwelling suspect nothing; they live in it, sleep in it, even dance in it with a sense of total security; until one fine night, with beams, trusses and floorboards completely eaten away, the entire house collapses and crushes them.

Let's not forget the patron Astucio. His silvery locks demand respect; his smile is full of benevolence; he instinctively patronises everyone; patronage is his mission. Twenty-five years ago he patronised Beethoven and gently strangulated him by saying, "It's beautiful, but it's only a beginning. This is just a *transitional school.*" Whenever he hears a piece by one of his present-day protégés, he applauds ostentatiously and says to his neighbours (while still applauding), "It's dreadful! For a start there isn't a single note of his own in it. It's copied from Gluck, who copied it from Handel." Then he adds, with rather more animation, "And *he* copied it from *me*." He's the doyen of the tribe.

Then there is the little dog Astucio. He seems to bite playfully, like puppies do when cutting their teeth. But in reality he bites with a concentrated fury which causes little apprehension because of its powerlessness. The best line to take with him when his nipping becomes a nuisance is to follow the example of the Newfoundland dog which, when pestered by a King Charles spaniel, picked the little dog up by the scruff of its neck, solemnly carried it, yelping, to the edge of a balcony overlooking the Thames and delicately let go.

But all Astucios, large or small, with or without wit, with or without teeth, with or without money, even when they're not behaving like white ants, know how to imitate corals and madrepores in constructing underwater ramparts which make it impossible to land on beautiful oceanic islands.[55] These ramparts are built up with extreme slowness, yet they rise continuously, inch by inch, until they reach the surface. The insects working on them are so active and so numerous! And the imprudent navigator who, not knowing the reefs around Tinian or Tongatapu,[56] puts to sea in that part of the world without due care, will one day perish, wrecked on a fresh outcrop of coral hidden from view by the waves. How many La Pérouses have fallen victim like this to the reef-building insects![57]

Marriages of convenience

In the last act of another opera by Monsieur Scribe (*Jenny Bell*),[58] we see a delightful young girl, obedient to her father's will, marrying a fat old imbecile of a goldsmith and virtuously pretending to be a loose woman in order to put off a young man whom she loves and who in turn loves her dearly. This ending seemed shocking to me, and put me in a temper. Yes, when I see examples of such stupid devotion, of such insolent paternal demands, of such infamous cruelty, of such fine passions being snuffed out, of hearts being so brutally broken, I'd like to be able to put all reasonable people, all virtuous heroines, all enlightened fathers in a sack weighted with a hundred thousand kilos of good sense and throw them into the sea, to the accompaniment of my most virulent curses.

· ·

You think I'm joking! Well, you're wrong. I *was* furious just now; I'm primed with such hatred for the father Capulets and the Count Parises who have or would like to have their own Juliets that the smallest dramatic spark sets me alight and causes an explosion. The grotesque virtue of *Jenny Bell* really exasperated me. Besides, there are so many father Capulets and Count Parises, and so few Juliets! Great love and great art are so alike! The beautiful is so beautiful! Epic passions are so rare! The daytime sunshine is so weak! Life is so short, death so certain! You hundredfold cretins, who devise these self-denials, these battles against sublime instincts, these marriages of convenience between women and monkeys, between art and base industry, between poetry and commerce, curses on you! Damnation take you! Why can't you just argue amongst yourselves, hearing nothing but your own rasping voices and seeing nothing but your own livid faces in icy perpetuity!

Great news

It has just been discovered that the English national anthem, *God Save the King*, attributed to Lully, who's supposed to have composed it to French words for the young ladies of St.-Cyr, isn't by Lully at all.[59] British pride repudiates such an origin. *God Save the King* is now by Handel: he wrote it for the English, to the hallowed English text.

There are people specially licensed to unearth these musical deceptions.

They proved long ago that *Orpheus* isn't by Gluck, nor *Le Devin du village* by Rousseau, nor *La Vestale* by Spontini, nor the *Marseillaise* by Rouget de l'Isle.[60] In fact some people even go so far as to claim *Der Freischütz* isn't by Castil-Blaze!!![61]

More news

Mme. Stoltz,[62] they say, is going back to Brazil! She has just signed her contract: 450,000 francs, insurance against seasickness, six maids and eight horses!!! A clear view of the bay of Rio, night and day! Real sunshine! Genuine enthusiasm! Rivers of diamonds! Sashes embroidered by the hands of Marquesas! Doves and negro slaves released after every performance! Not to mention free men becoming slaves! Joking apart, how could the diva resist the truly magnificent offers made her by Rio?

Well, fellow-Frenchmen, at least let *us* put up some resistance, and not allow our heaven to be ransacked in this manner and our stars removed by these Antipodean peoples who are all upside-down.

Barley sugar—Heavy music

People in the fashionable world imagine that all these theatres which have blossomed recently, where comedy is a serious business, are ill-kept, ill-furnished, ill-lit haunts of ill repute. In general they are quite right, but it takes all sorts to make a world. Some are indeed haunts of ill repute, but others are not haunted at all. Some are ill-furnished, others merely famished. One of them indeed—the Folies-Nouvelles theatre—is quite a stylish little place, simple, attractive, brightly lit, and patronised by a well-dressed and well-mannered audience.[63]

A custom has developed there (this may explain the good manners of its clientèle) of eating large quantities of barley-sugar sticks in the intervals. As soon as the curtain falls, the young lions in the pit stand up, give a friendly wave to the gazelles in the gallery, and cram their mouths with long different-coloured objects which they suck with quite remarkable earnestness.[64]

I'm wrong in saying these sugary objects are of different colours: a particular colour is settled on for each interval, and doesn't change until the following act. After the initial scene-setting, everybody sucks yellow; as the climax approaches, pink is on every tongue; and at the dénouement, green triumphs, and everyone sucks green. It's an extraordinary sight, which takes some getting used to. Why this pleasant custom exists at the Folies-Nouvelles, how it came to be established, what keeps it going . . . these are questions to which truly wise men can only reply as they reply to so many simple questions:

I haven't the faintest idea!

And just to show how badly informed we are in Paris about even the most essential things, a fortnight ago I didn't know where the Folies-Nouvelles theatre was, and it was only by asking people all along the boulevard who looked as if they might be willing to help, "Monsieur, may I venture to ask you to be so kind as to take the trouble to direct me to the Folies-Nouvelles theatre?" that I eventually found it. And this theatre is not only most attractive, as I said, but it has music. It has a jolly little orchestra, well directed by a skilful virtuoso, Monsieur Bernardin, and several far from incompetent singers. I went there that evening, on the recommendation of one of my colleagues, to attend a "venture into serious music" in the form of a new opera entitled *The Caulker*.[65]

Serious music at the Folies-Nouvelles—that's a pretty strange idea, I said to myself all along the boulevard. But it's certainly one way of justifying the jolly little theatre's name. Anyway, we shall see. Well, see we did, and our fears were quickly dispelled. The directors of the Folies are men of too much wit and good sense to fall into such grave error, in a manner so

Figure 11. *Lions* and *Lionesses* ("Lionnes"). Gustave Doré (1832–83). Bibliothèque Nationale de France.

"As soon as the curtain falls, the young lions in the pit give a friendly wave to the gazelles in the gallery" (page 47). 'Lions' and 'lionesses' were terms for fashionable young men and women.

prejudicial to their interests. We should make it clear at once that they never dreamed of such a thing. What on earth was my colleague thinking when he spoke to me seriously of *The Caulker* as serious music! If its composer had played a silly prank like that, all the yellow, red and green sticks of barley sugar would have disappeared and been replaced by common black liquorice, the young lions in the pit would have gone scarlet with fury, and the gazelles in the gallery would have hidden their muzzles behind veils.

Just imagine! Putting on serious music without having to—that would have been a real *folie*! Those words "serious music", or "heavy music", a phrase used by some people to mean the same thing, send shivers down my spine! They remind me of the hard, cruel, "heavy" ordeals which I have had to endure on my travels! The most recent of these was the only one that didn't end in tears; indeed it ended very satisfactorily—without ever getting started.

It was in a great northern city whose inhabitants have an almost frenzied passion for boredom. The city has an enormous concert hall, to which people rush in droves whenever they can be sure of catching something really heavy. Far from having to *be* paid, they actually pay to get in. Nobody seems to have thought of inscribing on the wall of this temple the famous motto which shines in letters of gold in the concert hall of another great northern city:

Res severa est verum gaudium[66]

which a malicious joker of my acquaintance has translated as "Boredom is the true pleasure".

Well then, I thought it my duty one day to go and hear one of the heaviest and most celebrated items in this great city's musical repertoire. Since all the seats were sold, I set out to find one of those touts who sell tickets near the hall at exorbitant prices. I was doing a deal with one of them when a member of the orchestra that was going to perform the *rem severam* caught sight of me and said, "What are you up to?"

"I'm haggling for a ticket, since I've never heard the masterpiece on today's programme."

"And why must you hear it?"

"For several reasons: conformity . . . desire to try something new. . . ."

"Really? Didn't I see you in the hall a fortnight ago, listening to the whole of our most recent masterpiece?"

"Yes. What of it?"

"Well, that should give you an idea of the old masterpiece we're going to play today. They're exactly the same, except the old masterpiece is twice as long as the new one and seven times as boring."

"Seven times?"

"At least."

"That's enough."

So I put my wallet back in my pocket and went off much relieved.

That is why "heaviness" in music sometimes fills me with such alarm. But on this occasion my terror turned out to be needless panic, with nothing but my colleague's letter to justify it. *The Caulker* is an entirely good-natured little opera, humming with nice big cheerful waltzes and nice little tunes which are gay, wanton and full of vitality. Not for the world would the composer of this amiable score, Monsieur Cahen, have wanted to appear "heavy" in the eyes of the honest folk who come to applaud it. And what a reception his work had! What a success! At the dénouement, the young lions and the gazelles showed rapturous enthusiasm, and the little green barley-sugar sticks were going in and out of every mouth like locomotive pistons.

The Evil Eye

Monsieur X*** directs a frightful little theatre in Paris which decency forbids me to name. This theatre and its director both possess the "evil eye". Anyone who shakes the director's hand usually dies within the year, and anyone entering the theatre is invariably laid low by violent diarrhoea.

At a house which I visited recently, our host, who is simple and sceptical enough to doubt the influence of the evil eye, decided to tease one of his guests, unlike himself a man of great intelligence and a firm believer, by playing a trick on him. Each guest's name was written in the usual way on a slip of paper placed in front of his napkin. He arranged for the slip at his unsuspecting victim's place to be turned back to front, and showed him to his seat, saying "Here's your place". The poor chap sat down without a qualm, unfolded his napkin, mechanically turned over the slip of paper which he thought bore his name, and discovered instead that of Monsieur X***, written on a ticket from the evil eye theatre. He recoiled in horror, intelligent man that he was, and there and then, without any warning, was violently sick . . . and before dinner, too!

Ordinary music lovers and serious music

A strange air of gloom had been apparent for some time in the Temple district, on the banks of the Ourcq canal, around the Rue Charlot, and even on the Place de la Bastille, among the inhabitants of those areas, young and old—splendid fellows, and normally so cheerful.

Each day with doleful eye and head downcast,
Immersed in dismal thought the hours they passed.[67]

No more games of quoits, no more pipe-smoking. Cigar butts lay on the asphalt with not one cigar-lover bothering to pick them up. No midnight customers came to buy from the muffin seller—her wares were getting stale, her big knife rusting and her oven going out. No urchins or wolf-whistlers went in pursuit of their pretty, provocative prey. No more love, so even less gaiety. The flower-sellers were ignored.

The worthies of the Rue St.-Louis met to consult with those of the Temple district and the St.-Antoine quarter, and decided as a matter of urgency to draw up a detailed official report of the progress of this malady. They sent it by express courier to the Commissioner of Police, who, as you can imagine, could not fail to be shaken to the core by the news. The mayors whom he hastened to inform of it were even more shaken. I must admit the bad news was imparted to them in a somewhat precipitate fashion. You have to manage mayors' feelings carefully.

But the mayors of Paris arrondissements have always felt a real affection for these unfortunate children of the Temple district, so they got over their alarm and hurried to meet in council. The session had scarcely begun when more couriers rushed in, with an immeasurably greater air of consternation than the first, reporting demonstrations by sizeable numbers of people at various points in the capital, characterised by profound gloom and fathomless despondency.

These demonstrations, which were not causing trouble of any kind, were headed by mere youngsters—weedy, pale, skinny lads wearing peaked caps. One had positioned itself on the Boulevard du Temple, opposite the house at number 35, where two popular stars of the Théâtre-Lyrique live, Monsieur and Mme. Meillet; another was blocking the Rue Blanche, from the Rue St.-Lazare to number 11, the home of the revered diva Mme. Cabel;[68] the third demonstration, fourteen times the size of the other two combined, surrounded the mansion of Monsieur Perrin,[69] Director of the Opéra-Comique and the Théâtre-Lyrique.* There the demonstrators remained, their eyes fixed on the windows of the landmarks I've just described. There was an expression of mournful reproach in their looks, and the crowd, surrounding the young leader they had chosen, "mirrored his silence, ranged all about him".[70]

---

*It will be evident that my story does not relate to the present. Everything to do with the management of this theatre and the behaviour of its clientele is quite different now.

This new news set the seal on the mayors' agitation, and greatly increased the anxiety of their chairman. Several voices were raised almost simultaneously from the body of the council demanding to be heard. All of them were given the floor, and all with one accord fell instantly silent: *vox faucibus haesit.*[71] Such was the emotion each felt. But the chairman, who had retained some presence of mind, called back the bearers of this new news and questioned them in turn:

"What is the reason", he asked sharply, "for this sadness, this melancholy, this dumb despair? For these dejected looks, these demonstrations, this passive protest? Have symptoms of cholera broken out again in the Temple district?"[72]

"No, Mr. Chairman."

"Are the alcohol sellers putting less wine than usual in their water?"

"No, sir, they're mixing their cocktails the same as usual."

"Have false rumours been circulating about the siege of Sebastopol?"[73]

"No."

"Well what is it then? And why have they chosen these three particular places as rallying points for their demonstrations? It's very worrying."

"Mr. Chairman, we couldn't understand it at all at first, but in the end we got it. With respect, sir, it would appear these people are devotees of the Théâtre-Lyrique."

"So?"

"Well, sir, they're passionate lovers of music, but of one sort only—light music, music as genial as their manners and behaviour. They believed implicitly what they'd been told about the Théâtre-Lyrique, that it was created and brought into being just for them, to satisfy this need for aesthetic sensation that has tormented them so long. They'd managed to cling to this hope until the Théâtre-Lyrique's latest reopening; but then they found themselves forced to abandon it. Now they think they've been duped.

"'We see it plainly now', they say; 'this isn't a light music theatre, a theatre with straightforward tunes, the sort of theatre needed for the jolliest and simplest people in the world. Far from it, all the pieces performed there so far have been obscure highbrow works we don't understand at all. And it's obvious from their insistence on repeating the whole of last year's repertory that the performers and the Director mean to continue like this, putting on only the heavy sort of operas which are beyond our grasp and have no real attraction for us. If it weren't for the price of tickets, we might as well go to the Opéra itself.' That's what they're saying, Mr. Chairman; and doubtless you in your wisdom will find some way out of this grave situation."

And indeed the chairman, having sent for Monsieur Perrin, quickly agreed with that able administrator a course of action to get around the problem, if not to remove it. It was clearly impossible to force composers to abandon the lofty style and leave the poetic regions of their art in order to stay

Figure 12. Théâtre-Lyrique, Paris. From a 19th century engraving. Richard Macnutt Collection, Withyham. "A light music theatre, a theatre with straightforward tunes", located on the Boulevard du Temple, in the Temple district (see pages 50–54).

within the scope of the simple intelligence of the largest and poorest class. In these circumstances they agreed that at least they could have recourse to cheerful librettists, and commission them to produce pieces so entertaining, so lively and so funny that the gloom of the populace would be bound to melt at seeing them, despite the heaviness and erudition of the music, just as ice melts in the sun.

And they began with the opera *Schahabaham II*.[74] And its success exceeded all expectations. And the populace laughed like mad as with a single voice. Nowadays their looks sparkle with gaiety and demonstrations are increasingly uncommon. Monsieur Perrin's mansion is accessible again, and the people are once more hopeful of having "their" Théâtre-Lyrique back—as indeed they have!

Lamentations of Jeremiah

How wretched are critics! They have no fire in winter and no ice in summer—they're always either freezing cold or boiling hot. They suffer a constant torment of listening, and then they must perform a perpetual dance on eggs, terrified of breaking some by a false step in the direction of either praise or censure. Not nightingales' eggs—they're far too rare these days—just heaps of owls' and turkeys' eggs, which they'd dearly love to trample with both feet. And at the end of the day they can't even hang up their weary pens on the willow trees by the rivers of Babylon, and sit down and weep at leisure on the bank![75]

There's a gloom-laden lithograph which I cannot help lingering over whenever I pass the shop where it is displayed. It shows a troop of unfortunates clothed in damp and muddy rags, their leader sporting a brigand's headdress,[76] plodding in filthy worn-out boot-tops tied to their legs with straw. Most have one swollen cheek, all have hollow stomachs. Their teeth are rotten and they are dying of hunger. There is no form of sore or affliction they don't have. Their sparse hair sticks lankly to their scrawny temples. They carry shovels and brooms, or rather fragments of shovels and stumps of brooms, tools fit for such threadbare labourers. In torrential rain they flounder along dejectedly in the dismal sink of Paris, and in front of them a sort of warder, armed with a formidable stick, peremptorily waves his arm, like Napoleon at Austerlitz showing his soldiers the sun, and shouts at them, with squinting eye and twisted mouth, "Come on, men, look lively!" They're street sweepers. . . .[77]

Poor devils! Where do these unfortunate creatures come from? On what butcher's block will they meet their end? What reward does municipal munificence allot them for thus cleaning (or dirtying) the pavements of

Figure 13. *The Street-Sweeper's School* ("L'École du Balayeur"). Lithograph by de Villain after Nicolas-Toussaint Charlet (1792–1845). Bibliothèque Nationale de France.

'Perhaps there's a former artist among them—perhaps he's done them some caricatures.' Of the two lithographs by Charlet with the same title, this one seems closer to Berlioz's description: "there's a gloom-laden lithograph which . . . shows a troop of unfortunates clothed in damp and muddy rags" (page 54).

Paris? At what age are they sent to the glue factory? What becomes of their bones (their skin is good for nothing)? Where does this one spend the night? Where does that one go to feed himself during the day? What does he feed on? Does this one have a mate, or any young? What's this one thinking? What can that one be talking about as he busies himself, looking lively as required, with the tasks allotted him by the Prefect of the Seine? Are these gentlemen supporters of representative government, or of the full flood of democracy, or of military rule? All of them are philosophers, but how many are literate? How many of them write vaudevilles? How many have worked with the brush before being reduced to the broom? How many were pupils of Vernet before posing for Charlet? How many have won the Grand Prix de Rome at the Academy of Fine Arts?[78]

I'd never finish if I listed all the questions this lithograph raises. Questions of humanity, questions of hygiene, questions of equality and liberty and fraternity, questions of philosophy and anatomy, of science and sewerage, questions of literature and painting, questions of subsistence and substance, questions of affluence and effluence, questions of beauty and butchery!

But what's the point, you may ask, of this rigmarole about street sweepers? What have I in common with them? True, I've won the Prix de Rome, I sometimes suffer sores, I don't lack causes of affliction, and I'm a great one for philosophy. But the Prefect of the Seine wouldn't dream of allotting me even the most minor municipal tasks. I've never touched a brush in my life—it's all I can do to use a pen. I've never written a vaudeville—I couldn't even run up a comic opera.

It's the "demon within" (as imagination or caprice is called when one doesn't wish to use the proper word) that has dictated this elegy to me. But I don't have time to give way to these literary diversions; comic operas are raining down in torrents, on the Boulevard des Italiens, on the Boulevard du Temple, in the salons, everywhere.[79] And we critics are both witnesses and judges, even though nobody has made us swear on the Koran to tell the truth, the whole truth and nothing but the truth. A regrettable oversight, for if I'd sworn such an oath, I would keep it. I suppose one can always tell the truth without having sworn to do so. Well then, since comic operas are pouring down in torrents, and since we're armed with our stumps of pens, with which we earn our living in Paris by acting as clerks of the operatic court, let's do our duty and march towards the noble goal which ambition holds out before us. Let's not wait to be told a second time "Come on, men, look lively!"

How wretched are critics! They have no fire in winter and no ice in summer—they're always either freezing cold or boiling hot. They suffer a constant torment of listening, and then they must perform a perpetual dance on eggs, terrified of breaking some by a false step in the direction of either praise or censure. Not nightingales' eggs—they're far too rare these days—

Figure 14. Berlioz c1860–64. Photograph by Nadar (Félix Tournachon, 1820–1910). Richard Macnutt Collection, Withyham.

Berlioz not long after the publication of *The Musical Madhouse,* beginning to show the strain of his life as a critic, described in "The Lamentations of Jeremiah"—"how wretched are critics!" (see pages 54–65).

just heaps of owls' and turkeys' eggs, which they'd dearly love to trample with both feet. And at the end of the day they can't even hang up their weary pens on the willow trees by the rivers of Babylon, and sit down and weep at leisure on the bank!

More articles! More operas! More albums! More singers! More gods! More mortals! Since last year the earth has travelled some 150 million miles in orbit around the sun. It has set off on one trajectory and returned on another, according to the Academy of Sciences. And why all this restless motion? Why has it travelled such an immense distance? To what end? I'd like to know what it's thinking, this great round head which we infest, indeed I would—for I don't doubt for a moment that it *does* think. I am not such a Pyrrhonist as that;[80] it would be as ludicrous as if one of the lice that infest the great mathematician Monsieur X*** were to let himself doubt his host's ability to think.

So yes, I am curious about what this great head thinks of our little evolutions, our great revolutions, our new religions, our war in the East, our peace in the West, our Chinese turmoil, our Japanese haughtiness, our Australian and Californian gold rushes, our British industry, our French gaiety, our German philosophy, our Flemish beer, our Italian music, our Austrian diplomacy, our Great Mogul and our Spanish bulls, and above all of our Parisian theatres, which I must say something about, whatever the cost. To be precise, I wish to know the Earth's views only about those of our theatres which are described as opera houses. Indeed, even though we have a total of five of these at present, I'm only really interested in its opinion of three. One of these is entitled "Académie Impériale de Musique", another "Opéra-Comique", and the third "Théâtre-Lyrique".[81] It follows, of course, that the Théâtre-Lyrique is not comic, the Opéra-Comique far from academic and the Académie not at all lyrical. Where do you suppose lyricism has gone to roost?

I could, like so many others, consult the Earth's opinion on these grave issues; and inevitably the Earth would respond exactly as it has responded to those who have dared question it on previous occasions. But I'd be embarrassed to include myself among those nuisances by disturbing it again. Especially since in its present mood it might well give me a completely wrong answer. It would be quite capable of claiming that the academic theatre is comic, the comic theatre lyric and the lyric theatre academic. Imagine the perplexity such oracles would produce in the minds of the public (at least those of them who have minds)!

Anyway, we have at least three theatres in Paris which, as I said before, I must say more about, whatever the cost.

How wretched are critics! They have no fire in winter and no ice in summer—they're always either freezing cold or boiling hot. They suffer a constant torment of listening, and then they must perform a perpetual dance on eggs, terrified of breaking some by a false step in the direction of either praise or censure. Not nightingales' eggs—they're far too rare these days—just heaps of owls' and turkeys' eggs, which they'd dearly love to trample with both feet. And at the end of the day they can't even hang up their weary pens on the willow trees by the rivers of Babylon, and sit down and weep at leisure on the bank!

To think that quite probably on this very day, June 3rd, Commandant Page may be entering the Bay of Papeete![82] His ships' cannon may be saluting the Tahitian shore, answered by a thousand perfumes and the joyful cries of the island beauties running down to the beach! I can see him now, with his tall figure and his noble face bronzed by the heat of the Indian sun. He gazes through his telescope at the point with its coconut palms and the house of Henry the Navigator, built at the mouth of the sea route from Matavaï.

He's surprised that his salute isn't returned. But there go the gunners running in all directions from Monsieur Moerenhout's house, and into the two detached forts. Gunfire on all sides! Hurrah, it's the French! It's the Protectorate's new Commandant! Another volley! Hurrah, hurrah!

Now people are coming out of the barracks and French officers rushing headlong from the café. Monsieur Giraud appears at the doorway of his hut,[83] and everybody heads in the direction of the Port Captain's house along the Rue Louis-Philippe. And where are those two ravishing creatures going, who have emerged from a lemon grove and are hastily plaiting garlands of leaves and hibiscus flowers? They are two of Queen Pomaré's maids of honour who had been playing cards in a corner of the royal hut while Her Majesty slept.

At the sound of the cannon they instantly forget their game and cast furtive glances towards the Protestant church. No reverend fathers to be seen! No Pritchards! No one will know! They complete their toilette by letting fall their *maros,* useless tunics imposed on them in the name of modesty by Anglican missionaries. With garlands crowning their fine heads and adorning their splendid hair, they are arrayed in all their oceanic charms, like two Venuses entering the water. "O Pagé! O Pagé!" (It's Page! It's Page!) they cry as they slice through the gentle ripples of the bay like two mermaids.

They approach the French ship, swimming with their left hands while waving friendly greetings with the right, and in their melodious voices they send repeated *ioreanas* (hellos) to the crew. A midshipman gives a cry of … of admiration at this sight, and starts towards the two Nereids. A look from the Commandant fixes him at his post, where he remains silent, motionless but trembling. Monsieur Page, who speaks the Kanak language like a native, points to the bridge of his ship and shouts to the two native girls "Taboo! Taboo!" (prohibited).

They come no closer, but raise their upper bodies out of the water, revealing themselves like ancient statues, and join hands, smiling in a way

that would lure Saint Anthony to damnation. But the impassive Commandant repeats his cruel taboo! They throw him a flower with a final regretful
ioreana and return to land. The crew won't disembark for two hours. While
waiting, Monsieur Page sits on the starboard side of his ship and gazes at
the wonderful view of this earthly paradise, where he is to live and rule for
some years. He breathes in the intoxicating warm breeze which wafts from
it, drinks from a fresh young coconut, and says, "To think that in Paris at
this moment the temperature is 35 degrees, and people are just entering the
Opéra-Comique, where they'll stay cooped up until one o'clock in the
morning to find out whether Pierrot will end up marrying Pierrette, to
listen to the two little ninnies bawling their love to the accompaniment of a
bass drum, and to be able to inform some newspaper's readers on the next
day but one of the difficulties overcome by Pierrette in order to marry
Pierrot! What rabid anti-abolitionists these newspaper proprietors are!"[84]

To think that one can reflect in this clear-sighted manner twelve thousand miles away in the Antipodes! In a land whose civilisation is far enough
advanced to do without theatres and newspaper articles; where the climate
is so cool, and the lovely maidens sport such elegant headwear; and where
a queen can sleep! I blush with shame to be living among one of those
infant races which the wise people of Polynesia don't even condescend to
visit.

How wretched are critics! They have no fire in winter and no ice in
summer—they're always either freezing cold or boiling hot. They suffer a
constant torment of listening, and then they must perform a perpetual dance
on eggs, terrified of breaking some by a false step in the direction of either
praise or censure. Not nightingales' eggs—they're far too rare these days—
just heaps of owls' and turkeys' eggs, which they'd dearly love to trample
with both feet. And at the end of the day they can't even hang up their
weary pens on the willow trees by the rivers of Babylon, and sit down and
weep at leisure on the bank!

Even the hardest of hearts would be moved if it knew of the torments
which these poor fellows endure without anyone taking any notice, especially in Paris. But they have little desire to excite pity, so they keep quiet;
they even smile sometimes, and are seen coming and going with quite an
air of calm, especially at certain times of year when they are freed on parole. When the hour comes for them to pluck up their courage again, they
head for the theatres where they suffer such agony with a stoicism equal to
that of Regulus returning to Carthage.[85]

And no one recognises the true heroism in this. Worse still, when some
of the less steadfast among them are so racked by thirst for beauty, or at
least for common sense, that their looks of suffering, their bowed heads
and downcast expressions begin to attract the attention of passers-by, people
add insult to injury by offering them sponges dipped in gall and vinegar on
the end of pikestaffs, and laughing at them.[86] And they resign themselves to

it. Yet there are some violent spirits among them, and I'm amazed that their frustration hasn't yet brought about a disaster.

Several, of course, seek safety in flight. This old expedient still works. I must confess I've been cowardly enough to use it recently myself. Some piece or other had been announced for execution; the headsmen of Paris and their assistants had already been summoned. A letter arrived for me, giving the date and the time. There wasn't a moment to lose. I rushed to the Gare St.-Lazare and set off for Motteville. When I got there I took a coach to an unknown little seaport where one is almost sure of not being discovered. Detailed intelligence had led me to hope I would find peace there— peace, that heavenly gift which Paris denies to men of goodwill. Indeed, St.-Valery-en-Caux is a charming spot, hidden in a cleft at the edge of the sea; *est in secessu locus.*[87] One isn't exposed to barrel-organs or piano competitions there. They haven't opened an opera house yet; and if they had, it would already be closed.

The public baths are a modest establishment, and no concerts are given there; the bathers don't make music; one of the two churches has no organist, the other no organ; the schoolmaster, who might be tempted to corrupt the local people by instructing them in what is called in Paris "the art of singing", has no pupils; the fishermen who might allow themselves to be corrupted have nothing to pay him with. There are plenty of people plaiting ropes, but no one plaiting sounds. The only songs to be heard here and there are those of young girls busy sewing drag- and sweep-nets from seven to eight in the morning, innocent children who still have mere threads of voices. There's no National Guard, so no lottery music; the only sound is the echoing noise of the caulkers' hammering as they repair ships' hulls.[88] There is a reading room, but neither romances nor polkas with portraits and lithographs are to be found behind its windows. You run no risk of meeting an amateur quartet or being asked for a subscription to save some virtuoso from the misfortune of serving his country usefully. The men in that part of the country are all past the age of conscription, while the children haven't yet reached it.

In short it's an Eldorado for critics, a Tahitian island on the mainland, surrounded by water on one side only and without the ravishing Tahitian girls, I grant you, but also lacking the Protestant ministers, the nasal hymns, the massive Queen Pomaré growing ever fatter in her hut, and the French newspaper; for a paper in French is published in Tahiti, something studiously avoided in St.-Valery. Reassured by this information, I got off the omnibus (I must mention too that the conductor of this omnibus, whose job is to bring honest folk from Motteville to St.-Valery, plays neither the post-horn, like his counterparts in Marseilles,[89] nor that frightful little bugle used by the Belgians to do in travellers on their railways).

So I alighted from the vehicle in one piece and in good heart, and hastened to climb one of the cliffs which rise vertically each side of the town.

Figure 15. View of the coast at St.-Valery-en-Caux. Watercolour by N. Pérignon from H. Destailleur, *Collection de Dessins sur les Départements de France*. Bibliothèque Nationale de France. "St.-Valery-en-Caux is a charming spot, hidden in a cleft at the edge of the sea" (page 61).

Then from the height of this dazzling observatory I shouted to the sea, murmuring its everlasting hymn three hundred feet below, "Good day, mighty sea!" I bowed before the setting sun, performing its evening decrescendo in a sublime palace of pink and gold clouds: "Hail, Majesty!" And when the delicious cliff breeze scurried up to welcome me, I greeted it with a sigh of happiness, "Good evening, capricious breeze!" Yielding to the soft greenery of the mountain, I rolled on the ground and let myself wallow in fresh air, harmony and light.

There are many tales I could tell of this trip to Normandy. I'll confine myself to recounting the shipwreck of a small lugger which was captained by a clarinettist from Rouen and ran aground five miles out of St.-Valery harbour. An extraordinary thing! For what better skipper could there be than a clarinettist? This task was once rigidly restricted to sailors, but at last the dangers of this old-fashioned practice have been recognised. It's easy to see: a sailor, as a professional, naturally has his own ideas, his own system. He acts in accordance with that system, and would never consent to a manoeuvre he considers wrong or ill-timed. Everyone on board must obey him without argument or hesitation—he subjects them to military despotism. It's intolerable. And sailors are so jealous of each other. If one says something is white, that's enough for another to call it black.

Besides, has all this specialist knowledge that they boast of, or their nautical experience, prevented countless appalling disasters? The search still goes on for Sir John Franklin, lost in the Arctic seas, yet he was a master mariner.[90] And what about the unfortunate La Pérouse,[91] smashed to pieces on the reefs of Vanicoro—hadn't he been an assiduous student of mathematics, physics, hydrography, geography, geology, anthropology, botany and all that rubbish with which proper sailors insist on cramming their heads? Even so he led his two ships to perdition. He had a system; he argued that the height of the coral rocks which clog the sea in the New Hebrides archipelago, next to Vanicoro, needed to be checked. So he ordered his men to go carefully, finding out how the rocks lay, looking for channels and taking soundings—and he was smashed to pieces. What good was his learning to him? Oh yes, it's only common sense to mistrust specialists, men with systems, and to steer clear of them!

Think of Columbus, too![92] Ferdinand and Isabella and their learned counsellors were quite right in their stubborn refusal to entrust two caravelles to him. And wouldn't it have been more sensible of them to stick to their refusal? He did eventually discover the New World, of course, but if he hadn't shown maniacal obstinacy in pursuing his route westward he wouldn't have chanced upon some bits of floating wood, worked by human hands, twenty-four hours before discovering San Salvador. Without the minimal degree of confidence restored to his crew by this laughable incident, he would have been forced to swallow his pride and return to Europe, thinking himself very lucky just to get back. So it was pure chance that brought about this renowned discovery. Anyone at all who had had the simple idea of sailing directly due west, without being either a sailor or a geologist like Columbus, would have reached the Bahamas and then the American continent just as he did.

And Cook, the celebrated, astonishing Captain Cook![93] Didn't he go and get himself killed like an idiot by a Hawaiian savage? He discovered New Caledonia and laid claim to it in England's name—and now France occupies it. A fine service he rendered his country!

No, no, these men with systems are the scourge of all human institutions, nothing could be clearer. The little mishap at St.-Valery proves nothing. The clarinettist who was in command of the lugger had about ten women on board and had put up as much sail as he could carry to show off. There was a stiff breeze blowing, so he was making heaven knows how many knots, and everybody on the jetty was shouting "Look how well that little lugger's going!" When he arrived off Veule and wanted to go about for the return journey he ran aground, and the poor lugger was thrown over on its side. Fortunately the people of Veule didn't waste any time but plunged up to their waists into the water to bring the shivering passengers ashore. No doubt the clarinettist didn't realise that at low tide you should avoid approaching the sands at Veule, nor that his lugger drew so much water. That's all there is to it. Even the most skilful of sailors arriving at that part of the coast with that lugger at that time, and equally unaware of the local conditions, would have met with a similar accident.

The day after this mishap, which, I repeat, proves nothing against the fitness of clarinettists to command vessels, a letter from Paris found its way to me at St.-Valery bringing word that a new piece (new!) had just been performed at the Opéra-Comique. My correspondent added that this work was inoffensive enough for me to expose myself to it without much danger. So I returned (I had no choice!), but I didn't see the piece, and I'm sure I'll be thanked for making no mention of it. When I arrived it had already reverted to nothingness. I quizzed various usually well-informed people about it but they had no idea what I was talking about. Go ahead, enjoy your successes, produce your masterpieces, cover yourselves with glory! All you'll be left with, after only five or six days, will be. . . . Ah, Paris! How little you care about comic operas! To what utter oblivion you consign them!

All the same, I returned. I left the high cliffs and the mighty sea and splendid horizons and the pleasures of relaxation and tranquillity, for the flat, muddy, restless city—the barbarous city! And once again I dish out eulogy with a trowel. I give praise and more praise, just like before—even more than before!

How wretched are critics! They have no fire in winter and no ice in summer—they're always either freezing cold or boiling hot. They suffer a constant torment of listening, and then they must perform a perpetual dance on eggs, terrified of breaking some by a false step in the direction of either praise or censure. Not nightingales' eggs—they're far too rare these days—just heaps of owls' and turkeys' eggs, which they'd dearly love to trample with both feet. And at the end of the day they can't even hang up their weary pens on the willow trees by the rivers of Babylon, and sit down and weep at leisure on the bank!

The Germans use the term "recensors" to describe journalists whose job is to give a periodic account of what's going on in the theatre world, and to review literary works recently announced for publication. Our own word "critics" perhaps applies better than the German term to writers charged with this second part of the task, but it must be admitted that the modest title of "recensors" more aptly describes the many decent people condemned to the sterile, thankless and often humiliating labour which constitutes the first part. Nobody knows, apart from the unfortunates themselves, what excruciating suffering, what immeasurable disgust, what shuddering repugnance, what concentrated fury (which they cannot allow to explode)[94] the accomplishment of this task may cause them. How much energy lost! How much time wasted! What ideas stifled! How many steam engines, capable of tunnelling through the Alps, employed just to turn a millstone!

Unhappy recensors, ineffective census-takers, so often censured themselves! When will they be. . . .

(Jeremiah is interrupted by a man of good sense)

"Pah! You're not going to start that litany all over again and give us a fiftieth verse about *hanging up your pen on the willow trees by the rivers of Babylon and sitting down and weeping at leisure on the bank*? Can't you see how insufferable your wailings and groanings are? What the devil has brought you to this state of despair? If you've got up such a head of steam, you'd better take a cold shower. If you feel you have such Titanic power for digging through mountains, for God's sake give it free rein. Tunnel through the Alps, tunnel through the Apennines, tunnel through Mount Ararat, tunnel through Montmartre even, if you have such a thing about tunnelling, but don't come splitting our eardrums with your screeching, like an eagle in a cage. There are plenty of others cleverer than you around, whose dearest wish is to turn that millstone of yours."

Jeremiah: Whosoever says "Pah!" to his brother merits eternal damnation. But you are right, three times right, seven times right, O man of rightfulness. The eyes of my soul were dimmed, but you are the good fortune that restores me to myself, and now here I am, in La Fontaine's words, a simple bumpkin once again.[95]

———

A model critic

One of my reviewer colleagues had a theory that a critic anxious to preserve his impartiality should never see the pieces which he has to review, in order, he said, to avoid being influenced by the acting. Such influence can operate in three ways: first by making something flat and ugly seem beautiful, or at any rate passable; secondly by producing the opposite effect, distorting the shape of a work that really is noble and graceful so as to make it seem repellent; and finally by making it impossible to understand the work at all, either as a whole or in its details, by obliterating it altogether. But what made my colleague's theory especially original was that he didn't even *read* the works he had to review, firstly because new works are generally not available in print, and then again because he didn't want to let himself be influenced, either for good or ill, by the author's style. This perfect incorruptibility obliged him to "compose" incredible accounts of pieces which he'd neither seen nor read, and led him to expound some very striking opinions on music he hadn't heard.

I've often regretted not being able to put such a fine theory into practice myself, for the reader who disdainfully puts down his newspaper and thinks about something completely different after a brief glance over the first few lines of a review cannot conceive the anguish endured in listening to so many new operas, or the pleasure the reviewer would feel if he didn't have to see them at all. Besides, in reviewing a piece he knew nothing about, he would have scope to be original. He might even unwittingly, and without being guilty of bias, be helpful to the authors by inventing some novelty which might inspire his readers to want to see the new work.

Whereas by sticking to the traditional approach, as we usually do, and doing our best to listen attentively to the pieces we have to describe to the public, we're forced always to say almost exactly the same, since basically they always *are* almost exactly the same. As a result we involuntarily do great injustice to many new works, for how can people be expected to go and see them when we've explained truthfully and clearly just what they're like?

Dramatic emphasis

The devil has always been held in high esteem by composers of comic operas. Critics tend to be quite the opposite, and often go so far in their irreverence for the devil as to tweak him by the tail (isn't that so, dear colleagues?).

The Opéra-Comique, let's face it, has put on a multitude of works with the devil as their hero: *The Devil and All, The Devil as Page, The Devil*

Figure 16. Opéra-Comique, Paris (Théâtre Feydeau)—exterior. Engraving by Elizabeth Byrne after T. T. Bury, 1830. Richard Macnutt Collection, Withyam.

"The Opéra-Comique . . . has put on a multitude of works with the devil as their hero" (page 66). Like the Théâtre-Lyrique, the Feydeau theatre, home of the Opéra-Comique, was situated on the Boulevard du Temple.

Lame, The Pink Devil, The Devil in Love, The Devil of Seville, The Devil's Due, The Devil at School, The Devil's Bride.[96]

Devil take it! (This is me speaking now, in case you thought my exclamation was the name of another comic opera.) In 1830 the Opéra-Comique failed to get its hands on *Robert le Diable* ('Robert the Devil'),[97] which was really meant for it; but Monsieur Véron, a shrewd burgher of Paris who is full of devilment, managed with devilish cunning to have himself compelled by Ministerial order to open the great doors of the Opéra to the greatest devil that ever left Hell.[98] For it weighed on his mind that the Opéra-Comique already possessed a fine collection of devils of every hue, while he at the Opéra had nothing to show but *The Blue Devils.*[99]

Well, the insatiable Opéra-Comique could never get over the loss of *Robert le Diable,* and it was a long time, an age indeed, before that particular devil's tunes raised the rafters there. Nothing went right for it; it made devilish efforts to attract the public, and the public avoided it like the very devil. Young actresses were engaged, young composers were "set to work"; but no, all these youngsters only led them the devil's own dance before fading away in no time at all, while that devil of a *Robert le Diable* went on making a devilish din all over Europe and cast an infernal multitude into the abyss of the Opéra three times a week.

Here is a story which shows how respectfully and reverently the actors of the Opéra-Comique pronounce the evil spirit's name. One day (yes, in full daylight), in a ceremony replete with sadness and solemnity, one of them had to deliver the eulogy on a composer of great talent who would practise his art no more. He read the funeral address in a natural and fitting enough manner, so long as it encompassed only human and earthly matters. But when he came to a listing of the composer's works and had to pronounce the name of the spirit of darkness, which was the title of one of those works, a strange and wonderful transformation could be observed in his appearance and voice. His expression became sombre, he knit his brows, his look darkened, his gestures became stiff and angular, and in a grating, cavernous voice he pronounced the following sentence, with a shudder at the last six syllables: "Monsieur Gomis, on arriving in Paris, made his début at the Opéra-Comique with a work entitled *The D-d-d-devil of Seville*".[100] I need say no more, my theory is proved. How about that?

Success of a Miserere

A correspondent writes from Naples: "A *Miserere* by Mercadante was sung at St. Peter's Church on March 27th, in the presence of His Eminence the Cardinal Archbishop and his suite, together with the staff of the

Conservatoire.[101] The performance was excellent, and His Eminence was kind enough to give repeated indications of his satisfaction. The work contains beauties of the highest order. The audience expressed its wish to hear the *Redde mihi* and the *Benigne fac, Domine* repeated."

So did the audience shout "encore" and "da capo" like the first night claque in our theatres here? I'd be intrigued to know. How can you complain now about concerts during Lent, or about our young singers making their débuts in Paris churches? Ha! Wretched Catholic critics, your anti-patriotism makes you blind; you can't see that we're little saints!

The season—The bugbears' club

There's a certain time of year when music of all kinds is rife in the great cities, especially Paris and London, when walls are covered with concert notices and foreign virtuosi flock in from every corner of Europe to compete with each other and with local performers. These new-style advocates fall upon the unfortunate public and violently demand its verdict in their favour—they would willingly pay, not just to gain its backing for themselves, but to deny it to their rivals. But audiences, like witnesses, do not come cheap, and are not just to be had for the asking.[102]

This terrible time is known in the jargon of the music profession as "the season".

The season! It explains and justifies all sorts of things that I'd like to call mythical, but which are only too true.

Critics find themselves assailed by people in a hurry who have come from far away to make their reputations in the big city, and who, wishing to succeed quickly, try to bribe them with Dutch cheeses.

It's the season!

Five or six concerts are given every day, all at the same time, and their organisers are outraged to find the poor critics absent from some of them! So they write inquisitorial letters, full of spite and indignation, to the absentees.

It's the season!

An unbelievable number of people, considered in their own part of the world to possess some talent, come to prove that outside it they have none, or only that of making a cheerful audience solemn and a solemn one cheerful.

It's the season!

Among this great mass of musicians, men and women, treading on each other's toes, elbowing and jostling and sometimes even treacherously tripping up their rivals, one can still be lucky enough to discern some fully grown talents which tower above the host of mediocrities like palm-trees over tropical forests. Thanks to these exceptional artists, some truly fine music-making can be heard from time to time, a consolation for all the other horrors one has to put up with.

It's the season!

But once this time of year is over, you may fall prey to burning thirst after long abstinence and yearn desperately for a cup of pure harmony: impossible.

It's not the season.

Someone tells you of a new singer, extolling his voice and his technique, so you go to hear him. He has neither voice nor technique.

It's not the season.

A violinist arrives, preceded by quite a reputation. He describes himself as a pupil of Paganini, as usual; he is said to perform "duets on a single string", and, better still, always to play perfectly in tune, with a tone that sings like a swan of the Eridan.[103] Off you go, full of anticipation, to his concert. You find the hall empty; instead of an orchestra there's a puny upright piano to provide the accompaniment; the fellow isn't even capable of performing a solo properly on all four strings, he plays as tunelessly as a Chinaman, with a tone that sings like a black swan from Australia.

It's not the season.

During long country-house evenings (in winter for the English, summer for the French), the news of a gala concert being organised with a great deal of fuss in a neighbouring town creates an immediate stir amongst a group of passionate lovers of great masterpieces, for whom vocal solos and piano pieces aren't enough. Seat reservations are hastily arranged, and on the appointed day off they all go. True, the hall is full, but what an audience! The orchestra consists of ten or twelve real musicians and thirty dance-band players; the chorus has been recruited from local laundrywomen and soldiers of the garrison. They make mincemeat of a Beethoven symphony and bray out a Mendelssohn oratorio. And yet any complaint would be churlish.

It's not the season.

In the big city a new work by an old master grown grey in harness is announced for a change, to be sung by a prima donna whose name, long popular, still retains its lustre. Alas! The music of the new piece is colourless and the singer's voice hasn't had the same good fortune as her name.

It's no longer the season.

How few countries there are with seasons!

Do you know the land where the orange-tree blooms?[104] That land has had no season for a long while now.

If you've lived in the Iberian countryside, you'll know there's no longer any season there.

As for the unfortunate lands where only fir-trees, birches and snow-drops flourish, they do have seasons from time to time, but only when they are lit up, like polar nights, by the aurora borealis. Let's hope that if the sun eventually shines on them, they'll have six-month-long seasons, to make up for lost time.

It would be inconceivable to have a season in those far-off countries where business is everything, where everyone is busy, where all is hustle and bustle, where the serious thinker is taken for an idiot, where the poet who dreams is a good-for-nothing scoundrel, where men's eyes are fixed obstinately on the ground and nothing can force them to look up for an instant to the sky. These are the isles of Lemnos of today's Cyclopes,[105] with a mission of great importance, to be sure, but incompatible with that of art. The musical glimmers of these hard-working giants will for a long time be as useless and contrary to nature as the love of Polyphemus for Galatea, and completely out of season.

There remain three or four small corners of our little globe where art, cramped, jostled, polluted and suffocated by its multitude of enemies, nonetheless clings to life and can claim to have a season.

Need I name Germany, England and France? By limiting the number of countries with seasons to these three and designating them as centres of the civilised world, I hope to stay clear of the prejudices held by each of the three peoples who live in them. In France they naively believe there is no more music in England today than in the time of Queen Elizabeth. Many Englishmen think French music is a myth and that our orchestras fall thousands of miles short of Jullien's concert orchestra.[106] How many Frenchmen despise Germany as a wearisome land of unrelieved harmony and counterpoint! And if Germany is perfectly frank, it will confess to despising both France and England equally.

But these opinions, more or less tainted as they are with childish vanity, ignorance and prejudice, can do nothing to alter the facts. That which is, is; *Eppur si muove!*[107] Music goes in *cycles,* just like the earth and everything in it; and precisely because the variation of its seasons becomes more noticeable year by year, so these national prejudices must disappear the more rapidly, or at least lose much of their force.

While recognising how pleasant the seasons are in a large part of Germany, we still persist in considering the London and Paris seasons, though often gruelling, as pre-eminently important.

The "high" season in Paris hardly gets going until about January 20th and is sometimes over by February 1st, occasionally lasting until March 1st.

Seasons have been known not to finish until April. But those were trisextile years,[108] when several comets appeared in the heavens and some new works were included in the programmes of the Conservatoire Concert Society.

The 1853 season was such an exception, when we heard Mendelssohn's *Walpurgis Night* for the first time at the Conservatoire concerts, and almost the whole of the same master's *Midsummer Night's Dream*. Mendelssohn wrote the *Walpurgis Night* in Rome in 1831, so it took twenty-two years for this fine work to reach us.[109] It's true that the light of certain stars doesn't arrive until after thousands of years of travel. But Leipzig, where Mendelssohn's scores have been available in print for a long time, isn't quite so distant from Paris as Saturn or Sirius.

It's a principle of the Conservatoire to proceed deliberately in all things. All the same, despite this lack of agility and ardour, which can be put down to its age, it must be admitted there's life in the old dog yet.

It has made its concert hall into a museum, where every year it exhibits a great number of musical masterpieces in their true light—that is its glory. It's reproached for not letting others display their works there when the museum is empty and it's not exhibiting anything itself.[110] That's quite misguided: it has a fine hall, the only decent one in Paris for orchestral music, and wanted a monopoly of its use, understandably enough. Having obtained exactly that, it now hangs on to it, again quite understandably. Naturally it couldn't possibly leave the field open to competition. If others were on the inside and it were outside, it would think it quite natural that they should leave it dying of cold on their doorstep. It simply understands the good sense of the saying:

One should do to others only that which one would not wish done to oneself.

Nevertheless, perhaps it's time for it to think about varying its repertory, in case the public gets so tired of this Society that it starts making bad puns about the Concert *Satiety*. To some people such remarks might not seem entirely out of season.

. . . .

Paris isn't the only place in France where a clear musical cycle can be observed. Every four or five years there are seasons in Lyons and Bordeaux; there's a splendid one in Lille every eight years, and excellent seasons in Marseilles, where the fruits of musical art ripen more quickly than they used to.

But after the French seasons, "The London season! The London season!" is the cry on the lips of every singer, Italian, French, Belgian, German, Bohemian, Hungarian, Swedish and English; and virtuosi of all nationalities take it up with gusto as they board their steamships, like Aeneas's soldiers embarking on their vessels with shouts of "Italiam! Italiam!".[111] For there's no country in the world where they get through so much music in a season as in London.

Thanks to this enormous appetite for music, all artists of real talent are bound to be kept busy, after a few months getting themselves known. Once known and appreciated, they are expected each year with the same confidence as the pigeons' migration is expected in North America. And never as long as they live will you find them betraying the trust of the British public, that model of fidelity which always welcomes them, always applauds them, always admires them,

Heedless of the irreparable ravages of time.[112]

One must see for oneself the bustle and whirl of the musical life of London's favourite artists to get a true idea of it. And those musical maestros who have been established in England for many years, such as Mr. Davison, his admirable pupil Miss Goddard, and Messrs. Macfarren, Ella, Benedict, Osborne, Frank Mori, Sainton and Piatti, lead still more astonishing lives.[113] They're in a constant rush, conducting and playing in public concerts and private musical soirées, with hardly the time to say "Good day" to their friends through the doors of their carriages as they travel down the Strand or Piccadilly.

When the Paris and London seasons are finally over, do you suppose musicians say to each other "Let's have a break: it's the season for it"? Indeed they do. You'll find them all rushing to tear each other apart at seaside towns, and at the waters of Vichy, Spa, Aix and Baden. This last rallying point attracts them above all, and from all over the world pianists, violinists, singers and composers, seduced by the beauty of the countryside, by the elegant society to be found there, and even more by the immense generosity of the director of the festivities, Monsieur Bénazet, make their way there, crying "To Baden! To Baden! To Baden![114] It's the season."

For some years now the Baden seasons have been organised in a fashion that discourages all competition. Most of the famous men and renowned beauties of Europe assemble there. Baden is bidding fair to become Paris, Berlin, Vienna, London and St. Petersburg all rolled into one, especially when a recent decision taken by Monsieur Bénazet, which I shall tell you of, gets about.

It's not enough to set about charming elegant society by putting its members in company with the wittiest men, the most ravishing women and the greatest artists, and laying on magnificent entertainment for them; beyond that, these jewels of the fashionable world must be protected from the very approach of individuals who are disagreeable to see or hear, and whose presence alone is enough to put a damper on a ball or strike a jarring note at a concert. Ugly women, vulgar men, fools, scatterbrains and imbeciles, in a word all bugbears, must be kept out of the way.

This is something no impresario before Monsieur Bénazet had ever tried to do. But now it seems certain that neither Mme. ***, so stupid and ugly, nor Mlle. ***, whose appearance is so grotesquely outlandish, nor the deathly dull Monsieur ***, nor Monsieur ***, his worthy rival, nor many others just as dangerous, will appear again in Baden for a long time. After

E. BENAZET. — D'après un dessin de M. Lallemand.

Figure 17. Édouard Bénazet. After a drawing by Armand-Joseph Lallemand (1810–71). Bibliothèque Nationale de France.
"From all over the world [musicians], seduced by . . . the immense generosity of the director of the festivities, Monsieur Bénazet, make their way [to Baden]" (page 73).

some pretty difficult negotiations, and at considerable cost, Monsieur Bénazet has arranged for their absence for three seasons.

If this splendid example is followed, which it certainly will be, I know some people who are going to make a lot of money.

Every year from now on, in August and September, these bugbears, delighted at becoming rich, will form a club in Paris, where they can shower congratulations upon each other.

"We, like you, are under contract", they'll say to each other, "to the directors at Baden (or Wiesbaden, or Vichy, or Spa). We must lie low and keep quiet, so no one suspects our existence. We're under contract—it's the season!!!"

Minor irritations of major concerts[115]

It's at the annual Baden festival that these minor irritations make themselves painfully felt. Yet the musical director in charge has everything in his favour; no cheeseparing economies are forced upon him, nor is he fettered in any way. Monsieur Bénazet, convinced that the best approach is to allow him a free hand, doesn't interfere in anything—except paying the bills. "Be as lavish as you like," he says, "I'm giving you carte blanche." Quite right too! With music, that's the only way to produce anything fine and beautiful. You're laughing, I see; you must be thinking of Jean Bart's reply to Louis XIV: "Jean Bart, I've appointed you commander of the fleet!"

"Well done, Sire!"[116]

Go on then, laugh! Jean Bart was right all the same. Yes, sire, you did well; it would be a good thing if sailors alone were chosen to command fleets. It would be a good thing, too, if once a Jean Bart was appointed, a Louis XIV should never start checking on his manoeuvres, making suggestions, and burdening him with his own anxieties, as in the first scene of Shakespeare's *Tempest*:

Alonso, King of Naples: Good boatswain, have care. Where's the master? Play the men.
Boatswain: I pray now, keep below.
Antonio: Where is the master, boson?
Boatswain: Do you not hear him? You mar our labour; keep your cabins; you do assist the storm.
Gonzalo: Good, yet remember whom thou hast aboard.
Boatswain: None that I more love than myself. You are a counsellor; if you can command these elements to silence, and work the peace of the

present, we will not hand a rope more. Use your authority; if you cannot, give thanks you have lived so long, and make yourself ready in your
cabin for the mischance of the hour, if it so hap.—Cheerly, good hearts!—
Out of our way, I say.

Despite having so many resources at his disposal, and this precious freedom to use them as he wishes, it's still a hard task for the musical director
to make a success of a festival like Baden, so great is the number of small
obstacles and so damaging the impact that even the slightest of them can
have on the whole of an enterprise of this kind. The first trial he has to
undergo almost always comes from agreeing the programme with the singers, especially the women. As he's fully aware of this problem, he sets to
work two months in advance to resolve it:
"What will you sing, Madame?"
"I don't know. . . . I'll think about it. . . . I'll write to you."
A month goes by without the singer either thinking about it or writing. Another
fortnight is wasted trying to get a decision out of her. Then the director has to leave
Paris. He draws up a provisional programme, with the title of the diva's piece left
blank. At last the long-awaited decision arrives. It's an aria by Mozart. Good. But
the diva doesn't have the music of this aria, there's no longer time to get the
orchestral parts copied, and she neither would nor should sing with piano
accompaniment. A helpful theatre is willing to lend the parts. Everything is
under control; the programme is published. But when the singer herself sets
eyes on it, she at once takes fright at the choice she has made.
"It's an immense concert," she writes to the director; "such a rich
programme, with all those splendid things in it, will make my poor Mozart
piece seem very small and feeble. I've decided to sing a different aria, 'Bel
raggio' from Rossini's *Semiramide*.[117] You'll have no trouble finding the
parts for it *in Germany*. Otherwise just write to the Director of the Théâtre-
Italien in Paris; I'm sure he'll send them off to you at once."
As soon as this letter is received, new programmes are printed and slips of
paper are stuck on the posters to announce the scene from *Semiramide*. But
the parts for this aria cannot be found *in Germany*, and it doesn't seem right
to ask the Director of the Théâtre-Italien in Paris to send the entire opera
Semiramide, from which the aria required cannot be extracted separately, all
the way across the Rhine. The singer arrives; they all meet to rehearse:
"Well now, we don't have the music for *Semiramide*; you'll have to sing
with piano accompaniment."
"Oh, my God! But it'll be positively glacial."
"No doubt."
"What can we do?"
"I don't know."
"Suppose I went back to my Mozart aria?"
"That would be very sensible."

Figure 18. Théâtre-Italien, Paris (Salle Ventadour)—exterior. Engraving by J. Tingle after T. T. Bury, 1829. Richard Macnutt Collection, Withyham.

"Just write to the Director of the Théâtre-Italien in Paris" (page 76).

"Let's rehearse it then."

"What with? We don't have the music for it any more; it was sent back to the Karlsruhe theatre, as you asked. The orchestra has to have music, if you want it to play. Singers are sometimes so carried away by inspiration that they forget these vulgar details. It's all very prosaic and boring, I admit, but that's how it is."

At the next rehearsal the parts for the Mozart opera have been retrieved; everything's under control again. The programmes are redone, the posters recorrected. The conductor tells the players they're going to rehearse the Mozart aria, and they're all set. Then the singer comes forward and says, with that irresistible charm she's famous for:

"I've had an idea, I'll sing the aria from *Le Domino noir.*"[118]

"Oh! Ah! Ha! Ow! Ouch! Grrr! Monsieur Kapellmeister, does your theatre have the opera of which Madame speaks?"

"No, Monsieur."

"So now what?"

"Should I make do with the Mozart aria, then?"

"Yes, take my advice, do that."

At last a start is made; the singer has decided to make do with the masterpiece. She embroiders it liberally, as might be expected. Within himself the conductor hears that eloquent exclamation "Grrr!" sounding even louder than before, and leaning towards the diva, he says in his quietest voice and with a smile that doesn't seem a bit forced:

"If you sing it like that, take it from me, you may find the audience rather hostile."

"Do you think so?"

"I'm sure of it."

"Oh, my God! But give me your advice . . . perhaps I should sing the Mozart naturally, just as it's written. We're in Germany, after all; I didn't think of that. I'm prepared to try anything, Monsieur."

"Yes, yes, be bold; take a chance on it; sing Mozart naturally. It's true that some arias were meant to be ornamented and embellished by their singers; but in general they were written by singers' lackeys, while Mozart is a master; indeed he's regarded as a master of unfailing taste."

The aria is restarted. The singer, having made up her mind to drink the cup to the dregs, sings this miracle of expression, of feeling, of passion, of style, quite naturally, altering only two bars for honour's sake. Scarcely has she finished than five or six people, who have come into the hall just at the moment when the piece was restarted, rush up to her full of enthusiasm, exclaiming: "A thousand compliments, Madame; how purely and naturally you sing! That's just how the masters should be performed; it's delightful, admirable! You really understand Mozart!"

The conductor, aside: "Grrrrr!!!"

20 francs per ticket

Once when Vivier had employed this unusual form of words to adver-
tise the price of seats for a concert he was giving, a poor horn-player from
the Pigalle sold everything he could and rushed off to the famous virtuoso's
house.[119]

Arriving at 24 Rue Truffaut in Batignolles, he went in trembling all over,
climbed to the second floor and knocked at a small door (the millionaire
Vivier affects an appearance of great modesty). A bearded gentleman, with
a cockerel on his left shoulder and a long snake in his right hand, came to
open the door.

"Monsieur Vivier?"

"I am he, Monsieur."

"I'm told you're offering seats for the concert at twenty francs per ticket."
(Notice the flattery of "the concert"—as if there could be no other concert
but Vivier's in Paris). "I'm something of a horn-player myself, and not
without talent, although I've never been invited to play at the Opéra. You'd
make me, Monsieur, the happiest of men, Monsieur, by. . . ."

"Ah! You must have had an ambition to join the Spanish magistracy?"

"The magistracy? What do you mean?"

"Well, you said you wanted a place among the horns at the Opéra. Those
who've achieved that honour have always ended up giving the same answer when asked if they were really at our Académie de Musique: '*Oui, j'y
suis cor et j'y dors.*'[120] But enough philosophising." He handed the poor
devil a napoleon together with a concert ticket.[121] "Here's what you want!"

"You're giving me twenty francs, Monsieur?"

"Didn't you see the announcement in the papers? Wasn't it quite clear?
Didn't you just say to me that you'd heard I was offering twenty francs per
ticket? Well then, isn't that what you've got? What are you fussing about?
Perhaps twenty francs isn't enough, in your opinion? Good God! A funny
sort of horn-player you are!"

"But, Monsieur. . . ."

"Enough! You came here to rob me!" cried Vivier in a furious voice.
"Get out of here, or I'll call the police and have you hauled off to the
Bastille!"

War on flats

A lady with a passion for music entered the premises of our famous
music publisher Brandus and asked to see the latest and best songs,[122] adding that she was particularly keen on those which were not overloaded

with flats. So the shop assistant showed her a romance.

"This is an exquisite piece", he said, "but unfortunately it's in a key with four flats."

"Oh, that's no problem", answered the young lady, "if there are more than two, I just scratch them out."

———————

Travel
Scientific Correspondence

Plombières and Baden

First letter

To the Editor in Chief of the *Journal des Débats*[123]

*Plombières—The Vosges—The piscine—Pleasure trips—Visit to Mlle.
Dorothée—The peasants of the Vale of Ajol—The Emperor*

Plombières, 24 August

Monsieur,

A horizontal position is manifestly the most favourable for exercising
one's intelligence and expanding one's mind, and it's easy to see why. Our
brain is the boiler that produces the steam we call thought, which propels
and so often derails the train of human affairs; our blood is the boiling
water which is transformed into steam—any physiologist will tell you so.
The more freely the liquid flows in the boiler, the more steam, or thought,
it will generate.

Voltaire was ill in bed when he wrote *Candide*, but enjoyed robust health
when he set to work on the *Henriade*.[124]

Bernardin de Saint-Pierre is said to have brought a hammock back from
the Indies, which he liked to lie in while doing his writing; that was where
he dreamed up his delightful masterpieces *Paul et Virginie* and *The Indian
Cottage*. Later when he concocted his *Harmonies of Nature*, in which he
tries to explain the phenomenon of the tides by the melting of the polar ice,
the hammock was the worse for wear and he no longer used it.[125]

J.-J. Rousseau was lying stretched out at the foot of a tree in the Forest
of Vincennes when he improvised his famous *Prosopopoeia of Fabricius*,
but he was doubtless standing when he wrote the comedy *Narcissus or the
Self-Lover* and several chapters of his *Dictionary of Music*.[126]

Tempted by these illustrious examples of the procedure's effectiveness,
I've often thought of hanging by my feet when I feel drained of spirit and
intelligence. Only the fear of not being able to let myself down again has
held me back. But I know three or four imbeciles to whom I wouldn't mind
applying this form of inspiration, just for forty-eight hours.

Anyway, I was lying in the pine forest by the old castle at Baden when I read the letter in which you were kind enough to complain of my silence and inactivity. Maintaining my horizontal position, I at once began to compose a most lively and interesting response, eloquent, passionate, clear but distinctive in style, and full of striking and erudite detail. Carried away by the charm of the narrative I was preparing for you about my travels, I got up to go and write it down—for in the end it must always come to that, of course.

Imagine my despair, when I got back, at finding myself unable to recall either eloquence, or passion, or style, or memory! I had no recollection at all of the fine descriptions, with such rich imagery, that I had been thinking up an hour earlier in my horizontal position. In fact I was reduced to the intellectual mediocrity, not to say the utter mental blankness, of the perpendicular man. It was pouring with rain, so I could not go back to my pine forest to gather my ideas. You'll say that one can always lie down somewhere, on a bed or a settee or even the floor. Well, I did just that, but without the slightest effect. My blood had gone cold, the boiler refused to boil, I remained stupid. Nature is so capricious. . . .

So I'll tell you of my tour in the Vosges and the duchy of Baden as best I can, in the style of a guidebook, with due apologies. At any rate I'll impose as much order as possible on my narrative, and not tell you anything not directly relevant to the subject.

For a start, the name of the Vosges reminds me of quite a good joke of Monsieur Méry's.[127] After the 1848 revolution, the Republican government changed the name of the Place Royale to Place des Vosges; there was also talk of renaming the Rue Royale Rue des Vosges. Monsieur Méry, a logical man if ever there was one, on the assumption that the name of the Département should always be substituted for the adjective "royal", wrote a letter addressed "To the Director of the Vosges Academy of Music"— and it duly arrived.

You mention the waters I'm supposed to be taking—indeed I *am* taking them, for I'm not well—and you ask which I prefer. Well, I prefer the waters you don't "take", those of Baden. As for the others, since I've only tried one sort, I can't form any comparison.

I will not say to you, like Caesar, "Veni, vidi Vichy"; first because the *Journal des Débats* is a serious French-language newspaper, which would not let such an abuse of the Latin tongue appear in its columns, and secondly because I haven't actually seen Vichy at all. I went straight from Paris to the spa of Plombières, and returned there again later, for reasons which I'll explain.

Plombières is a spring formed by Nature in the centre of the Royal Mountains (or the Vosges Mountains, if you insist on giving them their old Republican name). It is gloomy in summer and frightful in winter; yet the

Figure 19. Plombières—general view of the town and baths, from the Épinal road, [1836]. Bibliothèque Nationale de France.

"Plombières is . . . gloomy in summer and frightful in winter; yet the surrounding country-side is delightful" (page 82).

surrounding countryside is delightful. So it's absolutely essential to get out of the place to enjoy oneself. But the Emperor was there,[128] and everywhere for miles around there was an air of festivity—in the mountains, in the woods and at the spa itself. Everywhere there were garlands, flower arrangements, waving flags, gleaming uniforms, rolling drums, peals of bells, military bands, shouts of "hurrah" making the valley ring, balls, concerts, balloon ascents, municipal deputations, merry troops of peasants in their Sunday best, proud beauties done up to the nines, actors from the Vosges Palace theatre in Paris, writers, artists, intellectuals, mayors, deputy mayors, subprefects and prefects, celebrities without authority, authorities without celebrity.

It was indeed a transformation, and a splendid one.

There's a craze among new arrivals here for enquiring into the etymology of the name Plombières.[129] All sorts of derivations are fetched up, some from German, some from French, some from Latin, and each more far-fetched than the last. For Heaven's sake! Plombières comes from "plomb", lead. Lead is a metal—I hope nobody will dispute that; but iron is another, and one which definitely has its price. Now the mountains which tower over this little place are full of iron ore—their ferruginous waters stain the ditches with iron oxide; and since iron, being a metal, leads one naturally to think of lead, isn't that quite enough to account for the name Plombières? This derivation, as simple as it is obvious, is the only one tenable. Let's not discuss it any further.

The population of Plombières consists of two very different classes of individuals in summer: visitors, either sightseeing or taking the waters, and natives. This latter class—small in number, although Plombières does have a few inhabitants—congregates after the start of the snows in a tomb-shaped monument which occupies the middle of the "town" and is called the Roman bath. There, from morning to evening, kept warm at no cost by the water circulating under the tiles of the upper hall, men, women and children busy themselves with fine needlework and embroidery.

What else to do but sew in such a dismal haunt?[130]

And don't imagine it's only weak or sickly men or legless cripples or hunchbacks or dwarves who apply themselves to this work. Dear me, no! Even strapping young fellows, veritable Herculeses, embroider away at the feet of that tiresome Omphale whose name is Necessity.[131]

The houses are all locked up, and their occupants return only at night. During the day the homes of citizens who rent their rooms in summer to people taking the waters are empty except for courageous old women on their own, trusting that their appearance alone would put to flight any thieves who turn up. For the older generation in the Vosges is pretty formidable.

Figure 20. Emperor Napoléon III. Lithograph by Marie-Alexandre Alophe, Paris, c1853. Richard Macnutt Collection, Withyham.
"The Emperor was there, and everywhere for miles around there was an air of festivity" (page 84).

The main street of Plombières is quite wide in places, wide enough for four large men to walk abreast. Women used to enjoy the same privilege, but no longer. Now no more than one woman can walk along it at a time—the law of the crinoline forbids it. Even so, these lionesses' finery is always crumpled and stained on both sides as a result of constantly rubbing against the walls.[132]

These details, Monsieur, and those which follow, are not copied from any of the numerous publications concerning Plombières, I assure you. Anxious to see things for myself, I have not read any of them; so what you're getting is the result of my own all-too-personal observations.

There's a "saloon" at Plombières where one could play billiards and read the papers, if both papers and billiards were not permanently "taken", as waiters in cafés say. Prayers are said on Sunday in a small and modest church, but there's no cemetery, or at least I couldn't find one. It seems (could it be due to the efficacy of the waters?) that nobody dies in Plombières. Doubtless that's why all the inhabitants have such an appearance of age, and possess such depth of experience . . . in business matters.

People taking the waters during the summer season divide their days between three occupations: the waters themselves, set meals and "pleasure trips". Ah, those pleasure trips! They're the really painful and gruelling part of the régime prescribed for the sick by their doctors, and by the sick in turn for those unlucky enough to enjoy good health. You'll soon see why.

People usually take the waters in the morning, either aristocratically in a bathtub inside a little room, as in Paris, or democratically in a large stone cistern teeming with all the gibbosities and infirmities and deformities of every sex and every age. This toad-hole bears a name which would be enough to make me detest it even if I didn't already abhor its very essence (which is not essence of roses, you may be sure), the name "piscine". Piscine! What euphony! What images that awakens! Piscine! A word of Latin origin describing a place where fish swim about. Piscine! It reminds me of the lepers of Jerusalem who went to a "piscine", according to the Bible, to wash their ulcers.[133]

Anyway, everybody goes there, except for a few eccentrics who aren't afraid of being thought squeamish. I'll restrain myself from giving you even an approximate idea of the sight and sound of all these creatures done up in a scruffy sort of sack, more or less well-fastened, more or less buoyant when in the water, and more or less clinging when out of it; or of the conversations, the political discussions, the facetious remarks, the commercial travellers' songs, the whole lot sprayed and splashed with hot water by boisterous children, the tadpoles of the toad-hole, who have thought up the most amazing ways of annoying their neighbours.

"So despite your distaste, you've seen the piscine?", you ask. No, Monsieur, I *haven't* seen it, and I earnestly hope I never will. Think what I'd have said about it if I *had* seen it. Piscine! Piscine! To add insult to injury they have invented the verb "to piscine" at Plombières: "we are piscining,

Figure 21. *Le Règne de la crinoline* ("The reign of the crinoline"). Anonymous lithograph from *Un Siècle d'Histoire de France par l'Estampe, 1770–1871 (Collection De Vinck)*, Volume 8, chapter 13. Bibliothèque Nationale de France.

"Now no more than one woman can walk along [the main street of Plombières] at a time—the law of the crinoline forbids it" (page 86).

Figure 22. *La saison des eaux* ("The season for taking the waters"). Drawing by Cham (Amédée de Noé, 1818–79). Bibliothèque Nationale de France.

1 Do like me, my dear, go to Goodwater—it's done my chest a power of good.
2 The management of Goodwater finding people who from their appearance might be expected to take the waters.
3 Waters of the Pyrenees. Recommended for people who wish to regain strength in their legs.
4 The inconvenience when two tourists meet on a major route in the Pyrenees.
"People taking the waters during the summer season divide their days between
. . . the waters themselves, set meals and 'pleasure trips'" (page 86).

he or she is piscining"! Luckily, Plombières now has reason to expect major technical improvement and refurbishment, with no expense spared; it has been given a promise, and this promise, coming from very high up, is already in the process of being made good. So we must hope that within a few years we'll be able to drown the memory of the piscine in rather less primitive and more decent baths.

The surroundings of Plombières include some delightful spots, as I've already said, with imposing views, pleasant retreats, and places to rest in the woods, all worthy of celebration by the Virgils and the Bernardins de Saint-Pierre of every age and every land. Such are the *Vale of Ajol,* seen from the *Old Bower,* the mountainside plateaux which lead there, *King Stanislas's Spring,* the *Fox's Spring,* the *Valley of the Rocks* and ten others which I won't mention.

It's the custom among those taking the waters to set out after lunch, that is to say about eleven o'clock, for one of these poetic spots, in little caravans assembled for these occasions, paradoxically described as "pleasure trips". They would indeed be delightful outings, if one could only go in one's own time, at one's own pace, in tolerable weather conditions, and almost or entirely alone. But usually one goes up in groups of eight or ten people, at least six of whom are on donkeys, accompanied by three or four donkey-men or women of most disagreeable manner, in sunshine strong enough to melt stone, without being able to stop where one likes or to frolic in the thyme or the heather, like the hare in the fable.[134] One is hauled along by the donkey-men, who, being paid by the journey, are anxious to make as many trips as possible during the day, and are therefore very aware that time means money.

In fact, these are really purgatory trips. What's more, the donkey is a stupid animal. Despite his air of humility and resignation, he shows himself to be far more stubborn than the mule. When he's carrying some overweight windbag of a Monsieur Prudhomme,[135] holding forth about his civic duties, and about the sword of honour he has received—it was "the greatest day of his life", and he promises to use it "both to challenge and to defend our institutions"—if you try to quicken his pace (the donkey's, that is) in order to get clear of him (the windbag) by falling behind, the wretched creature (the donkey) becomes utterly thick-skinned and deaf; insensible to blows, he proceeds with Stoic gravity and obstinately matches his pace to yours. If, on the other hand, he's carrying a graceful crinoline with whom you'd be happy to walk along and chat, you may address the most urgent entreaties to the hellish beast not to go too fast, but all in vain, for he bounds over rocks and brambles at a trot, and leaves you marooned, all alone on the bare mountain, in a blazing heat of fifty degrees centigrade, almost a mile from any shade.

Then there are a dozen other little vexations which I won't tell you about, but which take their toll.

Ah, the pleasure trip! The Lord preserve you from it! The only thing which led me to describe it as mere purgatory, when I'd have had every

Figure 23. *Les deux ânes et les deux à pieds* ("The two donkeys and the two walkers"). Gustave Doré (1832–83). Bibliothèque Nationale de France.
   "Ah, the pleasure trip! The Lord preserve you from it!" (page 89).

reason to compare it with Hell itself, was that in general, although one returns worn out and shattered, burnt, "dustied" (a word used in the Vosges to mean "covered with dust"), with one's head and throat on fire, one's feet in shreds, in the devil of a temper, miserable at the waste of a day, at seeing nature's beauties in quite the wrong way, at the interrupted reveries and the suppressed emotions, still one does—almost always—return.

I was subjected to this trial by fire one day when the pleasure trip organisers had decided on a pilgrimage to the *Old Bower* and a visit to Mlle. Dorothée. Mlle. Dorothée, who is a celebrity in Plombières and held in high regard from Épinal to Rémiremont, is an honest and likeable person, born a long time ago in the Vale of Ajol, where she has remained for all but a few years. Her connections with the fashionable world have caused her to acquire a very correct accent, a distinctive but unaffected manner of expressing herself, and a demeanour that is dignified and courteous without being obsequious. She hand-makes instruments—modest instruments, for modest music—which she calls spinets, no doubt because they are sold at Épinal, for they have nothing in common with the true spinet other than the use of four metal strings, which are stretched over a hollow piece of wood with a series of frets like the neck of a guitar and plucked with a quill.

Mlle. Dorothée also writes poems full of expressions of benevolence towards the travellers who go to visit her, and offers her guests delicious milk, kirsch, and excellent wholemeal bread on a stone table constructed seventy years ago by her father on a terrace overlooking the Vale of Ajol from a great height. The view from there is indescribable.

On the day when our little caravan, consisting of a bouquet (or should I say a sheaf?) of the most graceful crinolines of Plombières, set out for Mlle. Dorothée's retreat, the donkeys were again in the party, and, true to form, they managed to make things miserable for those of us on foot. Despite our yells, they finally left us behind. So three of us were abandoned to the fusillade of a raging sun, in the midst of a barren landscape, without the least idea which direction to take to reach our goal.

After some moments of bad temper, we were quite surprised to re-experience sensations which the donkeys' company would undoubtedly have denied us. We walked in silence, studying the distinctive features of the high mountain plateau on which we had been so inhumanly stranded, features quite absent from the great plains lower down. These high regions seem more richly endowed with air and light; a sense of mystery hangs over the landscape; the spirit of solitude dwells in it. This open and deserted cottage; this little pool where fairies must come to disport themselves secretly at night; this grove of immovable oaks. . . . No ugly horned animals chewing the cud and looking slovenly; no mangy dog barking; no goitred, ragged shepherd; no domestic fowl, chickens or turkeys, recalling the farmyard or the stable. Peace and quiet all around, with little pink tufts of heather waving gently in the breath of a light breeze.

Two larks flash past in amorous pursuit; one of them disappears in a cornfield, the other flies up in a spiral, preluding his great paean of joy. Goethe has said: "No one can fail to be stirred by profound emotion when an unseen lark overhead pours out its joyful song far and wide."[136] It's the most poetic of birds. Don't speak to me of your classical nightingale, *Philomela sub umbra*,[137] which needs resonant flower-filled glades as its concert hall, sings at night in order to be noticed, looks to see if it's being listened to, is always aiming for effect with its florid cavatinas, full of trills and roulades, and uses special tones to mimic the expression of a grief which it does not feel—a bird with big greedy eyes, which eats large worms and would gladly seek the support of a claque. It's the very model of a tenor earning a hundred thousand francs.

But watch and listen to the male lark—he's a true artist. Heedless of the effect he can produce, he sings because singing is his joy; he needs open air and unconfined space. See him in the evening of a fine day, when the approach of nightfall is just beginning to make itself felt, see him dart up to salute the sun as it sinks to the horizon and the star which glimmers in the sky's vault. He sings as he climbs towards the heavens. He swims in the ether—we understand and share his unbounded joy. He climbs and climbs, singing all the time. Little by little his exultant voice fades, but we know it has lost none of its power—only distance has softened its brilliancy. Up, up he climbs, then disappears, but we hear him still, until, lost in the blue of the sky, worn out with inspiration, drunk with freedom, fresh air, melody and light, he daringly folds his wings and plummets from an immense height straight down to his nest, where his mate and chicks, grateful for his lovely singing, revive him with their caresses.

The three of us listened. We kept on listening after this Pindar of birds, back in his beloved nest, had finished his last verse and was doubtless murmuring to his family in intimate tones that our coarse ears could not catch. But we were completely lost and rather anxious about the young crinolines. Luckily, we woke up an old lady whom we passed stoutly asleep in a ditch in the sunshine, and she offered to lead us over the fields. Scarcely had we accepted her services as a guide than the old lady got us on to the topic of the Emperor, asking if we had seen him, if we knew him, and so on.

"'Coz oy meself knows 'im well", she continued. "T'other day, 'a wuz passin' by 'ere, jes' like 'ee, fer to see Miz Dorothée; some folk from Ajol Vale come down to wait fer 'im by th' edge o' this 'ere wood. There wuz a great general way afore the rest o' th' troop with another gent. Them country folk says to 'im:

'Eh, sor, be 'ee th' Emperor?'

'Nay, there 'e be, comin' over th' field there.'

So th' Ajol folk run d'rec'ly to th' field and say to th' other gent:

'Tis 'ee be th' Emperor, then, sor?'

'Yes, my lads', says th' other to 'em.

'Ah, then give us tha' blessin', sor.'

An' down on thur knees they go afore th' Emperor. 'A wanted 'em to get up, but 'a couldn' make 'em. 'A twirled 'is moustache, an' 'twuz clear to see 'a had tears in 'uz eyes, the pore mun."

"And you saw this?"

"Fer sure oy saw ut, jes' like oy see 'ee. An' a ways on, up by that there farm, them didn' know thur way, and 'a went to ask ol' Nicolas who wuz winnowin' buckwheat afore 'uz door. Nicolas told 'em wheres 'a should head, an' th' Emperor put a coin in 'uz hand. Nicolas s'posed 'twuz twenty sous, but when them wuz all far gone, 'e opened 'uz hand an' looked an' saw 'a had a real gold napoleon, all gold;[138] 'a gave a holler, an' then 'a begun to swear—'a swore fit to terrify 'un. Fer joy, o' course, 'a swore fer joy; but all th' same, 'tain't fit even then to swear so."

Gossiping away like this in her rustic dialect, the good lady succeeded in getting us to Mlle. Dorothée's house pretty well unscathed, where we found our charming crinolines and our villainous donkeys, along with kirsch and milk.

Second letter

Arrival at Mlle. Dorothée's—The Vale of Ajol—Forever crawling—Old age, ill-health and death—The Stanislas Spring—The moraines—The glaciers—Set meals—Backbiting and gossip—The Grunwater—Dr. Sibille, and his cure for intestinal ailments—Fathers without bowels—The windbag's fright—Vivier's concert—The Emperor's soirée—Baden—Monsieur Clapisson's new opera: a hit—The concert—Mme. Viardot—Mlle. Duprez—Beethoven—Return to Plombières—Depression

Plombières, 30 August

We were greeted with the inevitable exclamations, pitched in a whole range of keys and timbres and rhythms, "Ah! There you are!"

"What happened to you?"

"We were so worried!"

"Were you indeed! It was you that dumped us there!"

"It was the wretched donkeys!"

"Oh, come now, sor, 'tis plain them on donkeys travels faster than them on foot."

"And my saddle slipped."

"Yes! We caught it just in time."

"We picked raspberries."

"What a view!"

"God, it's beautiful!"

"No, sor, I bain't stayin'! We be 'avin' to get back to Plombié d'rec'ly. I be awaited fer goin' to the Fox Spring. I 'ave to be gettin' back wi' me donkeys!"

"Well, be off with you then, my fine donkey-wallah, we'll return on foot. Do you think we've struggled all this way up just to spend two minutes and leave without seeing anything?"

In the end we were allowed to enjoy the view, and to admire the Vale of Ajol, which stretches wide and deep below Mlle. Dorothée's house. It is a vast cradle of greenery, with a reddish-coloured village set at the bottom of the cradle like a child's toy, and a thousand arabesques delineated by variously hued clumps of fir, beech, birch and ash—that elegant tree which is the pride of the Vosges vegetation; the whole so fresh and peaceful, covered with a light blue veil and well framed on all sides.

On seeing it, the first inclination of the spectator standing at the edge of the terrace is to launch himself into space to swim luxuriantly in this great lake of pure air. But he quickly suppresses the spontaneous urge impelling him forward; he clutches on to a tree so as not to fall over the precipice, and cries out like Faust, "Oh! That I had wings!"[139] Surely it's only natural to feel a sense of humility at this, saying to oneself: "The stupidest and heaviest bird of all, a goose, can do it, yet I can't!"

Oh mankind, so proud of your inventions and your machines for production and destruction and your familiarity with steam and lightning, which you make virtually your slaves, so puffed up with your scientific and mathematical discoveries. You build houses on wheels and floating palaces; you've even pressed the laws of gravity into service, illogical as it may appear, to lift great spheres up to the clouds. Their ability to ascend should have opened the way for you to travel by air, yet still you crawl on the earth. Dragging yourselves along on land or water with the aid of wind or steam is still only crawling. And until you find a sure way of transporting yourselves freely in space, either by flying or by piloting aerial ships or aerial towns, you will belong whether you like it or not to the class of crawling creatures and remain no more than over-ambitious caterpillars or jumped-up snails.

Stuck up on the outside of one of the walls of Mlle. Dorothée's modest house, garlanded with laurel, was a quatrain of alexandrine verses in a sylvan vein, concerning the Emperor's visit a few days before.

"It's very fine, Mademoiselle, it has both feeling and style. No doubt His Majesty was well pleased?"

"His Majesty seemed particularly moved at seeing the part of my house where Queen Hortense and the Empress Joséphine had taken their repose before him."

"He must indeed have been touched by such memories—he can't have expected to find them in such an out-of-the-way spot. And he came here on foot, in heat like this?"

"Yes, Mesdames."

"And did His Majesty also compliment you on your milk? It's excellent."

"The Emperor didn't try it."

"What! Didn't you offer him any?"

"I was so overwhelmed I didn't even think of it. Yet he did ask me whether we had any cows. . . ."

"Well then! That was clear enough."

"Oh dear! Yes, I think you must be right, he was thirsty, and that was an indirect way of letting me know—he didn't have the heart to ask me for some milk. Goodness, how ashamed I am! It was disgraceful of me. But he promised to come back, and I shall make profuse apologies."

"If the Emperor does come back, you can be sure this time he will have refreshments brought, and he'll have them there on the lawn right under your nose, since you didn't even offer him a cup of milk at this inhospitable table."

After tormenting our poor hostess's conscience like this, and condescending to write some verses in her album, to which she replied with a whole sonnet two days later, we made the return journey without incident, without getting too tired, and without losing our way this time, some of us singing, others dreaming and philosophising a little. A charming lady was absolutely determined to know "Why do we have to grow old, suffer illhealth and die?"

"Oh, I agree, old age, ill-health and death are all terms which refer to utterly deplorable experiences, and it would be much better to enjoy oneself the whole time. If you ask me, it's really an atrocious mockery that one should grow up, learn to recognise beauty and truth, and experience the flowering of one's intelligence and emotions, only to see the mirage gradually fade away and all one's hopes evaporate in the midst of this sublime ecstasy; one would only drive oneself mad by persisting in trying to work it out. But, Madame, there are many other inexplicable features of this mousetrap in which we are all caught, with love and art and the earth's poetry as its bait and death as its spring. Let me ask you a question: Do you know which bird is the most vicious?"

"No indeed, so many are vicious. Is it the vulture? Or the pigeon which kills its young?"

"No, it's the finch."

"The finch? That playful songster, so graceful and lively? Good heavens! Why?"

"*Nobody knows.*"[140]

"I see what you're getting at. But you're being unfair to the finch, while I'm being unfair to no one when I say old age, ill-health and death are atrocious and abominable."

"Not even to whatever vulture will eventually devour us? No indeed—and, I assure you, that gruesome bird is quite as loathsome to me as to you. But if you ask why it's so hateful and appalling, even in thousands of years' time, if the human race still exists, they'll still be saying, just like us today,

Nobody knows."

Two days later (for at least twenty-four hours' rest is absolutely essential after a "pleasure trip"), we had to haul ourselves off to the Stanislas Spring. To get there, you start by following a pretty and quite easy track, recently laid out on the Emperor's orders, and since the rest of the route is through woods, it's at least shaded, if not exactly cool.

Another philosophical question brought up during the climb: which is preferable, dying of heat or of cold?

Everyone agreed it was preferable . . . that *nobody knows.*

When we reached the spring, whose trickle of water was so meagre as to be almost imperceptible, we found another magnificent view, along with more milk and verses. Here are four about King Stanislas which I took from a rock with a weeping naiad beneath it. I pass them on to you quite fresh.

> Happy with what's left to me,
> Good king, could I each day reclaim
> The tears due always to your name,
> Then less would be my modesty.

To get to the Stanislas spring by the new path you have to cross an immense accumulation of grey rocks, a chaotic mass of boulders of every shape and size, jumbled and heaped on top of each other, which looks like some gigantic ruin and has a vivid effect on the imagination. These great piles of rocks are called moraines or "murghers".[141] People always ask who could have put them there. Popular legend has it that in the days when the fairies were at work, those dainty labourers took it into their heads to build a bridge at this spot to cross from one mountain to the next; so they came one night carrying stones in their aprons to lay the foundations. But their queen, catching sight of a rash fellow watching them from the nearby wood, let out a great scream, and all the fairies let go of the ends of their aprons which they had been holding and fled in alarm, dropping their stones.

Some people claim these rock-piles were produced by ancient glaciers which, in the course of their slow downward progress, transported these fragments from the mountain tops to the valley—just as glaciers in the Alps do with some granite blocks. The only thing the authors of this explanation omit to tell us is how glaciers could have created the numerous moraines found near the *tops* of the mountains around Plombières. And even if there were none on the mountain-tops and they were only in the valleys—which is not in fact the case, remember—one must still face the fact that the glaciers must have picked up these boulders somewhere higher up in order to carry them down. So what had brought them all together when the glaciers reached them? This time it won't do to say "*Nobody knows*". It's obvious, in fact, that these moraines are simply the debris of the earth's rocky crust, shattered by the sudden upheaval which, in a global convulsion, produced the Vosges mountains. This debris was scattered indiscriminately in all directions by the violence of the shock, and its weight and momentum caused it to accumulate in greater masses on the slopes and at the feet of the mountains.

Another windbag, who says he'd "have liked to be a famous geologist", is completely in agreement with my opinion on this subject.

"Besides", he added yesterday, with a degree of good sense that his attitudinising had not led me to suspect, "what has become of these supposed glaciers? Did the earth just get warmer? We all know it's actually getting cooler."

"Alas, Monsieur, we all know that we really know hardly anything, and the old folk of Plombières will assure you, if you take that line, that there *were* once glaciers on these mountains. In fact their ice was so hard it was used to make gun flints. So of course once the percussion cap had been invented and percussion mechanisms for guns had become the norm, Providence, which never does anything without reason, must have got rid of the glaciers."

"Well yes, that's certainly logical. That point hadn't occurred to me. God! How I would have liked to be a famous geologist! I've always had a taste for geology. But life's so short! It just shows how slowly one learns: I shall clock up sixty in eighteen months' time, and up to now it hadn't dawned on me you could make gun flints of ice. Nature is unfathomable. By the way, just now I used the word "geologist" to mean an expert in geology. Is that correct, Monsieur?"

"Theology makes theologian, astrology produces astrologer, entomology gives entomologist. So I think we should go halves in the matter; you say geologer, I'll say geologian, and we'll both be bound to get it wrong."

"That's fine by me too—I wouldn't have liked to be a great grammarian."

"Then you've nothing to worry about."

.   .   .   .

The third important daily routine at Plombières takes place, as I mentioned, at set meals. There are too many of these get-togethers, but they're generally well organised. There aren't many windbags in evidence, and it's pretty unusual to find them standing on the dignity of their "swords of honour" or holding forth about "our institutions". The only problem is being forced, as at Boileau's banquet,

To turn to one's left and eat sideways on.[142]

The service is extremely slow. The chickens consist of nothing more than two wings; if only one is left when you're served, you feel bad about taking it, because your neighbour then secretly thinks you selfish; if you're decent enough not to take it, you feel even worse. Excellent trout are served, and large numbers of frogs (to the horror of the English). My conclusion from all of this, in a nutshell, is that at Plombières, like anywhere else, the set meal is no more than a piscine for dining.

After dinner, everyone goes out into the street. The ladies show off their breathtakingly billowing outfits outside their houses, on benches and chairs. Others stand on their balconies, and all of them devour each other with their eyes with an ardour and enthusiasm for which parallels are hard to find, even in the lions' dens of Paris.[143]

"That young lady in blue, she's still pretty, of course, even though . . . her upper arm was showing at yesterday's ball, and you could see . . . well, such bad luck! But you wouldn't come to Plombières if you didn't have something wrong with you, would you?"

"Oh! That skinny lady has a funny idea of what's proper, allowing her daughter out in the evening in such a low-cut dress—all the way from her neck to . . . the middle of next week."

"You know what happened to that fat Russian Countess?"

"No."

"You mean you haven't heard about the hot-air balloon?"

"Not yet."

"Nobody's taken crinoline-mania as far as the Countess."

"No indeed, her circumference must be equal to the great bell of the Kremlin."

"Well, yesterday, on the ladies' promenade, a group of rascals launched a pink and white paper balloon, much larger even than your precious Moscow bell. No sooner had it appeared above the big ash-trees on the promenade than everyone started shouting 'Oh, heavens! The Countess has taken off!'"

There's a little river, or to be more precise a large stream, in Plombières. It's called Grunwater by sophisticated people, and Gruntwater by the locals.[144] The latter is its real name; the former, with all deference to the highbrows, is only a pretentious *correction* of it. The river does in fact flow very noisily, making a constant grunting sound. With its twisting and turning it imparts a sort of animation to the lower part of town, but both this and the clarity of its water are rather offset by the variety of rubbish which it always carries. Butchers throw in animal debris which is as disagreeable to see as to smell. Everywhere you can see long intestinal tubes with one end caught on a rock, and the other floating in the current and snaking about like an eel. It's quite revolting. The windbag, thoroughly intrigued by these vile objects, asked me one morning what could be the reason for their presence in the Gruntwater.

"Don't you know, my dear sir, that the waters of Plombières are excellent for curing intestinal ailments? Monsieur Sibille, the doctor who is superintendent of the waters, . . ."

"Pardon my interrupting, I just want to ask you something about the superintendent, this Monsieur Sibille; does he have a good reputation as a doctor?"

"Yes, and also as a wit and a perfect gentleman, which is much rarer. Unlike other doctors, who insist on choosing their patients carefully and only take on those who are fit, healthy and in good shape, he is prepared to look after genuinely ill people, even the weakest and sickliest and most hopeless cases, and he restores them to health in no time."

"Tell me, where does he come from?"

"Good heavens, where could he come from but Cumae in Italy? His family is extremely ancient; it was already famous in Rome in Augustus' time, and Virgil mentions the Sibilles of Cumae frequently in his poems."[145]

"I see. So tell me about these intestinal ailments."

"Well, Dr. Sibille's very sensible idea was this: wouldn't the cure be less taxing, as well as more reliable and effective, if instead of immersing the sick person in the water and weakening him by interminable baths, only the particular organ causing the complaint were immersed? It clearly makes sense. Inspired by this brilliant idea, the ingenious doctor soon devised a wonderful operation, which you won't find described in the Sibylline books, for he keeps it secret; it's completely painless, and enables the sick person's intestines to be gently extracted from his body. They are then exposed to the stream's healing current, and within thirty-six hours a cure is effected. Of course, the patient has to maintain a rigorous fast during this period."

"Naturally, and he'd be crazy not to put up with it. The end justifies the means."

"Afterwards the intestines are replaced, again without pain, and this marvellous treatment is complete. But I must tell you the whole truth: this great physical improvement is unfortunately sometimes accompanied by emotional side effects. You are aware that the Gruntwater is teeming with trout? Well the trout is a voracious fish, and it often happens that while the intestines are in the water . . . I'm telling you the truth . . . need I say more?"

"I shiver at the thought!"

"Yes, part of the digestive system may be missing afterwards, a few yards of intestinal tube. . . . The wise doctor, who knows what a dangerous setback the patient's imagination could cause in such a case, keeps quite quiet about this mishap. He replaces what's left of the tube and the patient recovers without knowing a thing. His digestion functions more quickly, that's all. But his emotional state is no longer the same: he's rude and abrupt, he mistreats his wife and children, he may even go to the grave extreme of wilfully reducing them to ruin and appropriating all he can of their inheritance. Good, respectable heads of families have been known to leave Plombières after their treatment as fathers almost entirely 'lacking in bowels'."[146]

"You astonish me!"

"Well, Monsieur, you yourself remarked yesterday concerning a geological question, quite rightly too, that 'nature is unfathomable'."

"Yes I did; but even so I'm appalled; and if ever I'm afflicted with an intestinal ailment, which God forbid, I shall certainly not resort to Monsieur Sibille with his daring technique—I'm too concerned that my children should continue to have a good father."

Vivier, that great enemy of all windbags, was in Plombières when the season was at its height. He had the ambitious idea of giving a concert there. Having made this decision, he booked the "saloon"; nothing more was needed but the music and the musicians. For you really can't do without them in a concert; it's not like so many operas where dialogue, often neither brisk nor lively, makes a perfectly satisfactory replacement for the music. Even if Vivier's French horn were to multiply itself so as to produce three or four sounds simultaneously it wouldn't be enough.[147]

It was decided to try Mlle. Favel, that delightful deserter from the Opéra-Comique in Paris, and she was begged to come to Vivier's aid.[148] At first Mlle. Favel said no, then renewed entreaties drew a feeble yes from her, and a few hours later she delivered a resounding formal no. Apparently Mlle. Favel has discovered a singing teacher (thereby surpassing Columbus's feat)[149] who has forbidden her to utter a single note before the year of our Lord 1860, promising that if she fulfils this condition he will furnish her with a talent at least equal to the genius of the leading goddesses of the age.

Trust is the ruin of many.[150]

Vivier next invited a young singer from Nancy, Mlle. Millet, who possesses a thread of a voice as thin as the trickle of water from the Stanislas spring, together with an accompanist, Monsieur Humblot, an excellent musician and skilful pianist, a former student at the Paris Conservatoire, who teaches at Épinal. As for a grand piano, it was pointless even to think of it. There are plenty of Alexandre melodiums at Plombières (where aren't there these days?), but that poetic and religious instrument is no replacement for the piano, and they had to resign themselves to using one of those nasal-sounding pieces of furniture people insist on calling "upright pianos".

The concert took place. Despite their high price, all the tickets were sold. The windbag was in two minds, but was given to understand that this "occasion" enjoyed august patronage, and that his absence would be noticed, so in the end he resigned himself to going "in order not to cause a scandal". Vivier enjoyed a tremendous success, even though the menu of the musical feast offered to the public by its beneficiary was found somewhat lacking in sustenance. It consisted of prime venison and lots of nuts: hunting pieces with triple fanfares, by Vivier; barcarolles and comic songs from the light music repertoire, by Mlle. Millet. Nothing else.

Three days later, the Emperor held a private soirée, at which Vivier produced his most extraordinary tours de force, his ingenious semi-lyrical proverbs, his barrack-room idylls, in other words all of his huge repertoire. The evening could not have been livelier. His Majesty fell into a mood of irrepressible jollity, as did his guests, and several times complimented the spirited violinist-actor-pianist-mime-singer on the matchless originality of his pieces and on the verve with which he performed them. There was dancing during the intervals. At two o'clock in the morning, after the dancers had left, the Emperor, who had pretended to make his departure, came back to chat for a while with the diners. At half past two we retired, charmed by the Imperial hospitality and exhausted with laughing and applauding. At four o'clock I left for Baden.

· ·

The first event at Baden was the opening night of a French opera in two acts by Messieurs Saint-Georges and Clapisson, entitled *The Sylph*.[151] The two principal roles are very well acted and sung by Montjauze and Mlle. Duprez.[152] It is lively and gay, studded with graceful melodies and well-managed scenes, and the score is skilfully orchestrated. As it seems impossible to me that this work will not very shortly be produced in Paris, after the welcome it received at Baden, I shall say no more about it here.

So to the concert organised through the good offices of Monsieur Bénazet for the benefit of the French flood victims,[153] and its lengthy preparations. In the morning I had to go to Karlsruhe to rehearse the musicians of the ducal chapel there, returning in the afternoon for a rehearsal with those of Baden; in the evening I had to sort out the music from Strasbourg and elsewhere, give instructions to the carpenter about erecting the platform, etc., etc.

On the eve of the concert there was a great influx of people into the Assembly Rooms. I met German friends from Berlin and Weimar, as well as well-known music-lovers from Russia, England, Switzerland and France, celebrated Parisian performers, members of the Institut in Paris and colleagues from the Paris press. The concert took place in the presence of this élite audience. Ten thousand six hundred francs in takings—performances of rare beauty—the delightful Karlsruhe chorus admirably trained by its skilful chorus-master Monsieur Krug—the orchestra irreproachable—Mme. Viardot sparkling with life and musical humour in her Chopin mazurkas, her Spanish airs, her cavatina from *La Sonnambula,* and even in her weighty

Figure 24. Baden—the Fremersberg road. Lithograph by Jules Coignet, 1859. Bibliothèque Nationale de France.

"For some years now the Baden seasons have been organised in a fashion that discourages all competition" (page 73).

Graun aria[154]—Mlle. Duprez innocent and touching in that fine piece from *Iphigenia in Aulis*:

Adieu, conservez dans votre âme
Le souvenir de notre ardeur,[155]

and also showing brilliant virtuosity in Verdi's piquant *Sicilienne*[156]—great applause for Messieurs Gremminger and Eberius of the Karlsruhe theatre—the scene from *Orpheus* done full justice—the Adagio of Beethoven's *Fourth Symphony* purely and poetically played by the orchestra. How this last swells the heart—if only one could express one's feelings! It is music of a higher sphere. Beethoven is a Titan, an Archangel, a Throne, a Domination. Seen from the height of his work, all the rest of the musical world seems Lilliputian. He could, indeed should, have paraphrased the words of the Gospel and said "Man, what have I to do with thee?"[157]

· ·

The following day I suffered a renewed attack of stomach pains, brought on by various causes among which severe exhaustion bulked large. Trusting, not without reason, in the efficacy of the Plombières waters, I went back there to seek urgent relief.

But what a change! No more need to sit sideways at the set meals; no more crinolines—the fat Countess from the Kremlin really has flown; no more uniforms, or military music, or celebrities, or authorities; the flower arrangements all vanished without a trace; Mlle. Dorothée's alexandrines reduced to just eleven feet;[158] nobody standing in their doorways to gawp at their neighbours after dinner; the clogs of passers-by echoing noisily in the deserted Plombières street. It's raining. The days succeed each other indistinguishably. I take an umbrella and go for a walk in the woods, listening to the harmonious, melancholy sound of water dripping on the leaves while the Grunwater grunts in its bed on the valley floor. A robin, that pleasing precursor of autumn, pokes its pretty head curiously between two branches, fixes its intelligent gaze on the motionless walker and seems to say, "What's this strange fellow doing in my territory in weather like this?" So I return, and write to you. All is gloom.

Three weeks ago we were all so flourishing in Plombières that even the sick had an air of being in fine fettle. Today people who are perfectly healthy have an air of sickness. It's still raining—it never stops. The Emperor has left. The windbag obstinately remains.

I wish I were back in Paris.

Farewell, Monsieur.

H. Berlioz

Aural aberrations and delusions

One day, at a concert in which one of Beethoven's most marvellous violin and piano sonatas, the *Kreutzer,*[159] was being played, I sat next to a young foreign musician recently arrived from Naples, where, he told me, he had never even heard of Beethoven. The sonata made an impression on him that was both forceful and profoundly disturbing. He was delighted by the andante, in variation form, and the finale. But after listening with almost painful attention to the first movement he said to me:

"That's very beautiful, isn't it, Monsieur? Don't you think so?"

"Yes indeed, it's beautiful, grand, original, admirable in every way."

"Well, Monsieur, I must confess I don't understand it."

He was both embarrassed and annoyed. This is a bizarre phenomenon that can be observed even among people who have a very good natural ear, but whose musical education is incomplete. It's impossible to fathom why they find certain pieces incomprehensible; they just don't understand them. They can't appreciate the basic idea of the piece, nor its development, nor its mode of expression, nor its accentuation, nor its structure, nor its melodic beauty, nor its harmonic richness, nor its colouring. They simply hear nothing; as far as these pieces are concerned, some people are quite deaf. What's more, besides completely failing to hear what's there in abundance, they often think they hear things which aren't there at all.

One such listener found the theme of an adagio "pale" and "drowned by the accompaniment":

"Do you like this tune?" I asked him one day, singing a long, slow melodic phrase.

"Oh, it's delightful, it has such perfect clarity and shape; splendid!"

"Look at the score, then. You see, it's the adagio whose theme you found 'pale'. Perhaps seeing it with your own eyes will convince you it can't possibly be drowned by the accompaniment, since it's played *unaccompanied.*"

Another reproached the author of a romance for spoiling its melody with a modulation which was badly timed, harsh, jarring and ill-prepared.

"Dear me!" replied the composer. "Please do me the favour of pointing out this inappropriate modulation; here's the score—see if you can find it."

The amateur music-lover searched in vain, and found nothing: the piece was in E flat from beginning to end, it *didn't modulate at all.*

I'm only giving examples of the mistaken ideas arising from misconceptions formed by listeners who are completely unbiased, or even well-disposed and anxious to like and admire what they hear. You can imagine what aberrations and delusions are possible with bigoted, spiteful, opinionated people. You could play them a perfect D major chord and tell them it occurred in the work of a composer they detested. "Stop, stop," they'd cry, "it's atrocious, you're making our ears hurt!"

They're truly mad.

I wonder whether in the pictorial arts anyone has ever established the existence of a similar race of maniacs, for whom red is green, black is white, streams are flames, trees are houses—and they themselves are Jupiter.

———————

Philosophical Correspondence

A Letter to Monsieur Ella, Director of the London Musical Union, on the subject of *The Flight into Egypt, Fragments of a Mystery in Antique Style**[160]

Some judge of authors' names, not works, and then
Nor praise nor blame the writings, but the men.[161]

My dear Ella,

You ask me why the Mystery (*The Flight into Egypt*) bears the note "attributed to Pierre Ducré, imaginary maître de chapelle".

It's the result of a misdeed I committed, a serious misdeed for which I've been severely punished and shall always reproach myself. This is what happened.

One evening I was at the home of the Baron de M***, a sincere and intelligent friend of the arts, with one of my former fellow-students from the Rome Academy, the gifted architect Duc.[162] Everyone except me was playing cards—écarté, whist and poker. I detest cards. By dint of great patience, and after thirty years of effort, I've reached the point of not knowing a single card game, so I can't possibly be press-ganged by players in need of a partner.

So my boredom was pretty plain to see when Duc turned to me and said:

"Since you're not doing anything, you'd better write a piece of music for my album!"

"With pleasure."

I took a piece of paper and drew a few staves on it, and before long an andantino for organ in four parts was set down on them. I felt it had a certain naïve and artless mysticism about it, and at once the idea came to me of matching it with words in a similar vein. The organ piece disappeared and became a chorus of Bethlehem shepherds addressing their farewells to the infant Jesus at the time of the Holy Family's departure for Egypt. The games of whist and poker were interrupted to listen to my religious stanzas. The mediaeval quality of the verse was enjoyed as much as that of my music.

"Now", I said to Duc, "I'm going to put you on the spot by attributing it to *you*."

---

*Now part of my sacred trilogy, *The Childhood of Christ*.

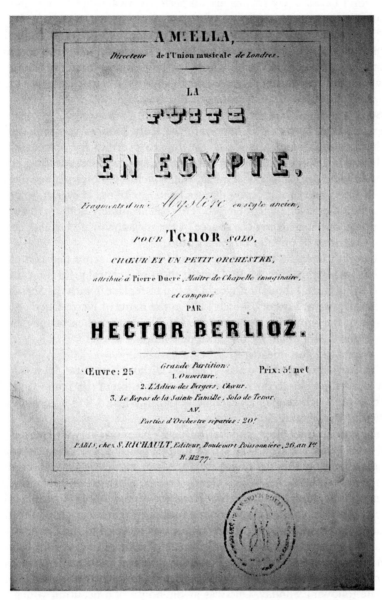

Figure 25. *The Flight into Egypt* ("La Fuite en Egypte")—title page of first edition of full score (Richault, Paris, 1852). Richard Macnutt Collection, Withyham.

"You ask me why ... *The Flight into Egypt* bears the note 'attributed to Pierre Ducré, imaginary maître de chapelle'" (see pages 106–9).

"Don't be silly! My friends are all perfectly aware that I know nothing at all about composition."

"Well that doesn't stop many people composing! All right then, since your vanity won't let you adopt my piece, I'll invent a name incorporating yours. It shall be Pierre Ducré, whom I appoint music-master of the Sainte-Chapelle in Paris during the seventeenth century. That will give my manuscript all the value of an archaeological curiosity."

So it was. But I had set out on the path of a Chatterton.[163] Some days later, at home, I wrote *The Repose of the Holy Family*—this time starting with the words—and a modest little fugato overture for a modest little orchestra in a modest little style, in F-sharp minor without a leading note— a mode which is no longer modish, but which resembles plainchant, and which the experts will tell you derives from one of the Phrygian or Dorian or Lydian modes of ancient Greece. This has absolutely nothing to do with the point, but is evidently the source of the melancholy and slightly home-spun character of popular laments of old.

A month later, by which time my old-fashioned score had completely gone from my thoughts, I found myself short of a choral piece for a concert I had to conduct. I thought it would be fun to replace it with the *Shepherds' Chorus* from my Mystery, which I left in the name of Pierre Ducré, music-master of the Sainte-Chapelle in Paris (1679). At the rehearsals the chorus was immediately taken by this antique-sounding music.

"Where did you unearth it?" they asked me.

"Unearthed is the right word", I replied without hesitation. "It was found in a bricked-up closet, during the recent restoration of the Sainte-Chapelle, written on parchment in an archaic notation which I had a great deal of difficulty deciphering."

The concert took place, and Pierre Ducré's piece was very well performed, and even better received. The critics heaped praise upon it two days later, congratulating me on my discovery. Only one expressed any doubt about its age and authenticity. Which clearly proves, whatever you may say, and Francophobe though you are, that there are *some* intelligent people everywhere. Another critic waxed emotional about the misfortune of this poor ancient master whose musical inspiration was revealed to the Parisians only after 173 years of obscurity. "For", he said, "none of us had even heard of him before, and even Monsieur Fétis's biographical dictionary of musicians, despite including so much abstruse information, makes no mention of him!"[164]

The following Sunday, Duc was at the house of a beautiful young lady who is very fond of early music and professes great disdain for modern works, at least when she's aware of their age. He asked his hostess:

"Well, Madame, what did you think of our latest concert?"

"Oh, very mixed, as usual."

"And the Pierre Ducré piece?"

"Perfect, delightful! That's what I call real music! Time has removed none of its freshness. True melody like that is all too rare, as our contemporary composers demonstrate. In any case, your Monsieur Berlioz will never produce anything to touch it."

At these words Duc could not help bursting out laughing, and was rash enough to reply:

"I'm sorry, Madame, but it *was* actually my Monsieur Berlioz who wrote the *Shepherds' Farewell*—right before my eyes one evening, on the corner of a card table."

The beautiful lady bit her lip, her pale complexion went pink with resentment, and turning her back on Duc she spitefully hurled this cruel sentence at him:

"Monsieur Berlioz is a charlatan!"

You can imagine my shame, my dear Ella, when Duc repeated this remark to me. I hastened to make honourable amends, by publishing this poor little work under my own humble name, although I did allow the words "Attributed to Pierre Ducré, imaginary maître de chapelle" to stand beneath the title, to remind myself of my disgraceful deceit.

Now people may say what they will; *my* conscience is clear. I no longer risk being held responsible for good, kind men working themselves into a state over imaginary misfortunes, or for pale ladies going pink, or for doubts being sown in the minds of critics not used to having doubts about anything. I shall sin no more. Goodbye, my dear Ella, and let my bad example serve as a lesson to you. Never take it into your head to set such a trap for *your* concert subscribers. Don't let yourself be described as I was. You have no idea what it is like to be called a charlatan, especially by a beautiful pale lady.

Your contrite friend,

Hector Berlioz

The débutante—The Director of the Opéra's despotism

It's no easy matter making one's début at the Opéra, even for a young singer of recognised talent with a beautiful voice who has been engaged in advance and handsomely paid by the theatre management, so that she may reasonably count on the goodwill of the Director and his desire to present her to the public as soon and as favourably as possible. The first necessity, whose importance can readily be grasped, is to choose the role in which she will appear. As soon as the subject comes up for discussion, a variety of voices make themselves heard, with more or less authority and force, giving the artist all sorts of contradictory advice:

"Sing this piece of mine!"

"Don't sing that piece!"

"You'll make a success of it, I guarantee."

"You'll come a cropper, I swear."

"All *my press* and *my claque* will be for you."

"All the public will be against you. But if you sing *my* piece you'll have the public on your side.

"Yes, but you'll have all my press and all my claque to contend with, and me into the bargain."

So the alarmed débutante turns to her Director for guidance. Dear me! What naïveté, asking a Director for direction! The poor man doesn't know himself which devil to please. He knows full well that these dealers in dud scores—popularly known as "bears"[165]—do indeed wield the influence they claim, and how important it is to humour them, particularly for a débutante. But one can't after all satisfy both white and black bears at once, so a decision is eventually reached in favour of the bear that growls loudest, and the piece for the début is announced.

The débutante knows her part, but since she has never yet sung it on stage, she needs at least one rehearsal, for which the orchestra, the chorus and the principal members of the cast must all be assembled. This marks the start of a series of intrigues, spitefulnesses, sillinesses, betrayals and acts of idleness and indifference fit to try the patience of a saint. One day the orchestra cannot be mustered, another day the chorus. Tomorrow the theatre is unavailable because of a ballet rehearsal; the day after that the tenor is going hunting, and when he returns two days later he'll be exhausted. The following week the baritone has a court case in Rouen which obliges him to leave Paris—he won't be back for eight or ten days. When he does arrive his wife is in labour and he can't leave her; but wishing to be agreeable to the débutante, he sends her some sugared almonds on the day of the child's christening.

So an appointment is made for a rehearsal in the practice room with the soprano. The débutante turns up at the specified time. The soprano, none too thrilled at seeing the dawn of a new star, keeps them waiting a little, but does eventually arrive. Only the accompanist fails to appear. Everyone leaves without any progress made.

The débutante wishes to complain to the Director. The Director has gone out, no one knows when he'll be back. She writes to him—the letter reaches him twenty-four hours later. The accompanist is reprimanded and receives a summons to another session, and this time he's punctual; it's the soprano's turn not to show up. No rehearsal is possible. The baritone can't be called, as Mme. Baritone is still unwell; nor the tenor, who's still tired. Perhaps this spare time could be used in going to visit influential critics (the débutante has been led to believe some critics *are* "influential"—in other words they wield particular influence on popular opinion).

"Have you been to see M***," she is asked, "that ruthless critic into whose clutches you're falling, you poor thing? Ah! You really must look out for him! He's a capricious bigot, with dreadful obsessions about music, all sorts of pet theories—he's prickly as a hedgehog, one just doesn't know which way to approach him. If you try to be polite to him, he gets angry. If you're impolite he's angry too. If you go to see him, he's bored; if you don't go, he thinks you disrespectful; if you invite him to dine on the eve of your début, he replies that 'he too is giving a *working dinner* that day'. If you suggest singing one of his romances (he composes romances)—and that's a perfectly right and proper thing to do, a charming form of temptation which is essentially artistic and musical—he laughs in your face and offers to sing yours when you write some. Yes, watch your step with this menace, and the others too, or you're lost." And the poor débutante, despite her fee of 100,000 francs, begins to feel 100,000 terrors.

She rushes off to see the reviled critic. The gentleman receives her coolly.

"Your début was announced only two months ago, Mademoiselle, so you have at least six weeks of trials to endure before making your first appearance."

"Six weeks, Monsieur!"

"Or seven or eight. But they'll come to an end eventually. What piece are you making your début in?"

When he hears the title of the opera chosen by the débutante, the critic becomes more serious and even cooler.

"Do you think I'm unwise to take this role?"

"I don't know if it will be a lucky choice for you, but for me it's fatal, since performances of that opera always give me violent intestinal pains. I'd promised myself never to expose myself to it again, and you're forcing me to break my word. Even so, I forgive you for the stomach-ache, but I don't know how I can forgive you for making me break my word and lose my self-esteem. For I shall be there, Mademoiselle, in spite of everything I shall be there to hear you; I must go and warn my doctor."

The débutante feels a shiver run through her veins at these menacing words. Not knowing what face to put on the situation, she takes her leave, begging his indulgence, and goes out utterly disheartened. But another "influential" critic reassures her. "Calm yourself, Mademoiselle, we'll support you, we're not men of no stomach like our colleague, and the opera you've chosen, although a little hard to digest, doesn't upset us too much."

At last the Director has hopes that it may be not impossible to assemble the artists before too long for a full rehearsal. The baritone has won his case, his wife is well again, his child has cut its first teeth; the tenor has recovered from his exhaustion, and has even put on a good deal of weight; the soprano is more relaxed, having been assured the débutante won't be a success; the chorus and orchestra have had no rehearsals for two months, so it's worth risking an appeal to their sense of duty. The Director, plucking up all his courage, even tackles the actors and stage hands one evening and addresses them in the despotic tone of that National Guard captain who gave his men their marching orders with the words: "Monsieur Durand, for the third and last time—I won't ask again—may I be so bold as to entreat you kindly to be good enough to take the trouble to do me the honour of *shouldering arms?*"[166]

The day of the rehearsal is fixed and prominently posted in the lobbies of the theatre and, incredibly, hardly anyone raises a murmur about this abuse of the Director's power. What's more, when the day comes, scarcely an hour after the specified time, everyone is present. The "Director of Successes" is in the pit surrounded by his forces and with a score in his hand; for this Director, an eccentric, has felt it necessary to learn music in order to be able to follow the melodic cues in the score and not let his people make any wrong entries.[167]

The conductor gives the signal and the rehearsal begins. "All right then! Where's the new singer? Call her." Everyone searches for her, but she's not to be found. Then one of the theatre's messenger-boys hands the Director a note which had "just been brought the evening before", as he puts it, announcing that the débutante has caught the flu and is unable to leave her bed, let alone rehearse. The whole assemblage is in a fury; the Director of Successes slams his score shut; the other Director departs the scene in a hurry; Monsieur Durand, who was just on the point of *shouldering arms,* tucks his rifle back under his arm and returns home grumbling.

The whole process has to start again, and the poor flu-stricken singer, when she eventually gets better, must think herself lucky that the baritone can have court cases and children only every ten or eleven months, that the tenor hasn't been gored by a wild boar, and that Monsieur Durand, not having mounted guard for a very long time, may kindly be good enough to take the trouble to shoulder arms once again. For to do him justice, he does get there in the end.

And in the end the débutante too makes her début, at least so long as no other obstacle crops up. Oh, but if that happens the Director, utterly exasperated, forgets himself to the extent of speaking point-blank to his staff, without any oratorical precautions and in a tone which admits of no dissent: "Ladies and gentlemen, I hereby inform you that tomorrow at midday there will be *no* rehearsal!"

————————

The song of cockerels—The cockerels of song

"What do you think of vocal trills in dramatic music?" I was asked one evening by a music-lover who had just had his eardrums shattered by a prima donna.

Figure 26. *Mr. Durand, pour la 3ème et dernière fois,* . . . Porter armes! Lithograph by Hippolyte Bellangé (1800–1866). Bibliothèque Nationale de France.
"Monsieur Durand, for the third and last time—I won't ask again—may I be so bold as to entreat you kindly to be good enough to take the trouble to do me the honour of *shouldering arms?*" (page 112).

"Vocal trills sometimes produce a good effect, as an expression of care-free joy or as a musical imitation of polite laughter; but when they're employed without good reason and trotted out at the end of every phrase in music that's meant to be serious, they grate on my nervous system and drive me wild. They remind me of the cruelties I used to inflict on cockerels in my childhood. The triumphal song of the cockerel annoyed me then almost as much as the jubilant trill of the prima donna makes me suffer today. And there have been many occasions when I have lain in ambush, waiting for the moment when the strutting bird, flapping its wings, would begin the ludicrous squawking that is absurdly described as its 'song', in order to bring it to an abrupt halt, often by striking it dead with a stone."

Later I cured myself of this bad habit, and confined myself to cutting short the cockerel's squawking with a gunshot. Today the blast of a 48-millimetre cannon would scarcely suffice to express the horror the cocker-els of song frequently inspire in me with their trills.

The vocal trill is on the whole as ridiculous, loathsome and stupidly clownish as the *flattés* and *martelés* and other horrors with which Lully and his contemporaries saturated their lamentable melodies.[168] When a trill is performed on a high note by some kinds of soprano voice it becomes frantic, demented and nasty (although nowhere near as much as the listener), and a 110-millimetre cannon would not be big enough to deal with it.

Trills performed by deep voices, on the other hand, especially on low notes, are irresistibly comic—they produce a sort of gurgling rather similar to the sound of water running from a badly made gutter. Musicians with any sense of taste use them very little. The ugliness of this effect of the human voice is beginning to be recognised. It already seems so ridiculous that singers produce it with an air of committing a shameful deed. One blushes for them. In two or three hundred years it will have disappeared altogether.

A Parisian composer of the Parisian school recently published a piece of *religious funeral music* for bass voice. At the end there is a long trill on the first syllable of the word "requiem":

Pie Jesu, domine, dona eis re-e-e-e-e-e-quiem!!!!

What a sublime example of its type!

Sparrows

Someone once described Paris as the city where music is loved least and where most comic operas are produced in the whole world. The first proposition is hardly sustainable. Clearly music is still loved more in Paris than in Constantinople, Ispahan, Canton, Nagasaki and Baghdad. But nowhere, in truth, are comic operas concocted in such prodigious quantity and of such good quality as in Paris.

What becomes of these innumerable productions is a mystery which I've not yet been able to unravel. If they were burnt, they would turn to ashes, and could be made into potash for commercial use. But I'm told there's no question of delivering them to the flames; on the contrary, they're carefully preserved—masses of music paper, orchestral parts, vocal parts, solo parts and full scores, which once cost so much to fill with notes but whose value a few years later is no greater than that of the dead leaves heaped up in the depths of the woods in winter.

Where are they hidden, these piles of paper? Where are the granaries, the warehouses, the cellars to stack them in? Are they in Paris, where the price of land is so high and the authors of comic operas themselves have such difficulty finding lodgings? Information is as lacking on this subject as about sparrows.

What becomes of the Paris sparrows? All the researches of scholars have so far been unable to throw any light on this question, yet it's not without importance—more so indeed than the comic opera question. For supposing a pair of these tuneful birds lives for five years, each pair producing two broods a season, and each brood consisting of at least four chicks, that makes four extra pairs a year; and with these pairs breeding in their turn while their parents continue to breed for four more years, by the end of a mere hundred years they must have given birth to an anthill of sparrows to make the imagination boggle: it would long ago have covered the entire surface of the earth. It can be proved mathematically, which proves once again that proofs prove nothing, for despite all such algebraic demonstrations, we can see that the sparrow population of Paris is no greater today than it was in the time of King Dagobert.[169]

Similarly, with every opera house (except the Opéra itself) producing a truly extraordinary number of little sparrows—I mean comic operas—every year, winter and summer, come wind or hail or thunder, regardless of whether there are singers for them, or the public stays away, or Sebastopol is under siege, or cholera is rife, or the East Indies are ablaze, or North America is going bankrupt and turning to organised piracy as its declared new economic policy;[170] with this alarming number of musical and literary productions, there are no more masterpieces than there used to be, not perhaps in the time of King Dagobert, but during the age of Sedaine and Grétry and Monsigny,[171] when opera houses were few in number and behaved with such laudable discretion.

This inexplicable circumstance naturally puts a high price on sparrows which sing well, when one is lucky enough to catch one of them by putting a grain of salt on its tail; especially these days, when real salt has become so scarce that one often finds oneself forced to use Glauber salts for comic operas.[172]

"And what are Glauber salts?", you may ask.

"Ask your doctor, and beg him never to make you take them."

Music for laughs

A new kind of so-called music is highly regarded in Paris at present. It's described as "music for laughs". It comes very cheap, like griddle-cakes from the pâtissiers of the Boulevard Bonne-Nouvelle. You can get it, if you wish, for six sous, or four sous, or even two sous. It has to be sung by people with no voice and no knowledge of music, and accompanied by pianists with no fingers and no knowledge of music, and it is popular with people of idiosyncratic temperament who take pride in having no knowledge of either French or music.

You can imagine how much in demand it is. The number of theatres attracting passers-by with this sort of music is increasing daily—both *intra muros* and *extra muros*.[173] Its admirers don't even bother to take precautions before going. They make no attempt to conceal themselves: even if the performances took place in broad daylight, I do believe, God forgive me, they would go without a moment's hesitation. What's more, even some of our concert halls are now putting on music for laughs. But it's been observed that the audience at these concerts always remains very serious and only the singers seem to find anything to laugh about. I say "seem to", because these poor people are generally as melancholic as Triboulet.[174]

One of them, who had sung music for laughs all his life without a single moment's enjoyment, died of boredom last year. Another has just become a professor of philosophy, I'm told. One alone is said to be luckier than his rivals. He lives enveloped in the esteem and consideration merited by the immense fortune amassed through his business as an undertaker. But this happy man enjoys himself so much that he no longer sings.

As evidence of the triumph of music for laughs and the incontestable influence it exerts, the Opéra-Comique decided to use it to make its patrons a little more serious. It had heard about the song *The Snake Man* which had been performed with such success at the Concerts de Paris, and about a comedy entitled *The Two Englishmen* which had a great many performances at the Odéon twenty-eight or thirty years ago, and also about two or three vaudevilles on the same subject. So the Opéra-Comique said to itself, showing good sense beyond its years: "if I ran up something new based on all of those, it would be pretty good; in fact it would be very good, and would make a companion-piece for another new work I've just concocted called *Pathelin of the Bar.*" And that's just what the Opéra-Comique has done. It now has two strings to its bow, and all that's missing is an arrow; but it's good at using any wood to make arrows, and the arrow comes to him who waits.

———————

National fatuities

(*Castigat ridendo mores*)[175]

I detest hypocrisy, and nothing infuriates me like the placarding of proverbs with moral pretensions, particularly on a theatre curtain. The Opéra-Comique's Latin motto claims that it *refines* our behaviour: "castigat" can have no other meaning. Isn't that a stupid piece of lapidary hypocrisy? And even if it were true, who looks to theatres to perform this refining function? Imbeciles! Refine your repertoire, refine your singers' voices, refine the style of your authors and composers, refine the taste of your public, refine the occupants of your boxes by admitting only pretty young women, and then your mission would be fulfilled—that's all we ask. Anyway, just how wise is the wisdom of proverbs?

Embrace much, grasp little[176]

This means one should occupy oneself with only a single task or enterprise—one should never have more than one vessel on the slipway or more than one iron in the fire or more than one regiment on the move. Caesar, who used to dictate three letters at a time in three different languages, was a fool; Napoleon, who found time to administer the Théâtre-Français while in Moscow, a dilettante.[177] And husbands saddled with plump wives shouldn't hug them, for in so doing they are indeed embracing much but grasping little.

A bird in the hand is worth two in the bush

Following this proverb would discredit and destroy all commerce, no more and no less. It would destroy agriculture too, for if the farmer took heed of it he would hold on to his grain instead of using it to sow his fields, and we'd die of hunger.

Boredom brings its own remedy

A false neo-proverb. Every day I attend operas, cantatas, soirées and sonatas of excruciating boredom, and far from the boredom bringing its own remedy, when I leave at the end of the ordeal I feel I could happily strangle people I'd have greeted politely when I went in.

Only a dog will betray you

The naïveté of this is beneath criticism: everyone betrays you.

One must howl with the pack

A host of present-day singers have recognised the aptness of this aphorism; they find fault only with the way it is expressed, which they see as too long by half.

These examples seem to me sufficient to show that Latin and French proverbs are nothing but national fatuities.

Ingratitude shows an independent spirit

There was once a man of great intelligence, with an excellent, cheerful disposition but such an acute sensibility that as a result of having his feelings bruised and battered by the world around him he had ended up as a melancholic. One great failing disfigured his rare qualities: he was a scoffer— Oh! but a scoffer such as there had never been before. He scoffed at everyone and everything: philosophers, lovers, men of learning, men of none, the devout, the godless, the old, the young, the sick, doctors (especially doctors), fathers, children, innocent girls, guilty women, marquesses, commoners, actors, poets, his enemies, his friends and finally himself. Only musicians, for some unknown reason, escaped his tireless mockery. Of course, musicians had been satirised already: Shakespeare trounced them pretty soundly in the final scene of Act IV of *Romeo and Juliet*:

Peter: What say you, James Soundpost?
3rd Musician: Faith, I know not what to say.
Peter: O, I cry you mercy, *you are the singer.*
. . .
2nd Musician: Come, we'll in here; *tarry for the mourners, and stay dinner.*[178]

It's hard to believe that, after having vilified so many people, the excellent fellow I speak of was never assassinated. After his death, it's true, they would have liked nothing more than to drag him through the mire, and his wife could calm their fury only by throwing them money from the windows of the death-chamber.

Although he was the son of a simple upholsterer, he had studied the classics thoroughly. He wrote both verse and prose remarkably well; so remarkably, indeed, that in the end, after a century and a half of reflection, the Parisians had the idea of putting up a bronze statue to him, with the titles of his numerous works on its pedestal. It was a splendid thought on their part. But the men responsible for carrying out this task, which was meant to celebrate a man of letters, were not too strong on spelling, so they wrote the name of one of the illustrious scoffer's masterpieces as *The Misser*.[179] This caused quite a scandal at the time among the knowledgeable grocers of the Rue Richelieu, and resulted in the man in charge of erecting the monument being obliged to have the botched inscription scratched out during the night.

A fitting outcome, sir, of matters here on earth.[180]

You mockingly created a character who sought employment as "corrector of Paris signs and inscriptions",[181] and here you are in the nineteenth century being described in an inscription as the author of *The Misser*.

This misanthrope (the reader would never have guessed) was named Poquelin de Molière.[182] The reason I have thought fit to speak of him here is that, as I mentioned earlier, this furious scourge of absurdities never laid his whip on the shoulders of musicians. Doesn't it seem ironic that musicians alone have made such desperate efforts, if not to remodel, at least to embellish and prettify the faces of the characters he has given the world, and to endow them with melodies giving them a sort of artificial charm which Molière would doubtless have had little inclination to allow them? So it's true that, for musicians at least, "ingratitude shows an independent spirit".

One of these ungrateful fellows opened fire on Molière with a degree of energy and success which fortunately has not been equalled since. His name was Mozart. He came to Paris when he was very young.[183] He expressed a desire to write a score for the Opéra (the Académie Royale de Musique). But as he played the harpsichord very well and had already published several sonatas for that instrument, the management of the Opéra, being discerning and sagacious men, pointed out the impertinence of his ambition and sent him packing with the advice that he confine himself to writing sonatas.

Mozart realised, with some difficulty it's true, that he was a mere whippersnapper, and returned crestfallen to Germany, where he had a Molière play that had made a strong impression on him in the theatre turned into a libretto. Then he wrote the music for it and had it staged in Prague, with prodigious success according to some, or no success at all according to others. So appeared *Don Giovanni*, whose glory has for some years caused that of *Don Juan* to look a bit pale by contrast. The great composers who were privileged to enjoy the confidence of the directors of the Opéra at that time wouldn't have been capable of such an act of ingratitude.

Much later, a little score written on another Molière play, *The Sicilian, or Love the Artist,* was acquired by the Opéra-Comique.[184] I don't know if it was performed. Later still came *Psyche,* by Monsieur Thomas. Monsieur Gounod's *Le Médecin malgré lui* is doing the Théâtre-Italien proud, and will do so for a long time yet. Finally *Les Fourberies de Marinette* by Monsieur Creste constitutes the latest assault upon the author of *Don Juan* to be recorded in the annals of musical ingratitude.

In sum—it's no good denying it—of all the musicians who've owed a debt of acknowledgment to Molière, Mozart was plainly the most ungrateful.

The futility of glory

The Director of the Opéra met Rossini one evening on the Boulevard des Italiens, and accosted him jovially, like someone bringing a friend good news:

"What do you think, dear Maestro," said he, "tomorrow we're doing the third act of your *Moïse!*"

"Really?" replied Rossini. "All of it?"

It's a splendid riposte—even more so because in fact *not* all of the third act was done. Such is the respect shown in Paris for the finest productions of the great masters.

Some works, indeed, seem predestined for the "palm leaves of martyrdom". Few have suffered such a long and cruel martyrdom as Rossini's opera *William Tell.* This would be hard to beat as an example for all composers of how little honour or respect is shown in our theatres to the most magnificently gifted and clever geniuses, however Herculean their labours, however immense their renown and however dazzling their glory. One might even say that the more indisputable and undisputed the superiority of great men who have deigned to write for the theatre, the more relentless and determined is the petty rabble in heaping insult on their works. I need only recall the treatment of Mozart's dramatic works in France or Shakespeare's in England, saying in Othello's words, "They know't, no more of that".[185]

But not even a musician with the liveliest imagination could have any idea of what is gradually happening to the works of Gluck in the theatres where they're still put on (I except that of Berlin), in the concerts where fragments of them are sung, and in the shops where they're sold in scraps. There's not a singer left who understands their style, not a conductor who

Figure 27. Gioacchino Rossini. Lithograph caricature by H. Mailly, 1850s. Richard Macnutt Collection, Withyham.
"The Director of the Opéra met Rossini one evening on the Boulevard des Italiens" (page 120).

AU THÉATRE-LYRIQUE.

— Quand je te dis que c'est Morphée !
— Mais, non, ma chère, c'est Orphée, je t'assure.
— Laisse-moi donc tranquille ! je sens bien qu'il m'endort.

Figure 28. *Au Théâtre-Lyrique* ("At the Théâtre-Lyrique"). Drawing by Cham (Amédée de Noé, 1818–79). Bibliothèque Nationale de France.
   —It's *Morpheus*, I tell you!
   —No, my dear, it's *Orpheus*, I assure you.
   —Well, just don't bother me—whatever it is, it sends me to sleep.
      [Morpheus, son of Hypnos (Sleep), was the Greek god of dreams.]
   "Not even a musician with the liveliest imagination could have any idea of what is . . . happening to the works of Gluck in the theatres where they're still put on" (page 120).

comprehends their spirit, feeling and traditions. They at least are not to be blamed, for it's almost always involuntarily that they pervert and stifle Gluck's most brilliant inspirations in these works. Arrangers, orchestrators, editors and translators, on the other hand, in various parts of Europe, have premeditatedly made of Gluck's noble, antique visage a mask so hideous and grotesque that it's already almost impossible to recognise its features.

A whole anthill of Lilliputians has swarmed over this Gulliver. Low-grade time-beaters, abominable composers, ludicrous singing teachers, even dancers, have all orchestrated Gluck, disfiguring his melodies and recitatives, altering his modulations and investing him with trite stupidities. One of them has added a set of *flute variations* (I've seen them) to the harp solo at Orpheus's entry into Hell, no doubt finding this prelude too dull and insignificant. Another has stuffed the chorus of the shades of Tartarus in the same work with brass instruments, even adding a serpent (I've seen it), apparently because no underworld scene involving the Furies would be complete without a serpent. At the other extreme is a fellow who has reduced the whole body of string instruments to a mere quartet. And then there's the Kapellmeister who has had the idea of getting the chorus to bark (I've heard this monstrosity), expressly requiring them not to sing in the scene of Orpheus in the underworld. He wanted them to sound like a chorus of Cerberuses, like ravening hounds—a sublime invention which Gluck failed to hit upon.[186]

I have in front of me a German edition of *Iphigenia in Tauris* where, among other mutilations, I notice that eight bars have been cut from the famous Scythians' Chorus, "Les dieux apaisent leur courroux", and the text of the translation has been stood on its head in the most painfully comic fashion. One example among a thousand is when Iphigenia says:

I have seen aroused against me
The gods, my country . . . and my father.[187]

The musical phrase ends with a sorrowful and tender accent on "and my father", the intention of which is unmistakable. But in the German edition this accent is completely misplaced, the translator having changed the order of the words to say:

My people, my father and the gods,

supposing it hardly mattered whether her father came at the end or not. This reminds me of an English translation of the German ballad *Erlkönig* in which the translator, following some extraordinary notion of poetic licence, judged it appropriate to change the sequence of the dialogue between the two characters. Where the German poet had placed the interjections uttered by the *father*, the English translation had the responses of the *child*. A London publisher, wishing to popularise Schubert's beautiful music for this ballad in England, managed more or less to fit the English translator's verses to it. You can imagine the farcical absurdity that resulted: the child screaming in a paroxysm of terror "Father! Father! I am frightened!" to music meant for the words "Be calm, my son, etc.", and vice versa.

The translations of Gluck's operas are studded with similar niceties.

And as ill-fortune would have it, the old French edition, the only one in which the master's thoughts are to be found intact (I'm referring to the full scores), is becoming rarer by the day, and is very poor in respect of both layout and accuracy. It's marred by a lamentable lack of coherence and innumerable faults of every kind.

In a few years' time two or three copies of these vast dramatic poems, these inimitable models of expressive music, will be all that remain in our great libraries, incomprehensible débris of another age, like so many Memnons no longer capable of producing harmonious sounds, colossal sphinxes guarding their secret for ever.[188] No one in Europe has ventured to undertake a new edition of Gluck's six great operas which is at the same time scholarly, properly laid out and annotated, and well translated into both German and Italian.[189] No serious attempt has been made to raise a subscription for this purpose. No one has considered risking 20,000 francs (it would cost no more than that) to combat in this way the ever more numerous agents of destruction which threaten these masterpieces. And despite the resources at the disposal of art and industry, this monstrous universal indifference to the key interests of musical art will cause these masterpieces to perish.

Alas! Alas! Shakespeare was right:

Glory is like a circle in the water,
Which never ceaseth to enlarge itself
Till by broad spreading it disperse to nought.[190]

As for Rossini, for some time now it seems that he has felt the brilliance of his fame to be too broadly based, and with colossal disdain he has obliterated any work of his that might cast a shadow on it. If it hadn't been for this prodigious, majestic indifference of his, the Paris Opéra might perhaps have been willing to deposit the scores of *The Siege of Corinth*, *Moïse* and *Le Comte Ory* in its archives, and abstained from mauling *William Tell* in the way it has.[191]

Can you think of anyone who hasn't fiddled with it or torn out a page or altered a passage, either from sheer caprice or because of some weakness of voice or mind? Must the Maestro forgive them all because they know not what they do?[192] But then again, is he in any position to complain? After all, hasn't *William Tell* just been put on again, almost complete? The first act wedding march which had been omitted for ages has been restored; all the big third act ensembles are back. The aria "Amis, secondez ma vaillance!" disappeared over a year before Duprez's début and was then reinstated as the work's final number, with all the rest cut.[193] Later its peroration was truncated to protect a singer from the danger he faced from the last phrase, 'Trompons l'espérance homicide'.[194] Now this peroration has been restored as well.

Condescension has even been pushed so far as to let us hear the magnificent final chorus at the dénouement, with its broad harmonies against which the reminiscences of Swiss national songs ring out so poetically; and also the trio with wind accompaniment, and even the prayer during the storm which was cut before the first performance. For right from the very first rehearsals the experts of the day had set to work on the work in their usual way, to give its author some good lessons, and many things which in their view were likely to compromise the new opera's success were ruthlessly torn out of it.

And now we see all these beautiful flowers of melody springing up again, without the work enjoying any less success than before—quite the contrary! There's scarcely anything, except the duet "Sur la rive étrangère", that was thought inadvisable to sing. You can't perform Rossini's masterpiece exactly as he composed it, for Heaven's sake! That would be going too far, and setting too dangerous a precedent. All the other composers would start to squeal under the surgeons' knives.

After one of the most murderous battles in our history, a sergeant in charge of burying bodies came rushing up to his captain in a panic:

"What is it now?" said the officer. "Why aren't you filling in that pit?"

"But sir, some of them are still moving, they can't be dead."

"Get on with it, confound you, and throw some earth over them at the double; if we took any notice of them, there'd never be anyone dead!"

Madame Lebrun

I remember seeing Monsieur Étienne at the Opéra one evening when they were playing a terrible thing called *The Nightingale*, with music by Monsieur Lebrun (some said Mme. Lebrun) and a "poem" concocted by this same Monsieur Étienne.[195] The illustrious Academician was at the front of the balcony boxes and was attracting the attention of the whole house by the ineffable joy he evidently felt at hearing his own verses sung. When it came to this fine passage in the magistrate's aria:

> I am the friend of all fathers,
> The father of all children,

Monsieur Étienne let out such a peal of laughter that I felt myself go quite red and walked out, much saddened.

That was the last time I managed to see almost the whole of this celebrated work, in which the nightingale sang with such gusto you could have sworn you were hearing a flute concerto played by Tulou.[196] This fine piece should be revived; I'm sure many people would enjoy it.

> Tell me the tale of the Ass's Skin—
> How much I would enjoy it,

as good old La Fontaine said.[197]

The Opéra regulars who knew Mme. Lebrun would certainly be delighted to receive such a favour. She was such an energetic person, especially in her conversation. Her nightingale was first cousin to Gresset's parrot.[198] F and B were her two favourite consonants. I still blush to recall the compliment she paid me in the church of St.-Roch when my first *Mass* was performed.[199] After an "O Salutaris" which was quite plain in every respect, Mme. Lebrun came to shake my hand and said in a ringing voice: "My dear boy, there were certainly no flies on that f***ing "O Salutaris" of yours; I'll be damned if any of those little b*****s in the Conservatoire's counterpoint classes could come up with anything half so well strung together and so jolly religious." It was a vote in my favour, since Mme. Lebrun's opinion was held in great respect at the time.

And how splendidly she used to descend from Heaven as Diana at the dénouement of *Iphigenia in Aulis* and *Iphigenia in Tauris*—for in both Gluck's masterpieces the plot is resolved by the intervention of Diana. I can still hear her declaim with majestic deliberation and in a slightly mannish voice:

> Scythians, return my images to the Greeks;
> For too long, in these savage climes,
> Have you dishonoured my cult and my altars.[200]

She sat with such poise in her 'glory', with a cardboard quiver on her left shoulder.[201] She could sight-read music from an upside-down score, she accompanied the most complicated arias on the piano, she would have conducted an orchestra if need be, and to cap it all she was credited with composing the music of *The Nightingale*. Her only fault was that she bore rather too close a resemblance to one of Macbeth's three weird sisters, especially in the last years of her life. Ah well! Mme. Lebrun died almost unknown, or at least forgotten by the current generation.

Sic transit gloria mundi![202]

———————

Time spares nothing

There's no denying that postilions are in a pretty bad way just now. Steam is asphyxiating them, immobilising them, giving them their marching orders. When electric power comes into its own, and that's not far off, things will be still worse. Electricity will strike them like lightning and turn them to dust. Then finally the day will come, as we know it must, of the dirigible airship, and even the name of these cheerful drivers of horses will become an old French-language word whose meaning is completely beyond the comprehension of most travellers.

If some learned scholar, passing over Longjumeau in the post-balloon from Paris, takes it into his head to look at the village through his telescope and exclaim, "That's where the postilion celebrated by an ancient composer came from!", the ladies playing shuttlecock in the grand saloon of the airship will interrupt their game to ask him what he means. And he'll reply:

"In the nineteenth century, Mesdames, the so-called civilised races crawled along the ground like snails. Travellers in those days of self-satisfied barbarism covered twenty-five or thirty miles an hour in heavy wagons propelled by steam along iron tracks, and took ludicrous pride in this "rapid" locomotion.

"But when people had to travel sixty or seventy miles from their native regions, a great many of them still shut themselves up in dreadful wooden crates with no room to stand up or lie down or even to stretch their legs. They suffered all the torments of cold, wind, rain, heat, foul ventilation, foul smells and dust. In addition to being shaken about like lead shot in a bottle they had to endure deafening and incessant noise. They slept as best they could at night, all on top of one another, passing on each other's infections, no better or worse than the livestock we cram into our little farm transport ships.

"These awful cumbersome boxes, called 'diligences' by some sort of inverted logic, were dragged along muddy ravines designated as royal, imperial or departmental roads by horses capable of covering up to six and a half miles an hour. And the man astride one of the quadrupeds given the task of hauling the contraption was called a postilion, a 'lion of the post'.

"Now there once lived a famous postilion in this hamlet of Longjumeau. His adventures formed the subject of one of those theatrical pieces called 'opéras-comiques', in which speech alternated with singing. The music of this work was written by a composer of effortless jollity, celebrated in France under the name of Dam or Edam (some historiographers give his name as Adam), and a member of the Institute—that much is certain.[203] Hence the renown of the hamlet of Longjumeau, which we caught sight of to the West just now but you can't see any longer."

Longjumeau! Longjumeau! *Fuit Troja!!*[204]

Figure 29. Adolphe Adam. Lithograph caricature by Benjamin (Benjamin Roubaud, 1811–47), from *Le Charivari*, 24 December 1838. Richard Macnutt Collection, Withyham.

"The music of [*The Postilion of Longjumeau*] was written by a composer of effortless jollity . . . some historiographers give his name as Adam" (page 127).

The rhythm of pride

A lady who's a great expert in theology and also plays the piano very well has recently published an intriguing booklet on rhythm, in which among other entirely novel ideas the following passage occurs:[205]

> Beethoven's music makes one love and take pleasure in despair *(the author perhaps meant to say this music makes one love despair and take pleasure in it)*; in it one weeps tears of blood, not for the sufferings of a God who died for us, but rather for the eternal damnation of the Devil. Its rhythm is that of a pride which seeks after truth, begs for it indeed, but is unwilling to accept that truth on the conditions on which it has deigned to reveal itself to us. It is forever the Jew saying to the Redeemer: Come down from the Cross, and we will believe in you. Follow our whims, flatter our evil instincts, and we shall proclaim you the true God, otherwise. . . . "Crucify him!" These works put Him to death in our hearts, just as the Jews put Him to death on the Cross.

What a pity I'm not a theologian and a philosopher! If I were, I'm sure I'd understand all that—which must be splendid. However I do have my doubts about one of the points of the author's doctrine. I have indeed often wept on hearing Beethoven's works; it's quite true that these tears are not prompted by the "sufferings of a God who died for us", but I can put my hand on my heart without hesitation and swear they weren't induced by the "eternal damnation of the Devil" either: I haven't been friends with him for a long time.

A remark of Monsieur Auber

A tenor whose voice is neither pleasant nor tuneful was singing the romance from Méhul's *Joseph* at a salon.[206] At the moment when he uttered the words

Into a damp and cold abyss
They plunge me, in their fury,

Monsieur Auber turned to his neighbour and said: "Joseph must have spent too long in the water closet."[207]

Music and dance

Dance has always shown itself a tender and devoted sister to Music. Music, for its part, constantly gives proof of its devotion to Dance. These two charming sisters are lavish in bestowing every courtesy upon each other. So it has been since time immemorial: they are always found in close alliance, ready to stand up and do battle against the other arts, the sciences, philosophy and even that fearsome foe, common sense. This fact was already recognised in the time of Louis XIV; Molière proves it in the first act of his *Bourgeois Gentilhomme*:

"Philosophy is something; but Music, Monsieur, Music. . . ."

"Music and Dance, Music and Dance—nothing else matters."

"There is nothing so necessary to men as Dance."

"Without Music no state can survive."

"Without Dance a man can do nothing."[208]

However, if either of these two Muses is ever inclined to take advantage of the goodness and affection of the other, I believe it must be Dance. Look what happens in the creation of ballets. Music goes to the trouble of composing a delicious morsel, well-conceived, melodious and skilfully orchestrated, lively, cheerful and stirring. Then along comes Dance and says: "Dear sister, your air is charming, but it's too short; lengthen it by sixteen bars, tack something on to it, I need it that much longer." Or: "That's a lovely piece, but it's too long. You must shorten it for me by a quarter." It's no good Music replying: "These bars you want me to add will produce a nonsense—an absurd and pointless repetition." Or: "The cut you're asking for will destroy the whole structure of the piece."

"Never mind," replies her nimble sister; "that's how it must be." And Music obeys. Elsewhere Dance finds the instrumentation too delicate; she needs trombones, cymbals, great thumps on the bass drum, and Music resigns herself with a groan to all sorts of brutality. Here the tempo is too lively for the dancer to have time for his *grands écartés* and his noble *élévations*. Music meekly breaks up the rhythm, waiting for the moment to resume her natural pace—she needs patience, for so high are the great dancer's leaps that quite often, as we know, he actually gets bored in midair. In another place the tempo will need to be speeded up more or less according to whether the ballerina wants to put her best foot forward or only her best toe. Music will be forced to go from allegro to presto and

Figure 30. Daniel Auber. Lithograph caricature by Benjamin (Benjamin Roubaud, 1811–47), from *Le Charivari*, c1840. Richard Macnutt Collection, Withyham.

See "A remark of Monsieur Auber" and "Another remark of Monsieur Auber", pages 129 and 132.

back, or from allegretto to prestissimo and back, and then the same thing over again, all within a few bars, without regard to the dislocation of the melodic design or even whether the result is playable.

But there's a much more serious issue. When a new ballet has had a success, some opera is chopped up, hacked to pieces and torn apart, even if it's a masterpiece commanding universal admiration, to serve as a curtain-raiser to make up the other half of an evening which the ballet is not enough to fill. But suppose there appeared a fine opera which was in only three acts, and therefore not long enough to hold the stage from seven until midnight. Would some fragment of a ballet be used to serve as a curtain-raiser for it? Good God, what a shocking idea! Dance would never stand for it.

Throw everything else overboard first: that's the spirit of Dance![209]

Dancer poets

A dancer once said of one of his own entrechats: "It's a handful of diamonds thrown towards the sun!" Another, on seeing Mme. Ferraris in *Le Cheval de bronze,* exclaimed: "She's a rose blown by the wind in a swirl of turquoises, rubies and gold dust."[210]

Another remark of Monsieur Auber

Not long ago a regular player in the Opéra orchestra, not recognising a young dancer who had just made her entry, asked one of his neighbours her name: "That's Mlle. Zina", came the reply; "you know, the one whose costume came undone on the evening of her début."

"A remarkable incident", added Monsieur Auber, who was nearby, in an undertone; "it was one of those rare occasions when success was the result of coming undone."

Concerts

It would be ungrateful of me not to mention the pleasant hours concert promoters have enabled me to spend in Paris this winter.

Almost every day for four months, I have been one of the actors in the following comedy:

The scene is a modestly furnished study, with a sick man coughing by the corner of his fireplace. Two pianists enter, followed by three more pianists, then another four pianists and a violinist.

Pianist no. 1 (to the sick man): I hear you're not at all well, Monsieur.

Pianist no. 2: Yes, I understand that your health . . .

Pianists nos. 7 & 9: We're told you're seriously ill.

Pianist no. 1: So I'm here . . . to ask you to come to my concert at Érard's recital hall.

Pianist no. 2: So I've made a point of coming to ask you . . . to be good enough to come and hear my new études in my recital at Pleyel's.

Pianist no. 8: As for me, the only reason that brings me here, my dear friend, is concern for your health. You work too hard; you should get out, take the air, enjoy yourself. That's why I'm here, to take you out; I have a carriage at the door, you absolutely must come to my recital at Herz's.[211] Come on! Off we go!

The sick man: When is your recital?

No. 1: At eight o'clock this evening.

The sick man: And yours?

No. 2: At eight o'clock this evening.

The sick man: And yours?

No. 8: At eight o'clock this evening.

The violinist (roaring with laughter): There are six or seven of them this evening, all at the same time. It was obvious to me that you'd follow your usual practice and not go to any of them, since you can't do them all. What's more, in my anxiety not to put you to any trouble, I've brought my violin with me, in its case. If you'll allow me, I shall play you my new set of caprices on the G string.

The sick man (aside): "A plague on your string, you poisonous devil, I hope it strangles you."[212]

. . . .

The fact is, sad to say, Paris concerts have become a pitiful nonsense. There are so many of them, they chase after you, besiege you, pester you and wear you out with such cruel persistence that the owner of a major literary meeting hall recently had the idea of putting up a notice outside the entrance saying: "No concerts given here". Since then his hall has been stuffed with readers and lovers of peace and quiet who go there for shelter.

Ever since Mme. Érard gave in and made her rooms available without charge to the ferocious virtuosi roaming wild in Paris, the revenue from pianos manufactured by her firm has fallen drastically, since nobody dares

go there any more, day or night, to inspect her instruments, for fear of
falling prey to one of these lions in full concert.

You'll notice that there are no longer enough halls, riding-schools, covered markets or corridors to satisfy all the concert-givers. The rooms at
Herz, Pleyel, Érard, Gouffier, Sainte-Cécile, the Conservatoire, the Hôtel
du Louvre, the Hôtel d'Osmond, Valentino, the Prado and the Théâtre-
Italien are not enough. Several virtuosi, in desperation, were beginning to
work in the open air, in some of the newer streets where the noise of the
few vehicles passing was insufficient to guarantee that the residents' ears
would be free from assault. As a result, the owners had to have signs painted
on their houses with enormous letters saying: "Music-making against this
wall prohibited."

Novice concert-givers are still busy—innocent souls!—distributing invitations around Paris: they slip them under people's carriage doors at night,
and then are astonished to find their hall deserted! It's worth giving a warning
to these worthy virtuosi—most of whom are foreigners, arriving from Russia, Germany, Italy, Spain, the Indies, Japan, New Caledonia, the Congo,
Monaco, San Francisco, Macao or Cuzco—that a concert audience expects
to be paid nowadays, just as the chorus, the orchestra and the claque have
always been paid. An audience of six hundred ears costs at least 3,000 francs.

The giver of a "benefit" concert recently had the idea of resorting to the
American system, which involves offering a cup of chocolate and a slice of
pâté with each ticket; but Parisian concert-goers, who aren't generally big
eaters, found the compensation inadequate, and immediately got one of
their leaders to ask the virtuoso Amphitryon if they could consume the
chocolate and the pâté without listening to the concert.[213] The indignant
beneficiary replied in the words of the ancient philosopher, "Eat, but listen!",[214] so no deal could be struck.

Nelson's bravery

There is a country next to our own where music is really loved and
respected, and as a result people wouldn't think of listening to a concert or
an opera performance that went on too long. In that country an evening of
music beginning at half-past six has to be over by nine o'clock, or half-past
nine at the latest, for at eleven o'clock everyone goes to sleep.

Here too everyone is asleep at eleven, but the music isn't over. To obtain
financial success, it's absolutely imperative for our composers to write those
great mongrels of operas which go on barking from seven o'clock until
midnight and sometimes even longer. People like going to them to sleep, to
test their endurance, to build castles in Spain, lulled by the unceasing sound

of cascading cavatinas, until some unexpected occurrence brings them back to reality, such as the claque forgetting to applaud; then they wake up with a start.

This tendency to debase music to serve ignoble ends, such as lulling the public to sleep in the theatre, accompanying the conversation in a salon, aiding digestion during banquets, or amusing children of all ages, is the surest sign of a barbarous nation. In this respect we in France are pretty lacking in civilisation, and our taste for art in general is very much like that of one of our kings, who was asked if he liked music and replied good-naturedly: "Well, I'm not afraid of it!" I'm not so brave as that king, and in all humility I confess that music often strikes terror into me. But even if, like Nelson, I tremble on the brink of battle, nonetheless, whatever you may think, I too am always at my post in the hour of danger, and I shall be found dead one fine evening in the sixth act of some opera about Trafalgar.

Grotesque prejudices

The utterances of prejudice are far grosser and stupider here in Paris than anywhere else—it would hold sway over every aspect of the art of music if it had its insolent way. Quite apart from what it has to say about harmony, melody and rhythm, one of its more outrageous assertions would have you believe there is only one possible form for texts intended for singing—that it is quite impossible to sing prose, and alexandrine verses are worst of all to set to music. Indeed some people maintain that *all* verse meant for singing should be, without exception, what is called "metrical" verse, that is to say verses with a uniform scansion all the way through, each one with the same number of long and short syllables in the same place.

As for setting prose to music, nothing could be easier; it's just a matter of knowing what prose to set. The great masses and oratorios, the master-pieces of religious music, were written by Handel, Haydn, Bach and Mozart to prose texts in English, German and Latin. "Yes," comes the answer, "it can be done in Latin or German or English, but not in French." These days, if something *isn't* done, people always say it *can't* be done. It's not even true that it isn't done; there is music written to prose texts in French, and there'd be a whole lot more if you cared to look. Every day, in the best-known operas, you can hear passages where the librettist's verses have been changed around by the composer, chopped up, mangled and jumbled by repeating some words and even inserting others, so that the verse has in fact become prose, prose which matches and fits the composer's intentions better than the recalcitrant verse.

Yet it can be sung without difficulty, and the piece is no less beautiful in musical terms; *for melody makes a mockery of your pretensions to steer and sustain it through literary forms prescribed by anyone other than the composer.*

A librettist once roundly criticised the verse text used for a new opera to me:

"What rhythms!" he said. "What a muddle! It might as well be prose. Here a long line, there a short line, no regularity in the placing of accents, long and short syllables scattered at random. What a mishmash! Just try setting that to music!"

I let him go on. Some days later, while walking with him, I hummed a tune he seemed to find charming.

"Do you know it?", I asked.

"No, but it's delightful; it must be from some Italian opera, for the Italians at least know how to write words that don't inhibit singing."

"It's the music of those verses you found so anti-melodic the other day."

I don't know how many times I've amused myself laying similar traps for people who advocate using nothing but metrical verse. I sing them a melody to which I've fitted some Italian words; then when they go on and on about the happy influence of the metre of the Italian verse on the composer's inspiration, I pour cold water on their enthusiasm by pointing out that the form of the verse couldn't possibly have had any effect on that of the music, since the tune they've just heard comes from a Beethoven symphony and was therefore written to no words at all.

This certainly doesn't mean metrical verse can't be excellent for music. I will go so far as to say it is quite often indispensable. In a piece like the Furies' Chorus in Gluck's *Orpheus,* the composer may adopt a recurring rhythm whose very insistence gives it its effect:

Quel est l'audacieux
Qui dans ces sombres lieux . . .[215]

Clearly this form must be reflected in the verse, or the words wouldn't fit the music.

If several different strophes are to be sung in succession to the same melody, it's equally desirable that they should all have the same scansion and rhythm. This will avoid the glaring errors of musical prosody inevitably produced in couplets which have a different metrical shape from the first, and will relieve the conscientious composer of the need to correct these faults by modifying his melody for each verse when he's particularly anxious not to do so.

But anyone who says that, in an aria or duet or scene where passion can and should be expressed in a thousand different and unforeseen ways, the verse must be absolutely uniform in metre and rhythm, and who claims that any other approach is musically impossible, proves without a doubt that he hasn't the least idea of what music really is. The adherence of Italian librettists to this system, even on occasions when music recoils from it, has undoubtedly been largely responsible for the outward uniformity of the bulk of Italy's musical output, a uniformity which can fairly be criticised.

As for the prejudice against alexandrines, which is shared by many composers, it's all the more strange since neither librettists nor musicians show any aversion to lines of six feet.[216] Now, what is an alexandrine when divided in two at the hemistich, but two non-rhyming verses of six feet? And what, I ask you, has rhyme got to do with the shape of a melodic line? What's more, it often happens that these librettists, for all their rigorous syllable-counting, produce an abominable line of thirteen feet when they mean to write two of six feet each, because they fail to take account of the non-elision of the end of the first line with the beginning of the second. A gaffe of this kind was committed by the librettist of *Le Pré aux Clercs,* when Hérold asked for metrical verse (which in this case was appropriate) in six-foot lines for one of his most attractive pieces:[217]

C'en est fait, le ciel même
A reçu leurs serments,
Sa puissance suprême
Vient d'unir deux amants.[218]

The first two lines together do give the composer twelve syllables as a result of the elision between them, but the other two clearly combine to make thirteen, since there can be no elision between "suprême" and "vient". As a result this extra syllable has to have an extra note in the music which spoils the symmetry of the phrase and produces a most awkward little hiccough. There's barbarism for you!

In a generally excellent book entitled *An Essay on French Metrics,*[219] Monsieur Ducondut has proved beyond question that, contrary to prejudice, the French language lends itself without difficulty to any verse form or any metrical scheme. If forms which seem particularly appropriate to music have not so far been utilised, we should look to the poets for the explanation, rather than blaming any deficiency in the language. The examples he gives of metrical verse of all kinds provide ample support for his theory. But because it argues that observance of the rules it lays down is absolutely necessary in writing poetry for setting to music, I must stress that the theory itself is fundamentally wrong. Music's capriciousness, even when least in evidence, makes it hard to pin down; and apart from the exceptional cases I mentioned earlier, it's perfectly senseless to talk of using nothing but metrical verse for singing, and to think the monotonous rhythm of such verse will make the composer's task any easier by imposing an invariable form from the outset. The truth would be precisely the opposite—but luckily there are thousands of ways for melody to slip away from such restraints.

"Music", says Monsieur Ducondut, "consists of phrases made up of bars of equal length, which are themselves divided into strong and weak beats; it has notes which are sounded and released, together with rests and rhythm. The regular recurrence of all these elements in the corresponding parts of the melodic pattern, along with the symmetry of the phrases, constitutes musical metre. Poetry intended for setting to music must conform to this process—or discord will occur between the two associated arts."

That may be so, but this musical process is far from having the absolute regularity he attributes to it, and which is to be found in his verses. One bar is equal to another bar—equal in duration, I grant, but this duration is not equally divided. In one bar I'll use only two notes for two syllables; in the next I'll write four or six or seven notes for four or six or seven syllables if I wish, or just for a single syllable if I prefer the series of notes to be vocalised. What then becomes of the poetic metre, which you've gone to such trouble to achieve? The music brushes it aside, destroys it, obliterates it. Poetry is the slave of the metre it imposes upon itself; music is not only its own master, but itself creates the metre and can modify it in a thousand little ways without losing any of its essential elements. And what about *tempo*, which authors of theories of poetics never mention and which alone can give metre its character—who determines that? The composer of course. For tempo is the soul of music, whereas poets have never even dreamed of finding a way to prescribe the speed or slowness with which their verses should be recited.

No written language has signs to indicate the division of time. Only music, modern music, possesses them; music can designate silence, and specify its length, something which spoken languages are quite incapable of doing. Finally music—just to dispose of those extraordinary ideas of the Greeks, recently resurrected by grammarians and poets who know nothing about it—stands on its own. It has no need of poetry, and even if all human languages should perish it would still remain the greatest and most poetic of the arts—and the most free. What is a Beethoven symphony but sovereign music in all its majesty?

. . . .

A similar prejudice keeps cropping up about gifted musicians and their supposed inclination to let the instrumental part dominate at the expense of the voices. Whenever a composer comes along who knows what he's doing, who's fully in command of his art and as a result knows how to deploy the orchestra with subtlety and refinement, making it speak with eloquence and move with grace, whether frolicking like a delightful child or singing with a mighty voice or roaring like thunder—if he doesn't follow the example of ordinary composers who hurl themselves at the orchestra kicking and punching, he will be said to be very talented but to have "put the statue in the orchestra". This idiotic criticism of Mozart's operas, made eighty years ago by that phony fellow Grétry, remains and will long remain a reproach applied by the mass of connoisseurs, or the connoisseurs of the masses, to those composers who in fact are the most entitled to praise. Anyone who dared to respond truthfully to Grétry for this carping at Mozart would have said: "So it's your opinion that Mozart has put the pedestal on stage and the statue in the orchestra? You'll find there are many occasions when such a preposterous comment would not be a criticism; but that's what you mean it to be. Well, it's an unjust criticism, quite misdirected in fact. Mozart's orchestration is charming, not perhaps very colourful, but tasteful, finely crafted, forceful when necessary, and perfect; as perfect as yours is tumbledown, decrepit and absurd.

"But the vocal part in his operas still remains predominant almost throughout; the action is still full of human feeling; his characters are still free to sing the true melodic line and thereby play the dominant part. Take the orchestra away, Monsieur Grétry, and replace it with a harpsichord, and you'll find—to your great disappointment, I imagine—that the main interest of Mozart's opera is still on stage. His pedestal has no fewer human features and is more beautiful to look at than all your statues."

That's how one could have replied to the phony fellow and his phony remarks about Gluck and Mozart. It might be added that if any composers could be said to have put the statue in the orchestra on occasion, it's the Italians. Yes, it was the masters of the Italian school who, with as much good sense as grace, first had the idea of giving the melody to the orchestra with the words accompanying it in recitative, both in comic scenes where *canto parlato* is indispensable and in many others where it would be quite contrary to dramatic sense to give the singer a real melody. I could quote innumerable examples of this excellent procedure from the Italian masters, from Cimarosa to Rossini. Most modern French composers have had the sense to follow them. The Germans, on the other hand, very rarely resort to this shift of the musical focus. Yet they're the ones most often accused of putting the statue in the orchestra, simply because they don't treat their orchestras like mere playthings. Such is the force of prejudice.

Parisian prejudice also insists that a musician is capable of doing only what he's already done. Anyone who makes his début with a lyric drama will unfailingly be accused of brazen cheek if he presumes to write a comic opera, just because he has shown conspicuous qualities in the serious form. If his first effort was a fine mass, people will say: "What does he think he's doing, composing for the theatre! It'll be nothing but plainsong. Why doesn't he stick to the cathedral?"

If he's unlucky enough to be a fine pianist they exclaim with horror: "Pianist's music!". Once that's said, the fellow finds himself pretty well written off by a prejudice he'll have to wrestle with for many long years. As if a great talent for performance necessarily precludes an ability to compose, and as if Bach, Beethoven, Mozart, Weber, Meyerbeer, Mendelssohn and others weren't great composers as well as great virtuosi.

If a composer starts by writing a symphony, and the symphony causes a sensation, that's it: he's classified, or more like trapped, as a symphonist. He mustn't think of writing anything but symphonies; he must keep away from opera, for which he isn't suited; he can't possibly write for voices; and so on. What's more, everything he does write thereafter is termed 'symphonic' by prejudiced people; words are twisted in their meanings when applied to him. What would be correctly called a cantata if anyone else wrote it is a 'symphony' if it comes from his pen—an oratorio is a 'symphony'; an a capella chorus is a 'symphony'; a mass is a 'symphony'. Anything a symphonist writes is a symphony.

He would have avoided this trouble if his first symphony had gone unnoticed or had been nothing out of the ordinary. He would even have found a number of theatre managers prejudiced in his favour: "This young man", they would have said, "has had no success in the concert hall, so he's *bound* to succeed in opera. He doesn't know how to get the best out of instruments, but he's *sure* to know all about writing for voices. He's a poor harmonist, according to other musicians, so he *must* be cram-full of melody."

In the opposite situation they would have been sure to say: "He's a master of orchestration, so he can't know how to handle voices. His harmony is remarkable, so his melodic gift must be unreliable—if he has one. And he refuses to write like everyone else, he believes in *expression* in music, he has a system: he's dangerous."

The proponents of these fine theories have two powerful protectors in Heaven whose names resemble that of the patron saints of cobblers: they are called, so I'm told, Saint Cretin and Saint Cretinian.[220]

Non-believers in musical expressiveness

"Music", according to Potier,[221] "like justice, is a very fine thing—when it's right."

I was speaking just now of composers who believe in musical expressiveness, but who act upon that belief with discretion and good sense, aware of the limitations which the very nature of music imposes on its expressive ability, and beyond which it can never go.

Yet there are many people in Paris and elsewhere who don't believe in it at all. Like blind men denying the existence of light, they seriously maintain that *all words go equally well with all music*. To them it seems perfectly natural for an opera libretto which has been found wanting to be replaced by another in an entirely different genre without disturbing the score. They convert Rossini's comic operas into masses: I know of one which is sung to the music of *The Barber of Seville*. They would have no compunction in fitting the poem of *La Vestale* to the score of *Der Freischütz*,[222] or the other way around. No one raises a murmur about such absurdities, and yet practised by men holding positions of authority their influence on art can be appalling.

It's no good answering these wretched people like the ancient philosopher who walked around in order to prove the possibility of movement. They'd never be convinced.

So it's merely for the amusement of healthy minds that we here present the words of two well-known pieces, the first set to the air *La Grâce de Dieu*, and the second to the tune of the song *Un jour, maître corbeau*.[223]

WORDS OF THE MARSEILLAISE[224]
Set to the melody of the *Grâce de Dieu*

WORDS OF ELEAZAR'S AIR IN *LA JUIVE*[225]
Set to the melody of the song
Un jour, maître corbeau

Ra - chel, quand du Seig - neur la grâ - ce tu - té - lai - re, A mes trem - blan - tes

mains con - fi - a ton ber - ceau, J'a - vais à ton bon - heur vou - é ma vie en -

tiè - re, Et c'est moi, oui, c'est moi, qui te livre au bour - reau!

These two glaring examples, in which different music of a particular character has been substituted for the noble inspirations of Rouget de l'Isle and Monsieur Halévy and coupled with verses of great intensity and tenderness, form a pendant to the psalm setting by Marcello that I quoted at the beginning of the book.[226] In that all-too-celebrated piece a merry, playful tune was written by the composer for an Italian ode of elevated and grandiose character; and by fitting some jolly words to Marcello's music I produced a perfect match between music and verse.

This irreverent joke, which in no way diminishes my admiration for Marcello's fine works, will appear no more shocking to the non-believers in musical expressiveness than the parodies of the *Marseillaise* and Eleazar's aria, since according to them all words go equally well with all music.

Here is the Venetian composer's theme with both poetic texts:[227]

I cieli im - men - si nar - ra - no del gran - de Id dio la glo - ri - a, del
Ah quel plai - sir de boi - re frais, De se far - cir la pan - se, Ah

grande Id - dio la glo - ri - a, I cieli im - men - si nar - ra - no del
quel plai - sir de boi - re frais, As - sis sous un om - brage é - pais, De

grande Id - di - o la glor - ri - a il fir - ma - men - to lu - ci - do il
boire et de fai - re bom - ban - ce! As - sis sous un om - brage é - pais, Ah

fir - ma - men - to lu - ci - do all' u - ni - ver - so an - nun - zi - a, il
quel plai - sir de boi - re frais, As - sis sous un om - brage é - pais, Ah

fir - ma - men - to lu - ci - do il fir - ma - men - to lu - ci - do, *etc.*
quel plai - sir de boi - re frais, Sous un om - bra - - ge é - pais!

This music is more like the song of a cattle merchant returning in high spirits from market than that of a devout admirer of the wonders of the firmament. Non-believers in musical expressiveness refuse to admit there can be the slightest difference of character between two such sorts of music.

Marcello produced a great number of very fine psalm settings, veritable odes which earned him the splendid nickname "the Pindar of music", but they're no longer sung. He also had the misfortune to allow this grotesque melody to slip from his pen, and today you hear it everywhere—it's almost a popular song in Paris.

The non-believers are right then; as Cabanis exclaimed: "I swear God does not exist."[228]

Truth is false, falsehood is truth! Fair is foul and foul is fair![229]

Aux ar - mes, ci - to - yens, for - mez vos ba - tail - lons!...

Allegro

Ra - chel, quand du Sei - gneur la grâ - ce tu - té - lai - re...

Ah quel plai - sir de boi - re frais de se far - cir la pan - se...

! !

Mme. Stoltz and Mme. Sontag—Making millions

In 1854 the Opéra reopened after a long closure with a revival of *La Favorite*.[230] I wrote the following observations on the subject, which seem not without relevance today.

"The Opéra has reopened. Mme. Stoltz has returned, more dramatic than ever in the fine role of Léonor.[231] This glittering occasion was followed by two no less remarkable performances of the same work, after which the Opéra, to refresh itself, gave a performance of *Le Maître Chanteur* by Monsieur Limnander, a score containing some charming things which in my opinion are much too little noticed. After *Le Maître Chanteur* came *La Reine de Chypre*,[232] in which Mme. Stoltz once again won triumphal honours, with fanfares of trumpets, bouquets thrown from the boxes and wild acclamation on all sides. Everyone who had anything to do with the Opéra took part; and I wasn't there! La Fontaine's fable is quite right, absence is the greatest of all evils, especially for me with my unfailing bad luck.[233] When I'm in Paris, nothing could be more lifeless and dull than our opera houses. But the moment I turn my back on it they're full of fireworks, with spectacular successes rocketing to the artistic heavens in their thousands.

"Mme. Stoltz has lost none of her voice nor of her blazing energy, so everyone is saying. But for my part my advice to her is that she's overdoing it. She's hoisting too much sail, laying bare too much of her soul; she's killing herself, burning herself out. One must look to the morrow, and our Opéra audiences are not used to such luxuriance of dramatic energy or such profusion of passionate expression. They gave all that up for lost a long time ago: we shouldn't let them get used to it again. Mme. Stoltz could and should limit her ardour to a suitably lukewarm temperature, telling herself like Rossini: *E troppo buono per questi.*"[234]

There are notable examples afforded by some even more notable singers to prove my point beyond dispute. One of them omits certain phrases in her finest arias, and takes a few bars' rest so as not to tire herself. In almost all her other roles she doesn't bother to articulate the words; vocalising is easier, even when you don't know how. Another arms herself with a monumental calm, a marmoreal coldness, and delivers ardour as Bossuet delivered his sermons,[235] without gestures, without movement, without any variation of tone, constantly maintaining what she thinks of as her soul at the moderate temperature recommended by professors of hygiene. That's the way to keep house![236]

What's more, these thrifty singers live much longer than roses. They never accept less than hundreds of thousands of francs, they buy castles, or build them, in France, and they become marchionesses or duchesses. And yet Mme. Stoltz, who has probably only ever built castles in Spain and has no handle at all to her name, is forced to accept just tens of thousands of francs, a mere pittance, for burning herself up like this in the flame of her inspiration. So now, after only a month, she's already exhausted to the point of having to ask for time off and go to recover her strength in the calm refreshing air of England. I trust she'll at least profit from the good examples London will provide in abundance. That is the place to find sing-

Figure 31. Rosine Stoltz. Lithograph after Francis Grant, London, undated.
Richard Macnutt Collection, Withyham.
　　"Mme. Stoltz has returned, more dramatic than ever" (page 144).

ers whose souls never suffer from exposure. Musicians of fiery temperament learn to cool their passion in the Stygian waters of good old oratorio,
from which they emerge cold, stiff and bereft of all feeling.

But even that is better, much better, than rushing off across the Ocean to
the tropics and their more or less cannibalistic peoples. What would savages need music for? What attraction can there be in their strings of horses
and bouquets of diamonds, when cholera and *vomito nero* and yellow
fever are there too, mingling with your hordes of admirers and flashing
glassy eyes at you? Mme. Stoltz did come back from Rio de Janeiro, admit-
tedly, but Mme. Sontag stayed in Mexico, poor woman—she died there, so
she won't come back.[237]

Where the eaglet has passed the nightingale remains.[238]

Poor Sontag! How sad and absurd to go and die like that, far from
Europe which alone appreciated her artistry!

I've been reproached for not having paid tribute to her memory. It's not
from any lack of feeling at such a loss, I assure you. I fully appreciate the
extent of the misfortune which music has suffered in the loss of this incomparable singer. But the daily displays of insincere grief and the constant
abuse of death as an excuse to shower praise on mediocrities make me
nervous of funeral elegies, especially about people or things which really
do deserve admiration; they've become so commonplace. Anyway there's
only one kind of funeral oration I know how to do well: for mediocre
artists who are still alive.

And then, if I may say so, I couldn't in all conscience approve of Mme.
Sontag setting off on this chase after millions and pursuing it right to the
peaks of the Andes. I couldn't bring myself to believe her so greedy for gain
when she was an artist, a true artist possessing every sacred gift of art and
nature: a fine voice, feeling for music, dramatic instinct, style, the most
exquisite taste, passion, imagination, grace, everything—and something else.
She sang vocal bagatelles, playing with notes as no Indian juggler could
ever do with his golden balls; but she also sang music, great immortal music, as musicians can only dream of hearing it sung. She could interpret
anything, even masterpieces; she understood them as if she'd written them
herself.

I'll never forget my astonishment one evening in London. I was at a
performance of Mozart's *Figaro*.[239] I'd never before heard that heavenly
solo of a woman in love, during the night scene in the garden, performed
other than crudely; when Mme. Sontag breathed it, in a *mezza voce* so
tender, so soft and so mysterious, this secret music, even though I already
knew the key to it, seemed a thousand times more ravishing. At last, I
thought—I had to take care not to exclaim out loud—at last this wonderful page of Mozart's has been faithfully rendered!

HENRIETTE SONTAG.

Figure 32. Henriette Sontag. Anonymous lithograph portrait, printed by Sturm, Berlin, undated. Richard Macnutt Collection, Withyham.
"Mme. Sontag could, I believe, have sung Shakespeare. I know no higher praise" (page 148).

Truly this is the music of solitude, the music of voluptuous reverie, the music of night's mystery. This is just how a woman's voice should sound in such a scene. Here is all the light and shade of the singer's art, its half-tint—I mean its *piano*, that *piano*, or rather *pianissimo*, which composers can obtain from an orchestra of a hundred players or a chorus of two hundred voices, but cannot get for gold or for jewels, not by flattery or threats or caresses or flogging, from the majority of singers, whether competent or incompetent, Italian or French, intelligent or stupid, human or divine. They nearly all sing too loud to a greater or lesser degree, with quite exasperating obstinacy. They never venture below *mezzo-forte*, the precise mid-point of dynamics, apparently fearful of not being heard. No, wretched women, we hear you all too clearly! It was Sontag, a German, who finally showed us how to sing secrets, how to sing a stage-whisper, how to sing like a bird hidden in foliage saluting the twilight. She understood this exquisite nuance of tone which is enough all by itself to give sensitive listeners a thrill of pleasure unlike any other. Her *piano* was as refined, as pure and as mysterious as that of twenty good muted violins under an able conductor. In short she had mastered the whole art of singing.

Admirable Sontag! She would have been Juliet if there existed a truly Shakespearean opera on *Romeo*.[240] She would have carried off the balcony scene triumphantly; how splendidly she would have sung the famous passage:

I have forgot why I did call thee back . . .
I shall forget, to have thee still stand there.[241]

She would have been equal to singing the incomparable love duet from the last act of *The Merchant of Venice*:

In such a night as this,
. . .
Troilus methinks mounted the Troyan walls,
And sigh'd his soul toward the Grecian tents,
Where Cressid lay that night.[242]

Unlikely as it may seem, Mme. Sontag could, I believe, have sung Shakespeare. I know no higher praise.

And then to go and die—just for a few thousand dollars!

Auri sacra fames![243]

What does a mere singer want with so much money? When you have a town house, a country house, affluence, comfort, your children's future taken care of, what more do you need? Why not settle for five hundred thousand francs, or six hundred thousand, or seven hundred thousand?

Why do you have to have a million, or even more than a million? It's monstrous—it's a disease.

If you're ambitious to achieve great things as an artist, all well and good.
Make as many millions as you can, but make sure you stop in time to have
the energy to carry out your self-ordained mission—a kingly mission, on a
scale no king has yet contemplated. Yes, make your millions, and then
we'll see a true opera house where masterpieces are properly performed,
not three times a week, but every so often.[244] Philistines won't be admitted
at any price; there'll be no claque; only operas of genuine musical and
poetic worth will be given, and no one will worry about putting crude
monetary values on objects of beauty. It will be a theatre of art, not a
bazaar. Money will be the means, not the end.

Make your millions, and you can found a gigantic Conservatoire
where everything worth knowing in and about music will be taught. It
will produce artistic, educated musicians, not mere artisans. Singers
will learn their own language, its history and spelling, as well as vocal
technique, and even a little music perhaps. There will be classes for
every conceivable instrument, bar none, and twenty rhythm classes.
Immense choruses will be formed, consisting entirely of singers who
have good voices and actually know how to sing, as well as how to
read music and understand what they are singing. Conductors will be
trained to read full scores and not to beat time with their feet. There
will be lessons on the philosophy and history of art, and much else
besides.

Make your millions, and you can build fine concert halls tailor-made for
music, not for balls and patriotic banquets, and not destined to become
granaries for storing hay.

You can give real concerts there, from time to time: for music isn't meant
to take its place among the daily indulgences of life, like eating, drinking
and sleeping. I know nothing so odious as establishments which serve up
the same old musical stew every single evening. It's they that ruin and debase our art, making it dull, inane and stupid. In Paris they've reduced it to
just another branch of commerce, like wholesale grocery.

Make your millions and you can destroy with one hand while building
with the other. You can lead a nation to civilisation and culture. Then we'll
be able to forgive you your wealth, we'll even applaud you for your pains
in acquiring it, and for going to Mexico or Rio or San Francisco or Sydney
or Calcutta to earn it.

But what earthly hope is there of any millionaire singer, male or female,
fulfilling a dream like this! I'm sure that those who read this unseemly
outburst—if indeed I count any millionaires among my readers—will look
on me as a rare species of imbecile. Imbecile, yes, but rare, no. There are a
fair number of people of this stamp in the world, whose disdain of senseless millions is a hundred million times vaster and deeper than the ocean.

That's something you must resign yourselves to, poor millionaires. Don't all go and blow your brains out—if you have any!

The rough and the smooth

In the last century there was a much-loved singer who is completely unknown today. Her name was Tonelli.[245] Was she one of those ephemeral immortals, the scourge of music and musicians, who rejoice in the title of *prima donna* or *diva* and throw opera houses into complete disarray, until some composer or conductor of true steel sets his face against their pretensions and without effort or violence puts an end to their divinity? I think not. On the contrary, to judge from what Rousseau and Diderot had to say about her, she seems to have been a gracious and unspoilt young Italian girl, with sweet manners and a voice of such charm that, on hearing her in those mewling little operas known as *opere buffe,* the connoisseurs of those days imagined they were savouring heavenly strains of superb music with exquisite melodies.

Oh, what splendid, worthy fellows they were, the connoisseurs of that philosophical age, writing about music without any trace of feeling for it, without even rudimentary knowledge of what it is or how it is put together! I'll make an exception for Rousseau, who did have some rudimentary knowledge. And yet it's astonishing what crazy ideas that great writer has put into circulation, giving them even today an authority which no commonsense axiom will ever have!

Of course it's a great convenience to find ready-made opinions on art or science bearing the signature of an illustrious name. You can use them like cheques of unquestionable reliability. O you *philosophes*! You great buffoons! To return to Tonelli, just recall the excitement aroused in Paris by the 'buffoons' of the Italian opera during her reign. To judge from the ecstatic accounts of their supporters, and the rough treatment these aficionados handed out to a great French master, Rameau, you'd suppose, wouldn't you, that the works of Italian composers of that time, and of Pergolesi above all, were brimming with musical vitality and overflowing with melodic milk and honey, that their harmony was heavenly and their forms of classic beauty? I've just been rereading *La Serva Padrona,* and I can tell you this isn't the case at all—although you won't believe me anyway. To see this much-vaunted opera restaged and to attend the first night of its revival would be divinely hilarious.

All this won't stop Pergolesi's name from being famous for a long time yet, while another Italian, Della Maria,[246] who possessed in the highest degree the true gift of fluent and expressive melody, and who wrote such attractive little scores for the Feydeau theatre, scores whose charm still comes up fresh and smiling, is now almost forgotten. His pretty tunes are familiar, but his name is unknown. Rousseau, Diderot, the Baron Grimm, Mme. d'Épinay and the whole school of *philosophes* of the last century sang the praises of Pergolesi, but no *philosophe* of our time has even mentioned Della Maria. That's the reason. . . .

So see here, young students, young teachers, young virtuosi, young composers, members and prizewinners of the Institute, learn from this example! Try not to get on the wrong side of us present-day *philosophes*. Steer clear of our disapproval, don't do anything to upset us. If you give concerts, don't forget to invite us, and make sure they're not too short; ask us to your final rehearsals and your prizegivings; don't neglect to call on us at home to sing us your latest songs or play your masses and your polkas. For no philosophy endures, and we'll get our revenge by refusing to mention your name in our sublime writings. We'll declare a war of silence on you— the worst kind of war, believe me. No glory for you, no immortality, no nothing; and in three thousand years' time, even if you've each written three dozen comic operas, you won't even receive as much attention as poor Della Maria does today.

Dilettanti of the fashion world—The poet and the cook

One often hears people in the fashionable world complaining about the length of operas—how tiring these huge works are to their audiences, how late at night performances end, and so on. As a matter of fact, these malcontents have no right to complain; for them there are no five-act operas, only three-and-a-half-act ones. Society people aren't in the habit of arriving at the Opéra before the middle of the second act, and sometimes later. No matter whether the performance begins at seven or half-past seven or eight o'clock, they won't put in an appearance in their boxes before nine.

Despite this, they're definitely anxious to get seats for first nights; but this isn't by any means a sign of their eagerness to get to know the work being performed, which is of very little interest to them. It's merely a matter of being seen in the theatre that evening and being able to say "I was there", with some superficial observation on the nature of the new work and some kind of assessment of its merits, that's all. A composer nowadays who writes a splendid first act can be certain of seeing it played to a house three-quarters empty, and of being applauded only by the gentlemen of the claque, who are at their posts long before the curtain goes up. These days a new opera is given scarcely once every two years; so fashionable opera-goers would only have to depart from their usual behaviour once in two years to hear a production of such significance in full at its first performance. But the effort is too great, and the most miraculous inspiration of a great composer wouldn't get these people, who pass for polite society, to bring even their horses' dinners forward by as much as a quarter of an hour.

Of course the composer can console himself for this discourtesy and indifference with an even greater indifference, saying "Why should I care that the people in the orchestra stalls and boxes aren't in their seats? The support of so-called music-lovers like that isn't worth having."

It's the same almost everywhere. Think how often ordinary members of the audience at the Théâtre-Italien can be seen getting upset during performances of *Don Giovanni* at the precipitate emptying of the principal boxes as soon as the Commendatore's statue appears. There are no more cavatinas to listen to. Rubini has sung his aria,[247] nothing remains but the final scene (the masterpiece of the whole masterpiece), it's time to get away as quickly as possible to go and drink tea.

In a large German city where people are supposed to have genuine admiration for music, it's the custom to dine at two o'clock, so most daytime concerts begin at noon. But if the concert isn't over at a quarter to two, even if a vocal quartet sung by the Virgin Mary and the Holy Trinity accompanied by the Archangel Michael was yet to come, the fine dilettanti would still leave their seats, calmly turn their backs on the divine virtuosi and march impassively off to get their grub.

Such people are intruders in opera houses and concert halls;

Art is not made for them, they have no need of it.

They're the descendants of that fellow Chrysale from Molière's *Les Femmes savantes*:

Living on good soup, not fine language.[248]

In their eyes Shakespeare and Beethoven are far less important than a good cook.

———

Orange groves—The acorn and the pumpkin

Our writers of vaudevilles and comic operas never fail to include orange groves in every outdoor scene, if the action takes place in Italy.

A certain author had the idea of setting one near the main road from Naples to Castellamare. That particular grove intrigued me greatly. Where had it been hiding? I'd have been so relieved to find it and go to sleep in its perfumed shade in 1832 when I travelled on foot from Castellamare in a temperature of 223 degrees, hidden, like one of Homer's gods, in a cloud of burning dust.[249] Phooey! There are no more orange groves there than in the Tauris Gardens at St. Petersburg or on the Roman plain.

But it's an ineradicable belief in the heads of all Northerners who've ever read Goethe's famous ballad "Kennst du das Land, wo die Zitronen blühn?"[250] that orange trees grow in Italy like potatoes in Ireland. It's no use telling them Italy is a big country, stretching all the way from the Alps to the Isles of Lipari. Chambéry is in Savoy, Savoy is part of the kingdom of Sardinia, Sardinia is in Italy, yet the Savoyards aren't at all Italian. Just because there really are vast and magnificent orange groves in the island of Sardinia, or even if there's quite a pretty one in a park in Nice on the right bank of the Payon, that's no reason to expect to find the garden of the Hesperides at Susa or St.-Jean-de-Maurienne.[251]

Never mind! Perhaps today there *are* orange groves on the Castellamare road. Once they begin to grow somewhere, they grow fast. It's just a matter of getting started.

In any case, there are certainly no lemon groves. That would be a heretical idea.

"Why so?"

"Why? Haven't you read the fable of *The Acorn and the Pumpkin?*[252] Don't you know that lemons, instead of being round like oranges, are armed with a hard protuberance, which could put out the eye of a traveller sleeping under a lemon tree if it fell on his face? Providence knows what it's doing. The author of the tale I've just cited demonstrates this clearly. 'The reason God has hung a lightweight fruit from the branches of the oak tree,' he says, 'while the monstrous pumpkin, whose appearance seems more suited to a mighty tree, sits on the ground amidst the leaves of a miserable creeping plant, is to save people who are tempted to sleep under oak trees from having their noses squashed by falling pumpkins.'"

Of course there are many other trees in tropical countries, like coconut palms and calabashes, bearing heavy fruits which are dangerous to people's noses, but moralists aren't required to take account of what goes on in the Antipodes. And anyway, think how many people of every colour one sees down there with squashed noses, passed on from father to son!

"Duckings"

Anyone who leaves Paris for any length of time is regularly astonished, when he gets back, by the persistence with which the bakers still make the same brioches every day and the smaller theatres still produce the same new comic operas, as well as by the sheer obstinacy with which the Opéra itself still performs the same old works.

As for bakers and smaller theatres continuing to produce the same new comic operas and the same brioches, that's not really surprising. The means of ensuring the highest perfection in these agreeable products were discovered long ago, so why change them? Here indeed the best would be the enemy of the good. The important thing for the customer is a good oven, so that brioches can always be served fresh and remain very little time in stock. This is the opposite of the system at the Opéra, where some works are kept in stock until patrons can no longer bite into them, having lost all their teeth.

In swimming schools the term "ducking" is used for a manoeuvre whereby one swimmer jumps on top of another, puts a hand on his head and gives him a hefty shove down to the bottom. This is just what's been happening since time immemorial at the Opéra-Comique and the Théâtre-Lyrique. The moment a bather wearing his life-jacket (without which he'd never stay afloat) sticks his head above water another swimmer gives him a ducking. The unfortunate victim goes under at once. Sometimes he reappears in a half-dead state, if he's good at holding his breath—but this is rare. Usually he drowns.

The public enjoys these watery escapades enormously—without duckings to watch, hardly anyone would go to swimming schools. This is called "varying the repertoire". At the Opéra, where there are no duckings and the works performed either sink on their own or

Apparent rari nantes,[253]

floating as calmly as buoys in a harbour, they obstinately insist on merely "maintaining the repertoire". These different systems must all be good in the final analysis, since they all bring the public flocking in. Bakeries, large theatres, small theatres—they're all full. Consume, consume and you'll be happy—as long as you don't drown.

Sensitivity and concision—A funeral oration in three syllables

Cherubini was once strolling in the foyer of the Conservatoire concert hall during an interval. The musicians around him had an air of gloom; they had just learnt of the death of their colleague Brod, a remarkable virtuoso and principal oboe at the Opéra. One of them went up to the elderly maestro and said, "So, Monsieur Cherubini, we have lost poor Brod!"[254]

"Eh? What's that?"

The musician repeated, in a louder voice: "Brod, our comrade Brod. . . ."

"What about him?"

"He's dead!"

"Hmph! Feeble tone!"

———————

Figure 33. Berlioz in Vienna, 1845. Lithograph by Joseph Kriehuber. Richard Macnutt Collection, Withyham.

A portrait of the composer at the time of his travels in France (see pages 157–88). He was in Vienna from November 1845 to January 1846, between his visits to Marseilles and Lyons (June and July 1845) and to Lille (June 1846).

Travels in France

Academic Correspondence

To Monsieur Monnais, Academician at Large[255]

Marseilles—A concert—The coachman—His conversation—His post-horn—
The happy music-lover—The unhappy music-lover

Paris, 18 . . .[256]

I got up "with the rising sun, hale and hearty, full of fun", just like the
financier in *Les Prétendus*,[257] that masterpiece of grotesque flannel which
eclipsed *Iphigenia in Tauris* at the box-office, bringing Lemoine (for Lemoine
it was who composed *Les Prétendus*) more money than all of Gluck's operas put together. Further proof that one day succeeds another just like the
day before.

So I feel up to writing you a whole string of nonsense. It all comes from the
extravagant dream to which I was treated by our friend Queen Mab.[258] I dreamt I
had six hundred million francs, and between evening and morning, by means of
irresistible arguments, I had engaged the services of all the talented singers
and instrumentalists in the whole of Paris, London and Vienna, including
Jenny Lind and Pischek, for my own personal gratification.[259] The result was
that all the opera houses in those three capitals had to close immediately.

You were the general in command of my musical forces; we understood
each other wonderfully well. We had a magnificent theatre and a splendid
concert hall, where, twice a month only, masterpieces were performed exactly as their authors wrote them, with hitherto unheard-of fidelity, pomp,
grandeur and inspiration. We picked the audiences ourselves, and not for
anything in the world would we have let in any of the cretins of whom
there are so many. One of them, who for the sake of his self-respect had
bribed an usher and sneaked himself into a box for 50,000 francs, was
spotted by the performers just as the first act of *Alceste* was about to start,
and forced to leave to a chorus of jeers. You were hopping mad; I felt sorry
for the poor chap, feeling his humiliation was excessive, and it would have
been simpler to get four stewards to remove him without so much fuss.

And we spoke Dr. Johnson's English, and had Shakespeare's plays performed in our theatre, without corrections or cuts, by Brooke, Macready
and the leading actors of the three kingdoms;[260] and we were dizzy with
admiration.

We had also organised a band of whistlers, booers and catcallers to stop
symphonies being played in the intervals at the Théâtre-Français, or arias

and overtures in vaudevilles. After some tempestuous evenings, the forces of good sense and good taste prevailed, and it was finally recognised that these horrible stupidities could not go on. So the art of music no longer had to put up with such outrages.

Just at that moment I awoke with a start. Someone had come looking for me on behalf of the committee of the Association of Artist-Musicians to enlist my help with the preparations for a "fête dansante" they had suddenly thought of giving under the direction of Musard in the Mabille garden, involving every showgirl in Paris.[261] The contrast between my dream and this reality struck me as so utterly ridiculous that I laughed fit to burst, and have remained in the state of hilarity in which I propose to continue this letter, if you don't mind. And you won't mind, will you? We've known for a long time that our conversations always end in laughter, and however burdened I may be with frustration or care,

My sorrow vanishes the instant you appear.

What a turnaround! Do you remember the days when you used to derive so much pleasure from tearing me to pieces in your feuilletons in the *Courrier français*?[262] What fine absurdities you printed about my "leanings" and my "excesses"! I envy you the happy times you must have had laying into me like that. It must be really delightful to belabour someone in that way, quite coolly, not with anger but amusement, simply as a mental exercise.

Not that your mind has ever needed much exercise; it was all too nimble and alert, all too supple and keen-edged, as I recall. You caused me a lot of anxiety, I must confess; and I felt acutely ill at ease that evening when our friend Schlesinger, with his usual aplomb, introduced me to you at the Opéra masked ball.[263] Besides, it was an oddly chosen occasion, as the three of us had come to witness a spoof of myself and my *Symphonie fantastique* in the form of a musical interlude by Arnal and Adam.[264] The latter had written a grotesque symphony in which he burlesqued my orchestration, and Arnal portrayed me, the composer of the piece, rehearsing it. I was shown delivering an address to the musicians on the expressive power of music, in which I demonstrated that the orchestra can express anything, say anything, explain anything, *even the art of tying one's cravat.*

It was Monsieur Véron, then Director of the Opéra, who had had the idea for this entertainment.[265] Later he had me warmly praised in the *Constitutionnel.* He was consumed with remorse.

Arnal became a regular attender at my concerts; he felt obliged by his conscience to support them. He's a man of honour.

Adam is a good fellow. Ten years later he repented of having accepted the role of caricaturist; since then he has only "spoofed" the orchestration of Grétry and Monsigny.

. . . .

As for you, you seem to have remained just the same man of wit without malice as you were before I knew you, and I'm lucky indeed, now I do know you, to be able from time to time to indulge with you in those fine outbursts of Homeric laughter which blot everything else from memory.

Still, I must say I found no trace of your old sense of fun in the letter you wrote me last winter while I was in London, and to which this is a reply. I'm quite happy about that; for I too felt a strange pang when I set eyes on the beauty of France again, and laughter comes less easily. Besides, there's nothing like a bankruptcy for making one serious, and I've just been sorting out a pretty unpleasant one across the Channel.[266]

But since you've asked me for an account of my travels in England, I'll give you one of a musical journey which I undertook in France in 1845. Up until then I'd never set foot in a theatre or concert hall anywhere in France outside Paris.

I had just given four festival matinée concerts in the Cirque des Champs-Élysées,[267] and I felt that taking the waters and other amusements, which had put me back on my feet the previous year after the Festival of Industry, would again do me a lot of good. No sooner had the idea entered my head than I put on my hat and set off for some bathing . . . in Marseilles.

Once I'd had a good swim in the Mediterranean, I had an urge to get to know the town, and my thoughts turned first of all to the best-informed music-lover of the Phocaean city, an old friend of mine, Monsieur Lecourt, who plays the cello extremely well and knows all of Beethoven by heart, and who travelled 500 miles some years ago to hear the first performance of one of my works in Paris—a man of unwavering convictions who says exactly what he thinks, who calls a spade a spade both in his writing and in his conversation, and who thinks, speaks, writes and plays fair, with a heart of gold worn on his sleeve.[268] I had no difficulty finding his residence; it would have been harder to meet anyone in Marseilles who didn't know where it was. As soon as he set eyes on me he exclaimed:

"There you are! Welcome! What on earth can have given you the idea of coming to Marseilles to put on a concert? At this time of year! And in such heat! And with all the coffee and indigo arriving daily in the port! Dear me, you must be quite mad!"

"Actually it was the Director of your theatre who suggested it to me—it's an excellent idea. We're giving the concert in ten days' time."

"What lunacy!"

"Two concerts then![269] And if you provoke me any more, we'll give three, and you can play a cello solo in the fourth."

You should know, my dear Monnais, that Marseilles was the first town in France which understood the great works of Beethoven. It was five years ahead of Paris in this respect; Beethoven's late quartets were already being played and admired in Marseilles while we in Paris were still treating the sublime author of these extraordinary compositions as a madman. So I did have some reason to expect a number of competent performers and a moderately intelligent audience. In addition Marseilles has several amateur virtuosi whose support I was hoping for, and who indeed provided it unstintingly. What's more, the theatre possessed at that time a well-balanced company of singers, amongst whom I had spotted the names of Alizard, Mlle. Mainvielle Fodor and two Italian sopranos whose praises had often been sung to me.[270]

With the help of Monsieur Pépin, the theatre's able conductor, Monsieur Pascal, his first violin, and Monsieur Lecourt, who for all his views on the inappropriateness of my enterprise nevertheless helped actively to bring it to fruition, my orchestral forces were soon gathered. We were lacking only trumpets, since at that time the custom had already begun among the major provincial orchestras of playing trumpet parts on cornets, an unspeakable abuse which ought not to be tolerated at any time or in any circumstances.

I'd heard only rather lukewarm recommendations of the theatre chorus, but to make up for this I knew of the Trotebas Society, a men's singing academy which, despite the recent death of its founder, was still going strong. They came to my aid very willingly, taking part in some very long rehearsals with much assiduity and patience. This society, which is justly celebrated in the Midi, consists of sixty members, not good sight-readers, it's true, but with remarkable feeling for music and voices of fine, clear sonority. These gentlemen performed several pieces with verve and a feeling for nuance worthy of the highest praise. As for the sopranos, who came from the theatre chorus, I was obliged to put a stop to their caterwauling by telling them, before starting a piece where they only had to double the tenors an octave higher, "Ladies, there's a copying error in your parts: there are three hundred bars' rest missing at the start, please count them very carefully, and in silence." It goes without saying the piece was over before the three hundredth bar, so the ladies didn't spoil anything. Alizard took the singing honours.

There were about eight hundred people in the hall; but Méry was one of them, which brought the number of people of intelligence and taste to at least two thousand in my eyes.[271] The audience was attentive and at times very enthusiastic; but some parts of the programme gave rise to lively discussions after the concert, as always in France. This is how I know. I was returning from the sea one evening, and as there was no room inside the omnibus which takes bathers back to town, I had to climb up to the seat on top, next to the coachman. It wasn't long before the two of us fell into conversation. My Phaeton told me about all the brilliant literary acquaintances he'd made plying to and fro between Marseilles and the Mediterranean.[272]

"I know Méry well", he told me. "Sharp as a razor, he is; he'd make pots of money if he didn't waste his time writing a mass of them foolish nonsenses

Figure 34. Marseilles—view of La Canebière, the principal street of the city. Bibliothèque Nationale de France.

"Returning from the sea one evening [by omnibus], . . . I had to climb up to the seat on top, next to the coachman" (page 160). Perhaps Berlioz's omnibus is the one on the left of the picture.

what women read—though I even laugh at 'em meself sometimes, fool that I am. Even so, Méry is a good feller, sure enough, and from Marseilles too. I know Alexandre Dumas and his son well.[273] Dumas, now, he writes tragedies, as they call 'em, where all of 'em kill each other off like flies, and drink poison by the bottleful. But blow me if they don't say he's also taken a fancy to writing them novels what people read all the time, just like Méry. A shame, I call it!"

"You're very hard on these two poets", I said.

"Poets? What poets? A poet is someone who only writes verse. Monsieur Reboul from Nîmes is a poet; he don't write any prose.[274] But to do Dumas justice, he certainly can swim, sir; he swims like a king, and his son like a 'Dauphin'![275] Ha! Ha! I knew Rachel very well."

"Mademoiselle Rachel of the Comédie-Française?"[276]

"Yes, the one who played tragedies at the Comédie. Ha! Ha! It was at one of her performances I made my famous speech what caused such a stir in Marseilles."

"Really? You spoke in public?"

"I tell you, I'd speak to four publics if it was called for. Here's what happened: Rachel arrived at Marseilles and announced that she'd perform Monsieur Racine's *Bajazet,* and that she'd make her entrance along with four Turks. So off I went to the theatre, she made her entrance, and there were no more than three turbans to be seen. Well, I ask you! What a fuss we made in the pit;[277] it looked like this Parisian joker-woman was trying to make a mockery of us Marseilles folk. I made a sign, and everyone went quiet. Then I got up on a bench and said, loudly: 'One Turk short!' Well, after a speech like that, you should have seen the place, it was terrible! La Rachel had to leave the stage, the curtain came down, and the Director got a fourth Turk into his costume pretty quick; so when La Rachel reappeared, they were all present and correct."

"You don't say! There's no fooling with you Marseilles people."

"No indeed, for sure! We had a spot of bother only the other day with Félicien David, when he came here and announced his *Le Désert,* an old symphony*, with its Caravan March.[278] Well, we all rushed to the theatre, and there wasn't a single camel in this caravan."

"You must have made some speech that evening?"

"No, I didn't say a thing, I never opened my mouth. I would've spoken up, mind you, and stoutly too, if David were French; but he's one of us, from Provence, and we didn't want to give him a hard time. Though it's a bit much to announce a Caravan March without a single camel."

The speech-maker fell silent for a moment, but I happened to touch his post-horn which was rolling about on the top of the coach, and he spoke again:

---

*He meant ode-symphony.

"Ah! Know about that, do you?"

"What? Why do you suppose I might know about horns?"

"Come on! D'you think I don't know it's you what's giving them big concerts everyone's talking of?"

"Oh, how did you know?"

"Why, from the driver, of course; quite a music-lover, he is, so he went along to the theatre. He told me."

"Well then, since people are talking of my concerts, what are they saying? Fill me in a little, since you know so much about these conversations."

"Oh yes, I heard some good ones the other evening, when them Trotebas serenaded you. The Rue de Paradis was packed so full, all the way to the Bourse, that we were all wondering if there was an extra-special coffee sale, or if His Grace the Archbishop was giving benediction. Not a bit of it; it was the honours being paid to you. That's when I heard some of them music-lovers talking, during the serenade. One of 'em, Monsieur Himturn, what had come from Nîmes for your music, all fired up he was, he kept saying: '. . . and the *Hymn to France*! And the *Pilgrims' March*!' 'What pilgrims?' shouted another, 'I didn't see any pilgrims.' '. . . and *The Fifth of May*, and the Adagio of the symphony.'[279] Well, he was just head over heels about you.

"Then there was a lady saying to her daughter: 'You have no soul, Rose, you'll never understand: stick to your contredanses.' But worst of all were two timber merchants, yelling even louder than the Trotebas: 'To Hell with firebrands like him; given half a chance he'd have had a cannon in his orchestra!' 'Get on with you! A cannon?' 'Yes indeed, a cannon. There's an item on the programme called *Field Piece*; he was going to let off an artillery piece at us, a twelve-pounder at least!' 'My dear fellow, you don't understand. The Field Piece you refer to is obviously the *Scene in the Fields*, the Adagio of the symphony. You're making a pun on its title.' 'Oh, all right then, there may not be a cannon, but there's certainly thunder. You'd have to be pretty thick not to recognise those rolls of thunder at the end, just like on stormy days when it's about to rain.' 'But of course, that's exactly what he wanted. It's very poetic, and I was greatly moved!' 'What do you mean, poetic? If he was trying to put a walk in the country into music, he's made a very bad job of it. Do you call that realistic? What about this thunder? I always head for my cabin the minute it starts thundering!'

"So he was thoroughly unhappy, and the happy one was unhappy that his chum wasn't happy, while the unhappy one was unhappier still at seeing the other happy."

"What can you expect," I said to him as I got off the bus, "however hard you try, you can't make everyone unhappy."

And off I went, with a friendly wave from the driver which proved the truth of the coachman's remark. He was a music-lover—a happy one.

———————

Second letter

Lyons—Philharmonic societies—My music teacher—Two anonymous letters—
A hurt music-lover—Dinner at Fourvières—The Brains Club—Scandal—The
millstone

Paris, 18 . . .

Today I'm neither "hale", nor "hearty", nor "full of fun", and it was
some time after the "rising sun" when I made the effort to get up to write
to you. I had a rough evening yesterday, you see, and I badly needed my
sleep after such an ordeal! The special gala performance given by the Opéra
for the benefit of the Welfare Fund included me among its victims. I have
realised Balzac's ideal, and you may consider me today a living personification of his "suffering artist".[280]

Before recounting my visit to Lyons, let me tell you about this latest
event at the Opéra: it will form a prologue to my "Letter from the Provinces". The programme was all the more appealing for including less music. The notices promised us the second act of Gluck's *Orpheus,* but the
notices were lying; only the Hades scene was performed, amounting to less
than half of the second act. As for the excerpts from Rossini's *Semiramide,*
they turned out to consist of an aria and a duet preceded by the overture.
That was the whole musical freight of an evening which began at seven and
finished at midnight. No, I'm wrong, we should also count some Biscayan
airs interpolated into the ballet *The Apparition,* and *half* the minuet from
Mozart's G minor Symphony,[281] which the orchestra began to play as a
curtain-raiser and would dearly have liked to continue if the actors hadn't
come on stage and obliged them to fall silent.

At the Théâtre-Français they treat Mozart with exactly the same degree of
respect. Only there the orchestra, unlike that of the Opéra, has no dignity to
consider when interrupted like this in the middle of a passage of Mozart—no
"noblesse" which *"oblige".* You can tell it to "Play on!" when it stops, or
"Stop now!" when it's playing, without wounding its self-esteem; it knows
that its role is to be treated like dirt. Mozart and Haydn symphonies serve
solely to produce some kind of noise to give notice of the suspension or resumption of dramatic hostilities. At the Opéra, though, the orchestra's purpose and importance are quite different, and I'd never have believed it would
be prepared to behave in such a submissive and demeaning manner. Its reputation for modesty, not to say humility, is henceforth beyond reproach.

Mlle. Rose Chéri had resigned herself to appearing in the first item,
Geneviève by Monsieur Scribe, a delightful vaudeville, to be sure, but one
which was pretty well bound to be played to an almost empty house, since
the public isn't in the habit of showing up at the theatre before half-past
eight, especially in summer.[282] Believe it or not, I'd never seen that young

and charming celebrity before. So hidebound are all of us in Paris in our theatre-going habits that the first time I saw Mlle. Rachel herself was only after five years of immense popular acclaim, cavorting on a donkey in the forest of Montmorency.

"It just proves you're a Philistine, that's all", you'll say. To which I reply: Yes, except that I decided ages ago to make every effort to resist my passion for vaudevilles, for tragedies "retold" in sets with six columns,[283] and for angular couplets and alexandrine verses. I even waited a good three months before hearing Jenny Lind in London.[284] I only went in the evenings to marvel at the crowd pressing round the stage door to catch a glimpse of its goddess going in.

What can I say? I lack fervour; my religion is tainted with indifference, and goddesses find me only a lukewarm worshipper. Anyway, what's one voice more or less amidst this chorus of praise, panegyrics and anthems, of passionate odes and overwrought dithyrambs? The only forms of homage still capable of pleasing these superior beings are repugnant to our prosaic ways and shocking to humane ideas. One would have to cast oneself under the wheels of their carriage as if it were the car of the Juggernaut,[285] or go insane with love and be locked up in a lunatic asylum where the good goddesses could visit from time to time, enveloped in cloud, to gaze at their victims. No doubt it would be rather nice for them to see the entire public seized with a spasm of frenzy, with women fainting or having convulsions and nervous attacks, and men killing each other in a fury of adulation. Perhaps they'd even accept young virgins or newborn babies as sacrifices, as long as the victims were of noble birth and rare beauty.

But when one doesn't feel possessed of such religious exaltation, it's better to stay well clear of the temple, and to keep one's eyes prudently averted from these dazzling faces. This is really an act of reverence, despite its irreverent appearance; for one would risk giving offence by less than perfect worship. Imagine someone saying pathetically to the goddess Lind: "Divine one, pardon the inability of feeble mortals to find words worthy of the feelings you inspire! Your voice is the sublimest of heavenly voices, your beauty is beyond compare, your genius beyond measure, your trill radiant as the sun, Saturn's halo is not worthy to crown your head! Before you, we mortals can only prostrate ourselves; permit us to lie in ecstasy at your feet!" The goddess, taking pity on such paltry words of praise, might be forbearing enough to answer: "Who is this pipsqueak?"

Ah well, despite my good resolutions, such is the magnetic attraction exercised by these celestial beings on even the coarsest creatures, that one day, after having applauded her for all I was worth the evening before in Donizetti's *Lucia di Lammermoor*, I couldn't resist the desire to go and admire Jenny Lind at close quarters in Richmond, hoping to see her cavorting on a donkey like Mlle. Rachel. But when I reached the Thames some distraction made me take a different boat from the Richmond one, and believe it or not, I went to Greenwich. There I admired a very interesting collection of small animals that the "director" of a travelling menagerie was showing for a penny, then I lay down on the grass in the park and slept for three hours like a true cockney, perfectly content.

Never mind, joking apart, Mlle. Lind is an accomplished woman, quite aside from her colossal talent—a real, complete talent, unalloyed gold. You know how she treated Monsieur Duponchel when he went to London to offer her an engagement in Paris,[286] and how our dear Director was left stupefied when she told him what she thought of his Opéra and his splendid offers! Goodness me! That was Mlle. Lind's finest hour: never did she play her role of goddess better or to finer effect.

But to return to last night. Why on earth, I ask you, should that noble fragment of ancient poetry named *Orpheus* be flung in our faces between a comic play and a ballet, without any preparation and wretchedly performed? The idea was obviously thought up by someone who despises music and hates the great composers. And then to cast Poultier as Eurydice's husband, that demigod, the perfection of beauty and genius! It made one sick to see and hear it; sick for the singer thus put on the rack, sick for the violated masterpiece, sick for the deluded authors.

Such treatment of Gluck is beyond words; it's quite simply an assassination of art. Poultier has a pleasant enough voice for singing pieces requiring no epic style, but he's as out of place in Gluck as he would be in Shakespeare. He could play Hamlet, Othello, Romeo, Macbeth, Coriolanus, Cassius, Brutus, Cardinal Wolsey or Richard III at least as well as Orpheus. Our Director will no doubt take it into his head one of these days to give us a fragment of *Alceste* or *Armide* with Mlle. Nau in the leading role![287] The result will be appalling, so he'll then have the satisfaction of saying: "It's this music: it's no good any more. It's too old, it doesn't suit our times, it's ridiculous to admire that sort of thing nowadays!"

How about that as a way of wiping out what little musical taste we still have? What penalty would be imposed for such a crime, such a premeditated act of murder, if there were a *Penal Code of the Arts*? The truth is, if such a code existed, there would also be other institutions we don't have, which would place art beyond the reach of its enemies and so secure it from such outrages.

. . . .

But my subject is Lyons and my musical experiences there.

I must tell you first that I was born not far from that great city,[288] and as a compatriot of the people of Lyons I was fully entitled to count on their complete indifference. That's why, when I first had the idea of threatening them with a concert in August in a temperature of twenty-five degrees, I felt I had to lay siege to the city. I wrote from Marseilles to Georges Hainl, the musical director of the Grand Theatre at Lyons and the man in charge there,[289] to warn him of my forthcoming arrival, and to suggest ways of

Figure 35. Jenny Lind. Anonymous engraving, c1850. Richard Macnutt Collection, Withyham.

"Mlle. Lind is an accomplished woman, quite aside from her colossal talent—a real, complete talent, unalloyed gold" (page 166).

grappling with the problems of giving a concert during the dogdays: large posters, innumerable leaflets, advertisements in all the local papers, notices permanently displayed on all the Saône and Rhône steamboats, invitations sent to the singing schools and to all the better amateur musicians in Lyons, as well as to the Philharmonic Societies of Dijon, Châlons and Grenoble (where there isn't one), peals of bells and volleys of cannon, the launching of a luminous balloon, a salvo of fireworks at the moment of my disembarkation on the Quai Saint-Clair, preachers in all the churches recommending me to their flocks, etc., etc. When he read this glorious little proposal, Georges, who might well claim to be one of the cleverest, boldest braggarts in Lyons or even in the Dauphiné, was overwhelmed. His ears tingled, his pride was wounded to the quick, and showing my letter to the manager and the treasurer of the Grand Theatre he exclaimed "My word! I admit defeat; this fellow puts even me in the shade!"

But he was not at all discouraged, and my instructions were scrupulously followed—except for the peals of bells, the volleys of cannon, the aerostatic ascent, the pyrotechnic eruption and the catholic sermons. These additions were not by any means unthinkable, though, as was later proved. For two years ago, not only was Jenny Lind received at Norwich with similar honours, but the bishop of that city paid her a visit, offered her rooms in his palace, and declared *ex cathedra* that since hearing the sublime singer he *had become a better person**. Which seems to prove beyond dispute this algebraic proposition: $L:B = B:H$; or (for those who don't understand algebra), in terms of publicity and spinning a good line, L is to B as B is to H; or again (for those who need to have their 'i's dotted and their 't's crossed) Hainl and I are mere babes at this game.

Be that as it may, we laid siege to the public as best we could by conventional means; *non licet omnibus* to enjoy the patronage of a bishop.[290] Then, having done our level best in that department, we turned our thoughts to the heart of the matter, the orchestra and chorus. The Dijon and Châlons Philharmonic Societies had responded to our appeal, promising us about twenty amateur violinists and double-bass players. A skilfully effected raid on all the players and singers in and around Lyons, a military band from the garrison and above all the large and well-balanced orchestra of the Grand Theatre, reinforced by some members of the Celestins orchestra, furnished us with a total of two hundred performers, who bore themselves bravely on the day of battle, I assure you. I even had the pleasure of including amongst them an artist of rare merit, who plays every instrument and whose pupil I was at the age of fifteen. I met him quite by chance on the Place des Terreaux. He had just arrived from Vienne, and his first words on seeing me were: "Count me in! What instrument shall I play? Violin, double-bass, clarinet or ophicleide?"

---

*Perfectly true.

"Ah, dear maître, you obviously don't know me very well. You must play the violin. Do I ever have too many violins? Does anyone?"

"Very well. But I'll feel quite out of place in your great orchestra, I don't know anyone in it."

"Don't worry, I'll introduce you."

So the next day, at the start of the rehearsal, I pointed out my teacher and said to the assembled musicians:

"Gentlemen, I have the honour to present to you a distinguished teacher from Vienne, Monsieur Dorant.[291] A grateful pupil of his is here with us today—I am that pupil. You may shortly come to the conclusion that I'm not much of a credit to him, but please welcome Monsieur Dorant as if you thought the opposite, and as he deserves."

You can imagine the surprise and the applause. Dorant was all the more nervous as a result; but once he was immersed in the symphony, the demon of music seized him completely, and soon I caught sight of him fencing feverishly with his bow, and I in turn felt strangely moved to be conducting the *March to the Scaffold* and the *Scene in the Fields* played by my old *guitar* teacher, whom I hadn't seen for twenty years.

Trumpets are almost as rare in Lyons as in Marseilles, and we had great difficulty finding two. The attractions of the cornet and the success it brings its players at country dances are becoming ever more irresistible to provincial musicians. If we don't look out the trumpet will soon become as much of a myth in France's greatest cities as the oboe—a fabled instrument which in twenty years' time people will no more believe in than in the unicorn. On the other hand, the orchestra of the Grand Theatre at Lyons is exceptional in possessing a first-rate oboist who plays the flute equally well, and has a great reputation: his name is Donjon. I should also mention the first violin, Monsieur Cherblanc, whose fine talent does credit to the Paris Conservatoire.

As for Georges Hainl, the conductor of this orchestra, here's a brief portrait of him. As well as being a cellist of indisputable excellence, which has earned him a fine name among virtuosi, he has all the conducting, teaching and organising gifts a musical director needs. In other words, his conducting is clear, precise, warm and expressive; when he puts on new works, he can spot mistakes in performance and remedy them as far as his musical resources allow; and finally he knows how to organise the means within his grasp and make the best use of them, keeping his musical domain under control and quickly overcoming the logistical difficulties which crop up in any musical enterprise, especially in the provinces. It should be evident from this that he combines great enthusiasm with a sharp mind and inexhaustible energy. He has done more in a few years for musical progress in Lyons than his predecessors did in half a century.

On the day of my concert, he was conductor and performer in turn. He conducted the chorus, and then played the cello in most of the symphonic pieces, the cymbals in the *Roman Carnival* overture, the timpani in the

Scene in the Fields from the *Symphonie fantastique,* and the harp in the *Pilgrims' March* from *Harold in Italy.* Yes, the harp. This was actually one of the most amusing incidents at our final rehearsal. I need hardly tell you that harpists are as rare in Lyons as in Poissy or Quimper. The harp too will soon become a fabled instrument in our provincial towns, like the oboe and the trumpet.

I'd been given the name of an amateur player in Lyons who enjoyed a certain reputation on the instrument. "Before you try him," said Georges, "let's have a look at the part you want him to play."

"Oh, it's not difficult; it has only two notes, B and C."

He looked at it closely. "Yes," he said, "it only has two notes, but they have to be played *right,* and this amateur of ours won't be able to cope. Your d****d music, as usual, is the sort that can only be played by *musicians.* But don't worry about it, leave it to me."

Next day, when we came to rehearse the piece, Georges put down his cello and shouted "Bring me the harp!" This was done. He took hold of the instrument, taking no notice of the jeers and yells of laughter coming from every section of the orchestra (for they knew he couldn't play it), quietly removed the strings next to the C and the B, and then, having thus made sure he couldn't go wrong, he attacked his two notes with imperturbable *"rightness"*, and the *Pilgrims' March* unfolded from beginning to end without the slightest mishap.

This was the first time I'd ever heard the harp part played at sight like that. For such a phenomenon to occur it had to be entrusted to a harpist who'd never tried playing the harp before but who was a real musician.

I was speaking earlier about the Lyons singing academies. One of the smaller ones consists entirely of young German amateurs who have imported the traditions of their native land to Lyons, and get together from time to time to work hard on their favourite masterpieces. Almost all of these gentlemen work for banks or major commercial institutions in Lyons. They came to my aid with much good grace and were an enormous help. The same should be said for the other choral society. This one is very large and consists exclusively of craftsmen and labourers. It was founded by Monsieur Maniquet, whose energy, talent and dedication to the hard task he has undertaken should long ago have won him and the institution he directs the active support and encouragement of the municipality of Lyons.

Barielle, a member of the Grand Theatre company with a fine bass voice, sang my cantata *The Fifth of May* in impressive fashion.[292] In short, except for the *March to the Scaffold* which was spoilt by the weakness of the brass section, the concert went splendidly from a musical viewpoint and satisfactorily as regards . . . what really matters.[293] Georges, however, would have liked people killing each other to get in; and despite members of the audience having come from Grenoble, Vienne, Nantua and even Lyons itself, nobody was killed.

Figure 36. Georges Hainl, director of the Lyons theatre orchestra. Lithograph by "A.F." Bibliothèque Nationale de France.

"As well as being a cellist of indisputable excellence, . . . he has all the conducting, teaching and organising gifts a musical director needs" (page 169).

If only the Lord Bishop had pronounced *ex cathedra* that my music "made people better", no doubt the crowd would have been packed tighter. But His Eminence of Lyons remained quite aloof. Besides, not one little rocket was let off in my honour, and the bells stayed silent. What hope, then, of people fighting at the doors to get in to a concert—in August, in the provinces! However I did get a serenade, as in Marseilles, and two anonymous letters. The first contained only vulgar abuse, untranslatable into polite language, and reviled me for coming to pinch pennies from the pockets of the musicians of Lyons. The second, much more entertaining, was from someone I'd unwittingly offended during the rehearsals. It consisted of two aphorisms which I can recall word for word. Here they are:

Even a great artist can be polite.
A gnat may sometimes trouble a lion.[294]

Signed: A Hurt Music-Lover

What do you make of this epistolary concision? And of the threat? And of the comparison? I'm very sorry to have hurt a music-lover; and whoever he may be, I ask him to accept my humblest apologies. In any case, if I'm the lion in question, I must assume the gnat has forgotten its anger, for I haven't suffered any trouble at all so far.

. . . .

I broke off at this point, my dear friend, to write a review of the latest concert at the Conservatoire. These chores seem to come my way rather too often, and I'm beginning to tire of dishing out admiration. All the more so since in the eyes of most true Frenchmen, especially Parisians, this admirer role is laughable. That's the least of my worries, I admit, for I've always allowed myself the pleasure of laughing heartily at their laughter. But to be frank, being a professional worshipper wears one out dreadfully when one is conscientious about it. After spending several hours on one's knees, inhaling incense and singing *Credo*'s, *Gloria*'s, *Pange Lingua*'s and *Te Deum*'s, one feels an imperious need to get up and stretch one's legs, to leave the church, breathe in the fresh air and the scent of flowers in the fields, and revel in creation, without meditating on the Creator or singing any sort of canticles. Indeed (this is strictly between you and me), one actually feels a desire to sing all sorts of nonsense, such as Monsieur de Pradel's delightful song, "Hurrah for Hell, we're on our way".[295]

I greatly admire . . . —there I go, admiring again! Sheer force of habit!— I meant to say, I very much like the verse of that jolly bacchanal that goes:

Godlike we sing
With a swing,
Filling Hell with the ring

Of pleasing melodies;
While far from Hell,
Gabriel
Wearies God with the knell
Of tiresome litanies!
Hurrah for Hell, etc.

The good Lord, you see, gets tired of being worshipped, beleaguered by Gabriel and his celestial choral society. He yawns fit to dislocate his jaw at the eternal chants of *Sanctus, Sanctus, Deus Sabaoth* addressed to him. Can we complain, miserable worms that we are, we human riffraff, witless rabble, can we complain when earthly Gabriels weary us for a mere three hours with music which, on balance, may well be far superior to that of Paradise? What's three hours in comparison with eternity?

Speaking of that piece, I daren't quote its refrain here. We used to break a lot of glasses when we sang it in chorus during Sardanapalesque student evenings some twenty-five years ago.[296] Let me tell you how I found out it was by that celebrated improviser Eugène de Pradel—which brings me back to Lyons.

After the concert which I had the honour to give there,[297] with the Lord Mayor's permission, I was invited to dine in Fourvières by a group of artists and literary men called the *Brains Club*. The group's members had taken great care to keep out bores and imbeciles, with the result that the latter took offence at their exclusion and sarcastically bestowed upon this society of men of wit the title of "Brains Club", which it readily accepted. When an artist passes through Lyons whom they are pretty sure of, or in other words who is apparently no more idiotic than the greater part of the human race, who doesn't propose toasts at banquets and who talks as much nonsense as anyone else, the Brains Club always makes an effort to show him some civility.

So in my capacity as an ordinary man and a non-orator, I was invited to climb Fourvières mountain to dine at a height of three hundred and sixty feet—no, what am I saying, eight hundred and fifty three feet—above the Saône, in a booth rather like the one to which the Devil once brought our Lord Jesus Christ to show him all the kingdoms of the earth.[298] That particular Devil wasn't too bright, at least in geology, so our Lord didn't find it too difficult to demonstrate his asininity and send him packing with his tail between his legs. But to get back to the booth at Fourvières, from which one can also see all the kingdoms of the earth, at least as far as the Guillotière district of Lyons, I found all the brains of Lyons gathered there, numbering twenty-four. That makes one brain per *xx,xxx* people of Lyons—I've forgotten the population of that great city. But Frédérick Lemaître,[299] who was performing in the Midi at the time, Monsieur Eugène de Pradel and I shouldn't be counted among those two dozen Lyons brains.

VUE DE LA CÔTE DE FOURVIÈRE
prise au fond du Pont du Change

Figure 37. Lyons—view of the hill of Fourvières, looking across the Pont du Change, 1858. Bibliothèque Nationale de France.

"I was invited to climb Fourvières mountain to dine at a height of . . . eight hundred and fifty three feet above the Saône" (page 173).

So, knocking off three brains (what a pretty expression!)—Frédérick's, Monsieur de Pradel's and mine—if I may put it like that, the club found itself reduced that day to twenty-one members. I like to think a considerable number of members were absent. We drank a lot, laughed a lot, and at coffee, which we drank in a kiosk even higher than the booth from which you can see all the kingdoms, Monsieur de Pradel came and introduced himself to me, without fuss, without getting anyone else to present him, without embarrassment, and without stammering—he just held out his hand as he might have done to anyone.

This self-possession delighted me. I like people who aren't nervous on big occasions; so echoing Napoleon's remark after staring for some minutes at Goethe standing impassively in front of him, I said to Monsieur de Pradel: "You are a man!"[300] He was stirred to the depths of his being by these sublime words, but a poet's vanity kept him from letting this be seen. Indeed he showed no emotion at all, and coming straight to the point, which he'd been chewing over throughout the meal, he said to me: "Didn't you, in one of your feuilletons, attribute the song 'Hurrah for Hell!' to Désaugiers?"

"Yes, you're quite right. My mistake was pointed out to me afterwards; I now know it's by Béranger."[301]

"Pardon me, but it's not by Béranger."

"In that case, I wasn't wrong after all; it must be by Désaugiers."

"Pardon me again, it's not by Désaugiers either."

"But who did write it then?"

"I did."

"You?"

"Yes, me, upon my word."

"I'm all the more sorry for my mistake, Monsieur, since the song sparkles with vitality, and in my opinion is worth more than a long poem.[302] I'll be sure to take the first opportunity to restore you the credit for it." Here we were interrupted by one of the guests. This gentleman felt the need to impart his ideas about music to us, well-meaning ideas that he put in the form of ill-disposed advice directed at me, making me think one more should be subtracted from the number of club members, since this must have been a stranger who, like me, was only one of the Brains *en passant*.

Another interruption. Devil take the nuisances! They're looking for me to . . .

A day later

It was nothing. I was being called to the full rehearsal of a five-act opera—a mere five acts!!! As a result, I'll be quite serious today. "So much the better", you may say. For I suspect you think that I've indulged in quite enough digressions and amused myself quite enough with words, people and ideas, and even with things hardly fit for joking about—that in an academic, musical and moral correspondence like this I should speak of music and morality, instead of quoting Bacchic, Pantagruelic,[303] fantastic songs, very daringly cut and not at all decent, which scandalise devout souls, and cause young people of fifteen and sixteen to avert their eyes, while those of forty-nine and fifty find their spectacles quivering on their noses.

Listen, to be honest, it's Monsieur de Pradel's fault; I couldn't resist the pleasure of acquainting you with a verse of his song. And naturally I had to choose the one which has to do with music; hence "godlike we sing" and "filling Hell with the ring" and Gabriel's "litanies", which, I fear, may have startled you a bit.

But suppose I'd continued my quotation, and reproduced in its entirety the refrain of this damnable hymn:

Hurrah for Hell, we're on our way!
Come, damsels,
Sweet Mam'selles,
Let's drink today;
Sing "Hey!",
Come and play,
And swigging away
Let's stay
Gay.

That would have been truly reprehensible and would merit severe rebuke. But I took care not to. I have too much horror of scandal, and I'm too convinced of the truth of the Gospel's words: "Woe unto him that scandaliseth his neighbour; it were better for him that a millstone were hanged about his neck, and he cast into the sea."[304] As a result—although I'm not absolutely convinced I'm right to describe you as my 'neighbour'— since there's some room for doubt, and as I don't feel disposed at this moment to resolve the matter in the grim fashion spoken of by the Evangelist involving the sea, I've avoided every hint of scandal to the best of my ability.

Besides, if by mischance the opposite had been the case, how would I go about following the text of the holy book? No doubt it's a simple matter to hang a millstone about one's neck, or at least to tie one's neck to the said stone; but it's the rest of the operation which strikes me as awkward. I haven't the strength to go even from here to the Pont des Arts with such a jewel hanging beneath my chin—how would I get all the way to Le Havre?

This Gospel text would be just as troublesome to the commentators as to people wishing to cast themselves into the sea with the aforementioned object, if we didn't know it was written at a time when men were wonderfully strong and tall, beyond anything we can imagine today. The young lads in those days carried millstones round their necks and went off to drown themselves with commendable ease; while even the strongest of our present-day musicians, attached merely to a full score as so many of them are, would have great difficulty in emulating them.

Now, since I absolutely must be serious, I *seriously* wish you goodnight. This letter with its various sections is already very long; to lengthen it further would be the worst of my bad jokes. Farewell; in a few days I shall tell you about Lille, then my correspondence with you will be closed—Marseilles, Lyons and Lille being (apart from Paris) the only French cities where I've heard and performed music, since making this unfortunate art the object of my studies and of my unwavering affection.

Third Letter

Lille—An improvised cantata—Melancholy—The half-moon at Arras—Artillery pieces—Linstocks—The rocket—A terrific effect—The autograph collector

Paris, 18 . . .

I don't expect you have any desire to know why I went to Lille. I'll tell you anyway. It was nothing to do with the Festival of the North, directed by Habeneck, in which the *Lacrymosa* from my *Requiem* was performed twice, in grand and beautiful style, I'm told.[305] The Festival organisers forgot to invite me, which amounted to an invitation for me to stay in Paris.

No, I only went to Lille some years later.[306] The Northern railway, so celebrated for the little accidents to which it was prone, had just been completed.[307] His Grace the Archbishop was to give it his solemn blessing, which promised to be an occasion for copious eating and drinking. It was thought a spot of music would not go amiss—rather the opposite, since many people need it as an aid to digestion. So it was decided to approach me, as a first-rate digestive.

Don't laugh, that's exactly what happened. A cantata was needed, to be performed, not after dinner, but before the opening of the ball. Monsieur Dubois, charged by the Municipality of Lille with the musical arrangements for the ceremony, came to Paris in a great hurry and with the old-fashioned, antediluvian, scarcely credible notions he brought with him from the provinces imagined that, since he needed words and music for this cantata, it wouldn't be a bad idea to approach a literary man and a musician. As a result, he commissioned Jules Janin for the verses and me for the music.[308]

Only, when he brought me the words of the cantata, Monsieur Dubois informed me, as if the piece in question were a mere five-act opera, that my score was needed in two days' time. "Very well, Monsieur, I shall meet your deadline; but if you find you need it tomorrow, don't hesitate to tell me." I'd just read Janin's verses; they were fashioned in a certain manner which I shan't attempt to characterise, but which attracts music like ripe fruit attracts birds, quite unlike the great volleys of hemistichs which professional librettists fire off as they beat out the coverts in pursuit of it.

I wrote the voice parts for the cantata in three hours, and the following night was busy orchestrating them. You must admit, my dear Monnais, for someone who makes it his business never to perpetrate outrages upon the Muses, that's not bad going. *It isn't the time it takes that matters,*[309] you'll say, like that old curmudgeon Nicolas Boileau Despreaux, who maintained this old-fashioned commonsense argument which is now so completely won or lost that nobody bothers with it any more.

Certainly time isn't what matters, or rather time matters a lot, whatever may have been said, not by Boileau (I realise now that I attributed the quotation wrongly), but by Poquelin de Molière, another poet who was mad about common sense. It's my belief that, with very rare exceptions, *nothing is blessed by time that has not taken time to create.* This maxim, which you've never heard or read before, since I've only this minute translated it from the Persian, embodies a profound truth.[310] I just wanted to prove to you that I too am capable of dashing off a score, when I make up my mind to be content with a short-lived celebrity of a mere four or five thousand years for my work.

I'm quite aware that if I'd had three full days to devote to this piece, my score would live forty centuries longer. But in pressing and *unexpected* circumstances, like the inauguration of a railway, an artist shouldn't concern himself about whether forty centuries more or less will be familiar with his work. At such times one's country has the right to demand absolute devotion from each of its children. So I said to myself, "Come, child of the fatherland!", and devoted I was. I had to be!!!

What are you up to at this moment, my dear Monnais? Have you a good fire going? Is your chimney smoking? Can you, like me, hear the north wind whining in the rafters, beneath ill-fitting doors and between the cracks of the casements where the windows aren't airtight, wailing and groaning and howling, like several generations in agony? Whoo! Whoo! Whoo! What a *crescendo*! *Ululate venti*! What a *forte*! *Ingemuit alta domus*![311] Then its voice dies away.

My chimney resonates like a sixty-four-foot organ pipe. I never could resist these Ossianic sounds: they strike to my very heart and make me long to die.[312] They tell me that everything is transitory, that beauty, youth, love, glory and genius are all swallowed up by space and time; that human life is nothing, and death no more; that whole worlds are born and die just like us; that all is nothing.

And yet some of my memories rebel against this idea, and I'm forced to recognise that there is something in our *great passionate adorations* and our *great adoring passions*. I think of Chateaubriand in his granite tomb on the rock at St.-Malo;[313] of the vast forests and deserts he crossed in America; of his René, who was far from imaginary. I think how many people find all this quite laughable, while others find it quite beautiful. And the storm's whistling resumes its violent song in chromatic style: Aye!!! Aye!!! Aye!!! All is nothing! All is nothing! Love or hate, joy or sadness, admiration or derision, life or death—what does it matter? There is neither large nor small, neither beautiful nor ugly; the infinite is indifferent, indifference is infinite! A . . . las! A . . . las!

Talia vociferans gemitu tectum omne replebat.[314]

. . . .

This inappropriate philosophical sally, my dear friend, was simply to introduce a quotation from Virgil. I adore Virgil, and I love quoting him. It's a mania of mine—as you must have noticed.

But now the wind's decreasing,
Hear how its sound is ceasing,

and I no longer long to die. How wonderful the eloquence of silence, after recognising the power of sound! Once calm returns, all my beliefs are restored. I believe in beauty and in ugliness, I believe in genius, in cretinism, in stupidity, in intelligence, yours above all; I believe France is the home of the arts; I believe the statement I've just made is totally idiotic; I believe you must be tired of my digressions, and that you can't imagine why I'm digressing when my subject is music.

Good God! If you can't imagine, I'll tell you: it's quite simply so as not to draw attention to myself. My aim is not to make myself conspicuous, not to do anything that jars with the social milieu in which we live. There's another proverb, as true as all proverbs, which I've also just translated from the Persian and which says: "One must gibber with the mad"; make sure you learn from it.

Well now! (That's how Odry began the tale of his adventures in the forest where he was lost, a virgin forest inhabited only by parrots and orang-utans*, in which he set himself up as a "public writer-at-large" in order not to die of hunger. What a great man Odry was!)[315]

Well now, again, with the cantata written and copied, we set off for Lille. The railway made an exceptional concession for its inaugurators, in

---

*I know perfectly well it should be spelt "orang-hutan", but instead of these two Malay words meaning "man of the woods", I prefer to use the common spelling, as you do, in order not to seem patronising.

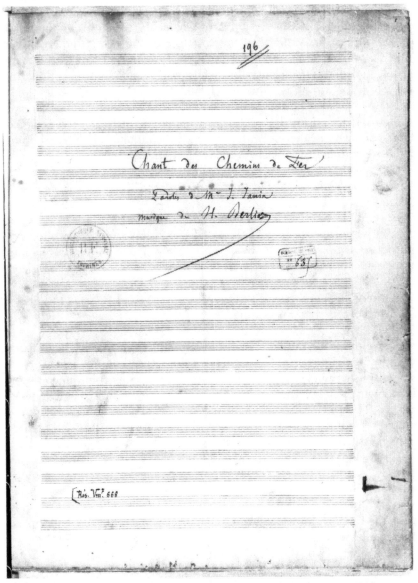

Figure 38. Hector Berlioz, *Railway Cantata* ("Chant des Chemins de Fer"). Autograph full score, 1846. Title page and first page of music. Bibliothèque Nationale de France.

"I wrote the voice parts for the cantata in three hours, and the following night was busy orchestrating them" (page 178). The manuscript shows clear signs of the haste in which Berlioz composed the piece.

Figure 38, continued.

that we reached Arras without being derailed once. Hardly were we within sight of the town walls than all the occupants of our carriage, male and female, let out a shriek of laughter—the sort of laughter that would split a wall of solid rock; and this without anyone having spoken a word.

Since everyone knew their Molière by heart, the memory of *Les Précieuses ridicules* had struck all of us simultaneously at the sight of the town walls, and through tears of laughter we all looked for the 'half-moon' captured by the Marquis de Mascarille at the siege of Arras, which, in the words of the Vicomte de Jodelet, was "to be sure, more like a full moon".[316] That's true success! Name me any comic playwright other than Molière who, without a theatre, without actors, without books, by the mere memory of a word, can make the children of his contemporaries' great-great-grand-children split their sides with laughter!

As soon as I reached Lille, Monsieur Dubois put me in touch with the singers who were to assist me in performing the cantata, and with the military bands which had come from Valenciennes, Douai and various other neighbouring towns. All these instrumental groups together formed an orchestra of about a hundred and fifty musicians to perform my *Apotheosis* piece on the public promenade, in the evening, for the princes and civil and military authorities gathered for the festivities.[317]

The cantata was quickly learnt by a choir of young people and children, almost all of them pupils of the institution referred to in Lille as the "Academy of Song", which I believe is part of the Conservatoire there. I speak in rather doubtful terms, since I have no precise knowledge concerning this establishment. I can tell you only that these young singers had excellent voices, and mastered the difficulties of the cantata in a very short time, so well had they been guided in their studies by Monsieur Ferdinand Lavainne, of whose high merit as a composer you are aware, and Monsieur Leplus, the able musical director of the Lille Artillery.

Studying the *Apotheosis* with the massed military bands gave us much more trouble. They had already started before my arrival, and because of a serious error in the tempo set by the conductor in charge of the rehearsal, the outcome was nothing but ear-splitting cacophony. Monsieur Dubois, my guide amid the trials and tribulations of the festivities, who had bravely assumed full responsibility for the musical aspect, seemed disturbed and anxious when I spoke to him about our military performers and this devilish great piece. I didn't realise that he'd attended the first run-through, nor that it had had such a disastrous outcome; it was only after the chaos had been sorted out that he told me of his fears and the reason for them. However that may be, they were quite quickly dispelled, and after the third rehearsal everything went smoothly.

As far as I can recall, none of the three military music ensembles belonging to the town of Lille itself, those of the National Guard, the fire brigade and the artillery, was willing or able to take part in this performance. I was

M. Berlioz allant embaucher des recrues pour son orchestre dans l'artillerie de la garnison...

Figure 39. "M. Berlioz seeking recruits for his orchestra from the artillery garrison." Cartoon by Nadar (Félix Tournachon, 1820–1910), published in *Le Journal pour Rire*, 5 January 1856. Richard Macnutt Collection, Withyham.
    "None of the three military music ensembles belonging to the town, . . . those of the National Guard, the fire brigade and the artillery, was willing or able to take part" (page 182).

told the reason at the time, but have forgotten it. This was a great pity, for these are excellent orchestras, and there are surely few military bands in France which bear comparison with them. I can appreciate their individual merits, since each of these bodies did me the honour of coming to play beneath my windows during the day preceding the concert—in truth a cruelly capricious gesture on their part.

I was given an excellent small orchestra (that of the theatre, I believe) to accompany the cantata; a single rehearsal was enough. So everything was ready when Monsieur Dubois introduced the National Guard Captain of Artillery to me.

"Monsieur," said this officer, "I've come to make arrangements with you about these pieces."

"Oh, do you mean pieces being put on in the theatre? I didn't know about that. But that's nothing to do with me."

"I beg your pardon, Monsieur, I'm speaking about artillery pieces!"

"Good God! What have I to do with those?"

"What you have to do", interjected Monsieur Dubois, "is to produce a deafening effect in your *Apotheosis*. Besides, there's no getting out of it, the cannon are on the programme. The public is expecting cannon and we can't deny them."

"Now my enemies in Paris, those fellow-critics of mine who are such good critical policemen, will say I include artillery in my orchestra! What fun they'll have! Why, it's a godsend for me—I enjoy nothing more than giving them a chance to utter some fine triple-charged stupidity about me. On with the cannon! First, though, what does your *choir* consist of?"

"Our choir?"

"Yes, your battery. What pieces do you have, and how many?"

"We have ten twelve-pounders."

"Huh! Pretty feeble. Couldn't you let me have any twenty-four pounders?"

"Good Heavens, we only have six twenty-four pounders."

"Well then, let me have those six soloists together with the ten chorus members. Then let's form up the whole mass of voices on the rim of the big ditch next to the esplanade, as close as possible to the military orchestra on the platform. You, Captain, will be good enough to keep an eye on us. I'll have a pyrotechnician beside me. At the moment when the princes arrive, he'll let off a rocket, and then the ten chorus members alone should fire one after the other. After that we'll begin the performance of the *Apotheosis*, during which you'll have time to reload. Towards the end of the piece, another rocket will be let off, you will then count *four seconds*, and at the fifth you'll oblige me by striking a good firm chord, with your ten twelve-pounder chorus members and your six twenty-four pounder soloists in unison, so that your combined voices coincide exactly with my final instrumental chord. Have you got that?"

Figure 40. Lille—view of the theatre. Lithograph by Deroy. Bibliothèque Nationale de France.

"I was given an excellent small orchestra (that of the theatre, I believe)" (page 184).

"Perfectly, Monsieur. We'll carry out your instructions to the letter, you may count on us."

And as he left I heard the Captain say to Monsieur Dubois:

"Magnificent! Only a musician would have ideas like that!"

The evening came, and the well-rehearsed, well-disciplined military band was in its place, as was my pyrotechnician. The Dukes of Nemours and Montpensier climbed up to a stand specially prepared for them facing the orchestra, attended by the general staff of the fortress, the Mayor, the Prefect, in a word all the local military, administrative, civil, judicial and municipal dignitaries. Just as I told the pyrotechnician to stand by, the artillery captain came rushing headlong up the stairs to our platform, and shouted to me in a shaking voice:

"For goodness' sake, Monsieur Berlioz, don't give the signal yet, our men have forgotten the *linstocks* for the cannon.[318] They're running to fetch some from the arsenal—just let me have five minutes!"

Ignorant as I am (whatever people may say) of everything to do with the mechanism, if not the character, of these particular voices, I was astonished that miserable little twenty-four and twelve-pounders couldn't be fired with a cigar or a piece of tinder, and that linstocks were as indispensable to cannon as mouthpieces to trombones; but I gave them their five minutes. Indeed I gave them seven. At the end of the seventh, another messenger came bounding up the same staircase which the frantic captain had just descended and pointed out that the princes were waiting and it was well past the time to begin.

"Off you go!" I said to the pyrotechnician, "too bad for the chorus members if there's nothing to fire them with!"

The rocket shot up with such force it seemed to be heading for the moon. Total silence. Evidently they hadn't got back from the arsenal.

I began. Our military band acquitted itself with prowess, the piece was deployed majestically without the slightest fault of musical strategy, and as it's quite lengthy, I was thinking to myself as I conducted: "We won't lose anything by having waited. The artillerymen will have had time to get their linstocks, and for the final chord we'll have a broadside to smash every window for miles." So at the appointed bar in the coda, I gave another sign to my pyrotechnician, another rocket shot up to the sky, and exactly four seconds after it went up. . . .

Believe me, I don't want to seem braver than I am, and it wasn't without reason that my heart had been beating faster as the big moment approached. You may laugh as much as you please, but I almost fell flat on my face. The trees shivered, the water in the canal rippled in the light breath of the evening breeze. Not a sound from the cannon!

A profound silence fell after the last bar of the symphony, a majestic, grand, immense silence, disturbed an instant later only by the applause of

Figure 41. *Concert à mitraille* ("Concert with grape-shot"). Woodcut after cartoon by J.-J. Grandville, 1845. Richard Macnutt Collection, Withyham.
    ('Luckily the hall is solid, it stands firm.')
    "Now my enemies in Paris . . . will say I include artillery in my orchestra!" (page 184).

the multitude, apparently satisfied with the performance. And the audience departed, without any idea of the importance of linstocks, nor any regret for the pleasure it had missed, oblivious of the programme's promises, and quite convinced that the two rockets it had heard and seen whooshing up with showers of sparks were simply a new orchestral effect I'd invented, quite pleasing to the eye.

The *Charivari* went overboard with this opinion, publishing a series of articles of the deepest seriousness about it.[319] What would it have done if the linstocks . . . Such is fate! I would have attained an entirely new status that evening, a reputation that would have been mine for ever; I would have received my *baptism of fire*! This is a striking new demonstration that, while we often hear of guns going off when they aren't loaded, we may sometimes also find cannon that *are* loaded *not* going off.[320]

With the *Apotheosis* thus peacefully concluded, we left our artillery pieces open-mouthed, still pointed, with their disappointed gunners by the edge of the canal. I had to hurry to the town hall, where another orchestra and another choir were waiting for me to perform the cantata. This time my expectations weren't let down in any way. Our singers and musicians had not a breath nor a semiquaver to reproach themselves about. The same could not be said for the audience. After the concert, while I was listening to the gracious words the Duke of Nemours and his brother, the Duke of Montpensier, were good enough to say to me, some autograph collector did me the honour of stealing my hat. I was pained by this, for the fellow's conscience will no doubt have reproached him severely for not taking a better one; as for me, I found myself compelled to go out bareheaded, and it was raining.

That's all I have to tell you about Lille and the inauguration festivities. "What," you'll say, "have you written this whole long letter just to let me know there are good choruses, excellent military bands and incompetent artillerymen in the capital of the Département du Nord?" Let me tell you, that shows real talent. What's so clever about writing a great deal when one has a great deal to say? It's in erecting a long arcade of columns leading nowhere that great art nowadays consists. You walk your innocent reader along the avenue of the Sphinxes at Thebes. He follows you patiently in the hope of arriving eventually at the city of a hundred gates. Then, all of a sudden, he reaches the last Sphinx; he sees neither gates nor city, and there you abandon him, in the middle of the desert.

H. Berlioz

———

All's well that ends merrily

A remarkable difference can be observed between the activities of musicians in Paris at the present time and the way they behaved twenty years ago. In those days they almost all believed in themselves and in the results of their efforts; today they've almost all lost that belief. Nonetheless they soldier on.

Their courage is similar to that of the crew of a ship exploring the seas around the South Pole. At first the hardy seamen brave the dangers of floes and icebergs quite cheerfully. Bit by bit, as the cold redoubles in intensity, the blocks of ice surround their vessel and its progress becomes slower and more difficult. The moment approaches when the frozen sea will hold it captive in a silent immobility similar to death.

The danger becomes plain; almost all living things have disappeared— no more great birds with enormous wings in the grey sky, from which a thick mist descends, nothing more except flocks of penguins, standing stupidly on islands of ice, fishing for their meagre prey, flapping the featherless stumps of wings which are incapable of bearing them aloft. The sailors have become taciturn, their mood is sombre, and the few words they exchange when they meet on the bridge of the ship are little different from the funereal phrase of the Trappist monks: "Brother, we must die!"

. . . .

But let's not fall victim to their melancholy. Let's chase away black thoughts and in lighthearted voice sing the gay refrain we all know so well:[321]

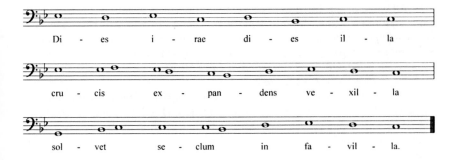

Di - es   i - rae   di - es   il - la

cru - cis   ex - pan - dens   ve - xil - la

sol - vet   se - clum   in   fa - vil - la.

The End

Notes

1. *Evenings with the Orchestra* was Berlioz's previous collection of musical essays and criticism, published in Paris in 1852.

2. The *Requiem*, the *Te Deum*, *Romeo and Juliet*, *The Damnation of Faust* and *The Childhood of Christ* are Berlioz's five most substantial works with chorus, apart from the operas. The *Requiem* ('*Grande Messe des Morts*'), Op. 5, was published in 1838. The *Te Deum*, Op. 22, appeared in 1855. The 'dramatic symphony' *Romeo and Juliet*, Op. 17, was first performed in 1839 and published in 1847. The 'dramatic legend' *The Damnation of Faust*, Op. 24, was first performed at the end of 1846 and published in 1854. *The Childhood of Christ*, Op. 25, described as a 'sacred trilogy', was performed in December 1854 and published the following year (see also pages 106–9).

3. A single *s*, as in *angoise*, would be pronounced as a *z* in French.

4. The reference to German musicians who are 'happy for only half the orchestra to play' relates to *Evenings with the Orchestra*, which is cast in the form of discussions among members of the orchestra of an opera house in northern Europe whenever second-rate operas are being performed—except for the bass drum, who is kept unremittingly busy throughout such works.

5. Berlioz sang in the chorus of the Nouveautés theatre in Paris in 1827 to make ends meet. The theatre specialised in comic opera and vaudeville.

6. The Saint-Simonians were followers of Claude Henri, Comte de Saint-Simon (1760–1825), who advocated a form of socialism based on large-scale industrial production controlled by benevolent leaders. Berlioz himself was briefly attracted to Saint-Simonianism in the early 1830s.

7. A sou was five centimes; thus there were twenty sous in a franc.

8. All of the operas listed were performed at the Opéra at various times between 1829 and 1857. Mme. Borghi-Mamo was a contralto whom Berlioz admired. Gustave-Hippolyte Roger (1815–82) was a leading tenor, first at the Opéra-Comique and later at the Opéra, who sang in several Berlioz works, including the Requiem, *Romeo and Juliet* and *The Damnation of Faust* (as Faust).

9. *Le Misanthrope*, Act I Scene 2.

10. In fact Balzac's analysis of Rossini's *Moïse* appears in his other musical tale, *Massimilla Doni*, not in *Gambara*. Gustave Planche (1808–57), despite having no formal musical training, effectively became the music critic of the literary journal *L'Artiste* during 1839, and published his critique of the *Eroica* in March of that year.

11. This refers to La Fontaine, *Fables* IV 7 (The Monkey and the Dolphin). In the fable, the dolphin, carrying the monkey on his back across the water, asks if he knows Piraeus (the port of Athens); the monkey replies that Piraeus is an old friend of his. So 'to mistake Piraeus for a person' is to show crass stupidity.

12. The Prado building was a dance hall in the Cité district of Paris, opposite the Palais de Justice.

13. Berlioz conducted the second performance of his *Messe Solennelle* at the church of St.-Eustache on 22 November 1827.

14. Adalbert Gyrowetz (1763–1850) was a Czech composer and conductor.

15. The king of Spain was Carlos IV (1784–1819).

16. Berlioz served as a music critic for the *Journal des Débats*, edited by Armand Bertin, from 1835 to 1863.

17. The ashes of the Emperor Napoleon I were returned to Paris on 15 December 1840.

18. The symphony Berlioz had been commissioned to write was the *Symphonie funèbre et triomphale* ('Funeral and Triumphal Symphony'), originally called *Military Symphony*. It was first performed in July 1840, as part of a ceremonial procession from the church of St.-Germain l'Auxerrois to the Place de la Bastille, with Berlioz conducting on the march (often walking backwards). Berlioz declined the opportunity of the second commission in December, preferring to let Auber, Halévy and Adam suffer by comparison with the success of his own earlier work.

19. The word used by Berlioz for francs is 'écus'; an écu was originally a French silver crown, worth three francs, but the word later came to be used for a five-franc piece.

20. 'People of France, let us return Napoleon's ashes to the Panthéon. Come, heroes, conquering spirits, we return your Emperor.' The Panthéon in Paris, constructed between 1754 and 1780 and originally intended as a church, during the Revolution became a temple to receive the ashes of France's heroes. In reality Napoleon's ashes were taken to the church of Les Invalides, not to the Panthéon. Berlioz's own remains are to be removed to the Panthéon on 21 June 2003, in the bicentenary year of his birth.

21. *La Rosière de Salency* was performed four times at the Odéon in October and November 1824, just before the première of *Robin des Bois*, Castil-Blaze's adaptation of *Der Freischütz* (see note 27).

22. Nathan Bloc was a violinist and supporter of Berlioz. As conductor of the Odéon orchestra he directed Berlioz's first concert in the Conservatoire concert hall on 26 May 1828. He later directed the orchestra of the Nouveautés, and in 1835 helped to establish a Conservatoire in Geneva, of which he became Director for thirteen years.

23. In a theatre of the time, the 'pit' was the ground floor (nowadays usually called the stalls in the U.K, the orchestra in the U.S.), or its occupants; unlike today, this was where the cheaper seats were located.

24. "Arm ye brave!" is from Handel's *Judas Maccabaeus*.

'A devilish violin sonata' refers to Tartini's Sonata in G minor, known as the 'Devil's Trill', which was first published posthumously in 1798.

'The fugue on "Kyrie Eleison" from a *Requiem*': a similar reference in the description of Euphonia, Berlioz's ideal musical city, in the Twenty-Fifth Evening of *Evenings with the Orchestra* makes it clear that the *Requiem* referred to is Mozart's.

'A psalm setting' refers to a setting of *Psalm 19* by the Italian composer Benedetto Marcello (1686–1739).

I have not been able to identify the other works mentioned.

On Gyrowetz, see page 11 and note 14.

25. The second performance of *The Damnation of Faust* took place in Dresden on 26 April 1854.

26. The flageolet is a small, high-pitched member of the recorder family with six holes, two of them thumb-holes at the back of the instrument. It was one of the instruments that Berlioz himself played, along with flute, guitar and percussion.

27. The 'famous critic' was François Henri-Joseph Blaze, known as Castil-Blaze (1784–1857), a critic and minor composer who 'rearranged' several operas by foreign composers, including Weber's *Der Freischütz*, which he adapted as *Robin des Bois* in 1824. His pastiche-opera *The Forest of Sénart*, first performed at the Odéon in January 1826, was based on Collé's *Henri IV's Hunting Party*, with music taken from Rossini, Beethoven, Meyerbeer and Mozart. He was a regular target of Berlioz's barbs.

28. Henriette Sontag (1805–54) was a German soprano admired by Berlioz—see pages 146–48.

29. Theodor von Döhler (1814–56) was an Austrian pianist and composer, mostly of virtuoso piano music.

30. The Peasants' March in *Der Freischütz* is Act I No. 1 (after the Introduction and Victory Song).

31. 'The suffering artist' is a reference to Balzac's novel *Le Lys dans la vallée* (1835).

32. Berlioz had been a member of the musical jury at the Great Exhibition of 1851 in London (at the specially constructed Crystal Palace in Hyde Park), as well as at the Universal Exhibition in Paris in 1855, to which this piece relates.

33. Sebastopol was besieged by British and French troops from September 1854 to September 1855 during the Crimean War.

34. Kamehameha III (1814–54) was king of the Hawaiian islands from 1824 until his death.

35. St.-Germain-en-Laye is a smart suburb about ten miles west of Paris, with a sixteenth-century royal château which was used as a military prison in the reign of Louis-Philippe (1830–46); under Napoleon III (1848–70) it was restored to house the French Museum of National Antiquities. Presumably the indignant piano-maker's point is that his pianos are used not only in all the far-off places he lists, such as Nagasaki (spelt 'Nangasaki' in the first edition), but even as close to home as the fashionable St.-Germain-en-Laye—although it is notable that he does not mention Paris itself.

36. The three other Frenchmen were the composer Halévy, a hearing-aid manufacturer named Marloye and a piano-maker named Roller; the Scot was Sir George Clerk, a long-standing Director of the Royal Academy of Music in London; the Belgian was François-Joseph Fétis, Director of the Brussels Conservatoire (see note 164); and the Austrian was Joseph Helmesberger, Director of the Vienna Imperial Conservatoire.

37. Jean-Zuléma Amussat (1794–1856) was a well-known surgeon with whom Berlioz studied when he first arrived in Paris in 1821 as a medical student; he later became Berlioz's own doctor, and both the composer's wives, Harriet Smithson and Marie Recio, were also his patients.

Joseph-Frédéric Charrière (1803–76) was an inventor and maker of surgical instruments.

38. A grand medal of honour for the manufacture of pianos of all types was awarded to the Paris Chamber of Commerce. Other piano medals of honour went to Alexandre (see note 43), Érard, Henri Herz (see note 211) and Pleyel.

39. Joseph d'Ortigue (1802–66) was a musician, scholar and critic, and a close friend and supporter of Berlioz. When Berlioz was away, d'Ortigue stood in for him as music critic of the *Journal des Débats*.

40. Pomaré IV was queen of Tahiti from 1827 to her death in 1877. She was born in 1813, not 1811 as Berlioz states.

41. The commander of the French garrison was Commandant Théogene-François Page (1807–67), French governor of Tahiti from 1848—see also page 59.

42. George Pritchard (1797–1883) was a Protestant missionary and British consul in Tahiti, whose overzealous activities led to a dispute between France and Great Britain. He was expelled from Tahiti by the French in 1844.

43. Édouard Alexandre (1824–88) was the son and successor of Jacob Alexandre (1804–76). Édouard was a friend and supporter (both moral and financial) of Berlioz, and was later his executor. Berlioz wrote three short pieces specially for the Alexandre 'orgue-melodium' (a form of harmonium), as well as articles about it in his *feuilletons* (musical and literary review pieces for journals).

44. On the 'pit', see note 23.

45. Adolphe Sax (1814–94) was the Belgian inventor of the saxophone (and numerous other instruments), and another friend of Berlioz, who helped to promote his instruments. A number of Sax's instruments—saxophones, sax-horns, saxotrombas and sax-tubas—are included, as is Alexandre's melodium, in the 'New Instruments' section of Berlioz's *Grand Treatise on Modern Instrumentation and Orchestration*, first published in 1844.

46. 'This distinguished . . . Aristarchus' refers to Paul Scudo (1806–64), the vitriolic critic of the *Revue des deux mondes* who was implacably hostile to Berlioz. Aristarchus of Samothrace was an Alexandrian grammarian of about 160 BC, regarded as the greatest critic of antiquity.

47. The young women Atala, Cora and Amazily figure respectively in Chateaubriand's *Atala*, Marmontel's novel *Les Incas* and de Jouy's *Fernand Cortez* (set to music by Spontini—see note 222).

48. A vivandière was a woman attached to a French regiment who sold food and spirits to the soldiers.

49. The Temple district was a part of Paris's 3rd *arrondissement* (ward), named after the fortress of the Order of the Templars on the Rue du Temple. Louis XVI (together with his wife Marie-Antoinette and their son and daughter) was imprisoned in the Tower of the Temple from 1792 until he was guillotined in 1793. By Berlioz's time the Tower had been razed, and much of the fortress enclosure was occupied by an open market, specialising in old clothes. The Théâtre-Lyrique was on the Boulevard du Temple at the eastern end of the Temple district, as was the Folies-Nouvelles. (See also pages 50–54.)

50. Halévy's opera *Jaguarita l'Indienne*, to a libretto by de Saint-Georges and de Leuven, was performed at the Théâtre-Lyrique in 1855.

51. Marie Dreulette (born 1827), later Mme. Cabel, was an opera singer who became a sensation in Paris after her appearance there in 1853 in Adam's *Le Bijou perdu*, followed by *Jaguarita l'Indienne*. She had a light voice with an exceptionally extended upper range.

52. 'All activity is broken off and suspended' (Virgil, *Aeneid* IV 88).

53. Eugène Scribe (1791–1861) was a French dramatist (and novelist) who wrote the libretti for some sixty operas by composers including Auber and Meyerbeer. His works became so popular that he set up a 'mass-production' system involving numerous collaborators working under his supervision.

The Court Concert is an opéra-comique in one act, subtitled *La Débutante*, produced in 1824 with music by Auber.

54. Ferdinando Paër (1771–1839) was an Italian composer of over 50 operas,

head of the Imperial chapel under Napoleon I, then Director of Music at the Opéra-Comique and the Théâtre-Italien from 1812 to 1827.

55. Madrepores are reef-building corals.

56. Tinian is one of the North Mariana Islands, in the West Pacific, east of the Philippines. Tongatapu is the main island of Tonga in the South Pacific.

57. Jean François de Galaup, Comte de La Pérouse (1741–88) destroyed the forts of the Hudson's Bay Company during the naval war of 1778–83 against Great Britain. He commanded a voyage of exploration to the north-west USA and north-east Asia in 1785, and sailed through the La Pérouse Strait between Sakhalin and Yezo. In 1788, during an expedition from Botany Bay, Australia, his two ships were wrecked north of the New Hebrides.

58. *Jenny Bell* was another opéra-comique with music by Auber, first performed in 1855.

59. The tune of the English national anthem *God Save the King* has been known since the middle of the eighteenth century, and has been used by about twenty countries for their official national song. The original authorship, of both its words and music, remains obscure.

St.-Cyr was a school for girls near Versailles, founded in 1685 by Louis XIV and Mme. de Maintenon.

60. *Le Devin du village* ('The Village Soothsayer') is an *intermède* by the political philosopher, educationalist and author Jean-Jacques Rousseau (1712–78); it appeared in 1752.

Claude Joseph Rouget de l'Isle (1760–1836) was a French army officer who wrote the words and music of the *Marseillaise* (under the title of *Chant de l'armée du Rhin*) when stationed at Strasbourg in 1792 as captain of engineers.

On *La Vestale* by Spontini, see note 222.

61. On Castil-Blaze, see note 27.

62. Rosine Stoltz (1815–1903) was the leading diva of the Opéra from 1838 to 1847, when she effectively retired following the disastrous flop of Rossini's *Robert Bruce*. She sang the part of Ascanio in Berlioz's opera *Benvenuto Cellini* in 1838. See also pages 143–46.

63. The Folies-Nouvelles theatre was built during the early 1850s in the Boulevard du Temple, and reopened under this name from 1854 to 1859, when it became the Déjazet theatre.

64. Lions and lionesses were terms used in French to refer to fashionable, ostentatious society people. On the 'pit', see note 23.

65. *Le Calfat* ("The Caulker"), text by Pol Mercier, music by E. Cahen, was first performed in November 1856.

66. 'True happiness is a serious matter'—from Seneca, *Letters to Lucilius* XXIII 4 (with the order of words slightly altered).

67. An adaptation of a passage from Théramène's speech in Racine, *Phèdre*, Act V Scene 6.

68. Auguste-Alphonse-Edmond Meillet (1828–71) was a fine baritone and comic performer who sang at the Opéra, the Opéra-Comique and (especially) the Théâtre-Lyrique. His wife, born Mlle. Mayer in 1829, was also a highly-regarded singer at the Théâtre-Lyrique. Berlioz wrote about both of them in several of his *feuilletons*, and they sang Joseph and Marie in the first three performances of his *The Childhood of Christ* in December 1854 and January 1855. On Mme. Cabel, see note 51.

69. Émile Perrin (1814–85) was Director of the Opéra-Comique from 1848 to 1857 and also of the Théâtre-Italien from 1854 to 1855. He later became Director of the Opéra (1862–70) and the Comédie-Française (from 1870).

70. The passage quoted is from Théramène's speech in Racine's *Phèdre*, Act V Scene 6.

71. '[Their] voices stuck in [their] throats'—Virgil, *Aeneid* III 48.

72. There had been a cholera epidemic in Paris between November 1853 and December 1854; it claimed more than 9,000 victims.

73. The siege of Sebastopol lasted from September 1854 to September 1855 (see also page 26).

74. *Schahabaham II*: opera buffa in one act by de Leuven and Carré with music by Eugène Gautier, first performed at the Théâtre-Lyrique on 31 October 1854.

75. This is a reminiscence of the start of Psalm 137: 'By the rivers of Babylon, there we sat down, yea, we wept, when we remembered Zion. We hanged our harps upon the willows in the midst thereof.'

76. The word for 'brigand's' used by Berlioz is 'Macairian', referring to Robert Macaire, the brigand hero of the 1823 melodrama *L'Auberge des Adrets* (see also note 299 on the actor Frédérick Lemaître, who first played the part of Macaire).

77. The lithograph Berlioz refers to is one of two works entitled *L'École du balayeur* ('The Street-Sweeper's School') by Nicolas-Toussaint Charlet (1792–1845). See Figure 13.

78. The Vernet family produced three generations of well-known French painters: Claude Joseph Vernet (1714–89), known especially for his seascapes; his son Antoine Charles Horace ('Carle') Vernet (1758–1835), a historical and animal painter; and his grandson Horace Vernet (1789–1863), who specialised in battle paintings and studies of horses. Horace was Director of the French Academy in Rome when Berlioz was there in 1831 and 1832; Berlioz was fond of him, and also apparently of his daughter Louise. It is presumably Horace that Berlioz means here, in the light of the reference to the Prix de Rome.

Nicolas-Toussaint Charlet (1792–1845) was a graphic artist and lithographer who excelled in military subjects, sometimes satirical, including of soldiers of Napoleon's Old Guard (the 'grognards').

In *Evenings with the Orchestra* (Tenth Evening) Berlioz had referred to another Charlet lithograph, *The Marauding Hussars* (although Professor Guichard in his note suggests persuasively that Berlioz may have been thinking of a different work by Vernet with this title). In the lithograph, two hussars are shown using feed to entice chickens out of a coop and chopping off their heads as they emerge. Berlioz compares the chickenfeed to prizes like the Grand Prix de Rome (which he himself had won in 1830), and the birds to the young prize-winners.

79. The Opéra-Comique was on the Boulevard des Italiens. The Théâtre-Lyrique was on the Boulevard du Temple, a short distance to the east, as was the Folies-Nouvelles.

80. Pyrrhonism is complete scepticism, named after the Greek philosopher Pyrrho of Elis (third century BC).

81. The other two are the Théâtre-Italien and the Folies-Nouvelles.

82. On Commandant Page, see note 41.

83. Monsieur Giraud must be the painter Charles Giraud, who painted a portrait of Queen Pomaré in 1851.

84. Berlioz calls newspaper proprietors 'rabid anti-abolitionists' because of their refusal to end the slavery endured by their music critics.

85. Marcus Atilius Regulus, Roman consul in 267 BC and 256 BC, won notable victories against the Carthaginians in 256 BC and rejected the opportunity of a truce by offering intolerable terms. He was then utterly defeated by the Carthaginians under a new Spartan general, Xanthippus. According to tradition, he was taken prisoner and released on parole after five years to accompany an embassy to Rome, having promised that he would return to Carthage if its peace proposals were declined. Instead of arguing for the peace, he went to great lengths to persuade the Senate to refuse the offer, and then returned as promised to Carthage, where he was put to death with the most excruciating tortures.

86. A reference to St. Matthew 27:48: 'One of them ran, and took a sponge, and filled it with vinegar, and put it on a reed, and gave him to drink.'

87. 'It is located in a remote spot'—Virgil, *Aeneid* I 159. St.-Valery is a fishing port on the English Channel between Dieppe and Fécamp, popular for its sea-bathing. Berlioz visited it for eight days in August 1854, after failing to be elected to the Institut. (The Institut de France consists of five Academies, founded between 1635 and 1795: the Académie Française and the Academies of Inscriptions and Literature, Sciences, Fine Arts, and Moral and Political Science.)

88. I have been unable to clarify Berlioz's reference to lottery music ('musique de la loterie'). Possibly he is referring to a lottery to raise funds, or to recruit, for the National Guard, accompanied by band music.

89. This is a reference to Berlioz's coachman in Marseilles—see pages 160–63.

90. Sir John Franklin was an English explorer (1786–1847) who joined the navy at the age of fourteen and was present at the battles of Copenhagen (1801) and Trafalgar (1805). He was Governor of Van Diemen's Land (the former name of Tasmania) from 1834 to 1845. In 1845 he set out with two ships, the *Erebus* and the *Terror*, in search of the Northwest Passage. They were beset by ice in the Victoria Strait in 1846, and Franklin died the following year; the rest of the men died attempting to get back to safety on foot. In 1859, a journal was found confirming the date of Franklin's death.

91. On La Pérouse, see note 57.

92. It took Columbus (1451–1506) seven years, until April 1492, to persuade Ferdinand and Isabella of Castile to agree to fund his plans for an expedition to reach India by sailing westwards.

93. Captain James Cook (1728–79) was killed by the (initially friendly) inhabitants of Kailua Bay in Hawaii in February 1779 after his attempt to discover a passage round the north coast of America from the Pacific. He had discovered New Caledonia (in the south-west Pacific, 1,100 kilometres east of Australia) in 1774; it was annexed by France as a penal settlement in 1853.

94. 'Which they cannot allow to explode' is a reference to pages 25–30.

95. From La Fontaine's *Fables* VII 10 (The Milkmaid and the Churn), about the girl who spills the churn she is carrying on her head and loses all its milk, as a result of getting carried away by the thought of everything she will buy with the proceeds of selling it.

96. Most of these operas were staged or restaged at the Opéra-Comique between 1831 and 1858, and in many cases reviewed by Berlioz.

97. *Robert le Diable*: Opera in five acts by Meyerbeer, with a libretto by Scribe and G. Delavigne, first performed with sensational success at the Opéra on 21 November 1831.

98. Louis-Désiré Véron (1798–1867) was Director of the Opéra from 1831 to 1835.

99. *Stello, or the Blue Devils* was published by Berlioz's friend Alfred de Vigny (1797–1863) in 1832.

100. Gomis was a Spanish composer (1791–1836) who died in Paris. His *Le Diable à Séville* was played at the Opéra-Comique in 1831.

101. Giuseppe Mercadante (1795–1870), Italian composer, including of some 60 operas, and Director of the Naples Conservatoire from 1840 until his death.

102. This is a reference to Racine's *Les Plaideurs* ('The Litigants'), Act III Scene 3: 'Witnesses are very expensive and not just to be had for the asking.'

103. Eridan was the ancient Greek name of the river Po (in Italy).

104. A reference to the song of Mignon in Goethe's *Wilhelm Meister's Apprenticeship* III 1 ('Kennst du das Land, wo die Zitronen blühn?')—the land in question is, of course, Italy.

105. The Cyclopes were one-eyed giants, traditionally regarded as the assistants of Hephaestus, the Greek god of fire, whose workshop is sometimes placed in the isle of Lemnos, between Mount Athos and the Hellespont (the Cyclopes are more usually located in Sicily). Polyphemus was the chief Cyclops, who fell in love with the nymph Galatea (Ovid, *Metamorphoses* XIII 780). In Homer's story he was blinded by Odysseus (*Odyssey* IX). This paragraph presumably refers to America.

106. Louis-Antoine Jullien (1812–60) was a larger-than-life London-based entrepreneur and concert promoter who founded a series of promenade concerts in London at which many leading musicians appeared. He wrote literally thousands of popular quadrilles. He set up the disastrous Grand English Opera venture, with Berlioz as conductor, at the Drury Lane theatre in 1847, after which he suffered a series of further bankruptcies. He finally went mad and died in an asylum.

107. 'And yet it does move'—the famous remark of Galileo Galilei (1564–1642) after his forced recantation in 1632, referring to his belief that the earth moves round the sun. (Berlioz quotes it in the form 'E pur si muove'.)

108. The Romans counted the sixth day before the Calends of March (24 February) twice in a leap-year, and called the extra day 'dies bissextus', the 'twice-sixth' day. Thus a 'trisextile year' (apparently an invention by Berlioz) would be a year with two extra days, a double leap-year.

109. Mendelssohn's *First Walpurgis Night*, Op. 60, for soloists, chorus and orchestra, based on Goethe's ballad, was published only in 1843. Berlioz himself was in Rome during 1831 (as a Prix de Rome prize-winner), and became a friend of Mendelssohn there.

110. Berlioz himself gave twenty-one concerts in the Conservatoire hall from 1829 to 1843, after which he was excluded from giving his own concerts there.

111. 'To Italy!'—Virgil, *Aeneid* III 523–24. In Berlioz's opera *The Trojans*, the cry of 'Italie! Italie!' recurs several times to remind Aeneas of his mission.

112. Modified from Racine, *Athalie*, Act II Scene 5.

113. James Davison (1813–85) was a critic and friend of Berlioz.

Arabella Goddard, a rising young pianist of the day, was highly rated by Berlioz (who spells her name Godard).

Sir George Macfarren (1813–87) was a composer and Professor (and later Principal) of the Royal Academy of Music.

John Ella (1802–88) was a violinist and concert director, and the dedicatee of Berlioz's *The Flight into Egypt* (see page 106 and note 160).

Sir Julius Benedict (1804–85) was a conductor and composer.

George Osborne (1806–93) was an Irish pianist and composer who later translated Berlioz's *Grand Treatise on Modern Instrumentation and Orchestration* into English.

Francis Mori (1820–73) was a young composer.

Prosper Sainton (1823–90) was a French violinist based in London, where he taught at the Royal Academy of Music. He was also the leader (concertmaster) of the Covent Garden orchestra, and played the solo viola part in Berlioz's *Harold in Italy* in 1853.

Alfredo Piatti (1822–1901) was an Italian cellist and composer based in London since 1846.

114. Berlioz first visited Baden (now known as Baden-Baden to distinguish it from other Badens in Austria and Switzerland) in 1853, and then each year from 1856 to 1863, to conduct his own and others' works; he was fulsome in his praise of Édouard Bénazet (1801–67), the administrator of the Baden Casino and Director of the annual festival. Bénazet commissioned Berlioz's last major work, the comic opera *Beatrice and Benedict,* which is dedicated to him and was first performed at the festival in 1862.

115. This piece evidently reflects much frustrating personal experience on Berlioz's part, even with singers he regarded as highly as Pauline Viardot.

116. Jean Bart, or Barth (1651–1702), served first in the Dutch navy, but joined the French in 1672 and became a privateer, scoring notable successes at sea against both the English and the Dutch. He was appointed by Louis XIV at Versailles in 1697 to command a squadron, after escaping English captivity in Plymouth.

117. 'Bel raggio lusinghier', sung by Semiramide herself in Act I of the opera, was first performed in 1823.

118. *Le Domino noir,* a comic opera in three acts by Auber to a text by Scribe, was first performed at the Opéra-Comique on 2 December 1837. The aria referred to is 'Ah! Quelle nuit', sung by the Abbess.

119. Eugène Vivier (1821–1900) was a famous horn-player and novelist, known as a practical joker. He could apparently play three or four notes simultaneously on his horn.

120. *Oui, j'y suis cor et j'y dors:* 'Yes, I play the horn and sleep there'—a typical and untranslatable pun on 'je suis corrégidor', a corregidor being the chief magistrate of a Spanish town.

121. A napoleon was a twenty-franc piece—see also page 93.

122. Gemmy Brandus (1823–73) was Director of the *Revue et Gazette musicale* from 1846 and successor of Maurice Schlesinger as head of a major music publishing company. He published several of Berlioz's works, including all four of his symphonies: the *Symphonie fantastique* (Op. 14), the *Funeral and Triumphal Symphony* (Op. 15), *Harold in Italy* (Op. 16) and *Romeo and Juliet* (Op. 17).

123. This letter originally appeared in the issue of 4 September 1856. Berlioz was in Plombières from 20 July to 8 August of that year shortly after being elected to the Institute at last (on 21 June). He returned on 16 August after conducting a concert in Baden.

124. Voltaire (1694–1778) wrote *Candide* in three days in 1768, when he was 62. He was 21 when he started to write *La Henriade,* in 1715. There appears to be no evidence to support Berlioz's claims concerning his state of health in either case.

125. Jacques-Henri Bernardin de Saint-Pierre (1737–1814) wrote *Paul et Virginie*

in 1788, *La Chaumière Indienne* ('The Indian Cottage') in 1791 and *Harmonies de la Nature* in 1796.

126. This refers to a passage in the eighth book of the *Confessions* of Jean-Jacques Rousseau (1712–78); the prosopopoeia (meaning 'personification') was published in his *Discours sur les sciences et les arts* in 1750. The comedy *Narcisse* was first performed at the Comédie-Française on 18 December 1752; it had only two performances. His *Dictionary of Music* appeared in 1767.

127. Joseph Méry (1798–1865) was a French poet, writer, translator (including of Virgil's *Aeneid*), journalist and wit—and not surprisingly a friend of Berlioz.

128. Napoleon III (1808–73), nephew of Napoleon I (Bonaparte), assumed the title of Emperor in 1852 and held it until 1870.

129. The name does in fact derive from the Latin word for lead.

130. Based on La Fontaine, *Fables* II 14 (The Hare and the Frogs).

131. Omphale was the Queen of Lydia to whom Hercules was bound as a slave for three years. He fell in love with her and led a submissive life spinning wool.

132. On 'lionesses', see note 64.

133. This is presumably a (slightly inaccurate) recollection of John 5:2–3 and John 9:7; the word used in English is 'pool'—there is no mention of ulcer-washing.

134. A reference to The Hare and the Tortoise (La Fontaine, *Fables* VI 10).

135. I have used the term "windbag" from here on to translate Berlioz's 'Monsieur Prudhomme', who is based on the character Joseph Prudhomme, a personification of the pompous and empty-headed bourgeois, created by the writer and caricaturist Henri Monnier (1805–77) in 1830. The reference to his sword of honour comes from Monnier's *Grandeur et décadence de M. Joseph Prudhomme*, a comedy first performed on 23 November 1852. Monsieur Prudhomme describes almost every experience as "the greatest day of my life".

136. *Faust,* Part I (at the city gate).

137. Virgil, *Georgics* IV 511—'Qualis populea maerens philomela sub umbra' ('As the nightingale, mourning beneath the shade of a poplar, ...').

138. A twenty-franc piece (see also page 79).

139. From the same passage of *Faust* as above (see note 136).

140. It is not clear whether 'Nobody knows' is a quotation, or just a regularly used phrase (like 'Who knows?' in English). It is virtually the same expression as 'Nessun lo sa' in Mozart's *Così Fan Tutte,* Act I Scene 1.

141. Berlioz uses the word 'murghers'. Guichard suggests it is a Provençal term, usually spelt 'murger', 'murgier' or 'merger'. I am not aware of any English equivalent.

142. Boileau, *Satires* III (Le repas ridicule) 55–56.

143. On 'lions' dens', see note 64.

144. The real French name of the river is neither Eaugronne nor Eaugrogne, the two forms given by Berlioz, but Angronne.

145. 'The Sibilles of Cumae' is a reference to the Sibyls, prophetesses of classical legend, one of whom was supposed to be based at Cumae in Campania (north of Naples). Virgil describes Aeneas consulting the Cumaean Sibyl in *Aeneid* VI.

146. The bowels were traditionally thought to be the seat of mercy; hence 'bowels' was used to mean compassion or sympathy.

147. On Vivier, see page 79 and note 119.

148. Mlle. Favel made a highly successful début in Dalayrac's *Nina* at the Opéra-Comique, reported by Berlioz in January 1852.

149. On Columbus's feat, see page 63.

150. This is only an approximation of the French, 'Il n'y a que la foi qui perd', meaning that people who are too trusting can easily be led astray.

151. Jules-Henri de Saint-Georges (1801–76) was a prolific producer of librettos, and briefly Director of the Opéra-Comique.

Antoine Louis Clapisson (1808–66) was a French composer, elected before Berlioz to the Institut in 1854.

152. Jules Montjauze (1824–77) was a tenor at the Opéra-Comique who enjoyed great success in *Jaguarita, the Indian Maid* (see above, pages 42–44).

Caroline Duprez (1832–75) was the daughter of the famous tenor Gilbert-Louis Duprez (see page 125 and note 193), and herself a soprano at the Opéra-Comique.

153. In 1856 the Seine reached a height of 7.5 metres and burst its banks in several places, causing numerous casualties.

154. Pauline Viardot-Garcia (1821–1910) was a Spanish mezzo-soprano and sister of the great Maria Malibran. She was much admired by Berlioz (both as a singer and in person) and sang Orpheus in his revival of Gluck's *Orpheus and Eurydice* in 1859. In her concerts she frequently sang her own arrangements for voice of six Chopin Mazurkas.

Carl Heinrich Graun (1703–59) was a German composer who composed, among other things, thirty-two operas.

155. 'Farewell, keep in your heart the memory of our passion'—Gluck, *Iphigenia in Aulis* Act III Scene 3, Iphigenia's farewell to Achilles.

156. *I Vespri Siciliani* ('Sicilian Vespers') Act V No. 18.

157. A reference to John II 4 ('Woman, what have I to do with thee?').

158. An alexandrine is a verse of twelve syllables in six iambic feet. Here (as elsewhere—see page 137) Berlioz seems either to be confused between syllables and feet or to be thinking of alexandrine couplets.

159. The "Kreutzer" sonata was Beethoven's Op. 47 in A major, dedicated to the violinist Rodolphe Kreutzer—Berlioz had recently heard it played by Camillo Sivori and Theodore Ritter.

160. On Ella, see page 73 and note 113. In 1855 he had given Berlioz a superb edition of the complete works of Shakespeare.

The Flight into Egypt is the middle section of Berlioz's 'sacred trilogy' *The Childhood of Christ*, Op. 25. It was published in 1852, followed by the full work in 1855. The *Shepherds' Farewell* which forms part of *The Flight into Egypt* was first performed in Paris in November 1850 at a concert of the Société Philharmonique.

161. Alexander Pope (1688–1744); *An Essay on Criticism*, 412–13 (quoted in English by Berlioz).

162. Joseph-Louis Duc (1802–79) was the official architect of the city of Paris. His works included the Bastille Column, in memory of the July Revolution, and the restoration of the Palais de Justice. Like Berlioz, he was a Prix de Rome prize-winner, and they overlapped in Rome during 1831. The *Apotheosis* which forms the last movement of the *Funeral and Triumphal Symphony* (originally called *July Symphony*, then *Military Symphony*) was dedicated to him.

163. Thomas Chatterton (1752–70) fabricated a number of poems purporting to be the work of an imaginary fifteenth-century British monk and poet, Thomas Rowley.

164. The Belgian François-Joseph Fétis (1784–1871) was a Professor at the Paris Conservatoire and Director of the Brussels Conservatoire. His *Biographie universelle des musiciens* appeared from 1835 to 1844.

165. I am aware of no English counterpart for the French word 'ours' ('bear') used for a manuscript that has 'gone the rounds'.

166. This (with minor differences) is the caption to a lithograph by Hippolyte Bellangé (1800–1866). See Figure 26.

167. The 'Director of Successes' is the leader of the claque, a body of hired applauders for theatrical performances. Berlioz gives a description of the operation of the claque at the Opéra, and some of its principal leaders, in the Seventh Evening of *Evenings with the Orchestra*. On the 'pit', see note 23.

168. *Flattés* and *martelés* are vocal ornaments of the Baroque period, involving the insertion of extra short notes before the main note sung.

169. Dagobert was king of the Franks from 628 to 639.

170. On the siege of Sebastopol and the cholera epidemic, see also pages 26 (and note 33) and 52.

The statement about the East Indies being ablaze refers to the Indian Mutiny of 1857–58.

'North America is going bankrupt' refers to the fact that some states, including Mississippi and Pennsylvania, had recently repudiated their public debts.

171. Michel-Jean Sedaine (1719–97) was a playwright and librettist. André-Ernest-Modeste Grétry (1741–1813) and Pierre-Alexandre Monsigny (1729–1817) were French composers, especially of operas.

172. Glauber salts: a strong laxative named after Johan Rudolph Glauber (1604–68), the German chemist who discovered it.

173. 'Within the walls . . . outside the walls'.

174. Triboulet is a character in Victor Hugo's *Le Roi s'amuse* (1832)—immortalised by Verdi as Rigoletto.

175. Literally, 'it refines behaviour through laughter'—a description of the true function of comedy by the French priest and writer of Latin hymns Jean Baptiste de Santeul (1630–97). (On this whole piece, see the Translator's Note, page xxi.)

176. The nearest English equivalent would be 'Grasp all, lose all'.

177. In October 1812, Napoleon issued a decree from Moscow concerning the management of the Théâtre-Français.

178. *Romeo and Juliet*, Act IV Scene 5.

179. The (meaningless) French word is 'L'Avarre', instead of *L'Avare* ('The Miser').

180. Molière, *Tartuffe*, Act V Scene 3.

181. The character referred to is Monsieur Caritidès in Molière's *Les Fâcheux* ('The Impertinents'), Act III Scene 2.

182. Jean-Baptiste Poquelin, known as Molière (1622–73), was the French comic playwright whose numerous well-known works include *Don Juan*, *Le Misanthrope*, *Tartuffe*, *Amphitryon*, *Le Médecin malgré lui*, *L'Avare*, *Le Bourgeois Gentilhomme* and *Le Malade imaginaire*. The libretto of Mozart's *Don Giovanni* is partly based on *Don Juan*. Molière's statue stands at the foot of the Rue de Richelieu in Paris.

183. Mozart first visited Paris in 1763, aged seven, and again in 1766.

184. There were several different opera and ballet versions of *Le Sicilien*, with

music by Lully, Dauvergne and Sor. Thomas's *Psyche* appeared in 1857, Gounod's *Le Médecin malgré lui* in 1858, which was also the year of Creste's *Les Fourberies de Marinette* (perhaps based on Molière's *Les Fourberies de Scapin*), which Berlioz is here supposedly reviewing.

185. *Othello*, Act V Scene 2 ('I have done the state some service. They know't, no more of that.')

186. The harp solo, the chorus of the shades and the scene of Orpheus in the underworld are all references to Gluck, *Orpheus and Eurydice*, Act II.

187. Gluck, *Iphigenia in Tauris*, Act I Scene 1. 'Les dieux apaisent leur courroux' ('The fury of the gods subsides') comes from Scene 3 of the same act.

188. The statue of Amenophis III at Thebes, known by the Greeks as the statue of Memnon, is said to have produced a musical sound when struck by the rays of the rising sun (Eos, the Dawn, was Memnon's mother).

189. Gluck's six great operas were *Orpheus and Eurydice*, *Alceste*, *Iphigenia in Aulis*, *Armide*, *Iphigenia in Tauris* and *Echo and Narcissus*.

190. *Henry VI Part One*, Act I Scene 2.

191. *The Siege of Corinth*, *Moïse*, *Le Comte Ory* and *William Tell* are operas by Rossini first performed at the Opéra in 1826, 1827, 1828 and 1829 respectively.

192. A reference to Luke 23:34.

193. Gilbert-Louis Duprez (1806–96) was the leading tenor of his day at the Opéra, in succession to Adolphe Nourrit. He made his début in Rossini's *William Tell* in April 1837, and also sang the tenor solo in Berlioz's *Requiem* in December of that year. In 1838 he created the role of *Benvenuto Cellini*: his discomfort with the part contributed to the opera's withdrawal after only three performances.

194. 'Let us cheat the murderous hope.'

195. *The Nightingale* was first performed in 1816, and frequently revived. Louis-Sébastien Lebrun (1764–1829) was a singer, teacher and composer. His wife was a member of the Opéra chorus; she sang the soprano part (badly, according to the *Memoirs*) in the Mélodie Pastorale trio with chorus from Berlioz's unfinished opera *Les Francs-Juges* at his Conservatoire concert on 26 May 1828, conducted by Bloc (see note 22). Étienne (1777–1845) was a journalist and author.

196. Jean Louis Tulou (1786–1865) was the excellent solo flute of both the Opéra and Conservatoire orchestras, also a Professor at the Conservatoire who composed numerous pieces for his instrument.

197. La Fontaine, *Fables* VIII 4 (The Power of Fables).

198. Jean-Baptiste-Louis Gresset (1709–77) was the author of a comic poem entitled *Vert-Vert*—perhaps best translated as *Blue-Blue*. Vert-Vert was the name of a parrot owned by an order of nuns in Nevers, who sent it to their colleagues in Nantes to show off its ability to speak the pious phrases they had taught it. Unfortunately on its journey by boat down the Loire it learnt a different, much 'bluer' repertoire from the boatmen, and scandalised the nuns with its language when it arrived.

199. Berlioz's *Messe Solennelle* had its first performance at the Church of St.-Roch on 10 July 1825. It was later withdrawn by him, and was thought to have been lost until the autograph manuscript turned up in an organ-loft in Antwerp in 1991 (an uncanny echo of Berlioz's own fiction about having discovered the manuscript of the *Flight into Egypt* from his *The Childhood of Christ* in a bricked-up closet at the Sainte-Chapelle—see page 108).

200. Gluck, *Iphigenia in Tauris*, Act IV Scene 6.

201. A 'glory' was a theatrical machine on which actors playing gods or goddesses would appear, surrounded by rays of light.

202. 'So passes earthly glory'. A quotation from Thomas à Kempis (1380–1471), *De Imitatione Christi* I iii 6, used at the coronation ceremony of the Pope.

203. The opera *Le Postillon de Longjumeau* by Adolphe Adam (1803–56) was first performed at the Opéra-Comique in October 1836, and was immensely popular for a hundred years. This piece is based on Berlioz's review of its 1852 revival at the Théâtre-Lyrique.

204. 'Troy is no more'—based on Virgil, *Aeneid* II 325, 'Fuimus Troes, fuit Ilium et ingens / Gloria Teucrorum' ('We Trojans are no more, Ilium is no more nor the great glory of the Teucrians'). These words were incorporated in the original closing scene of *The Trojans*, but later replaced.

205. *On Rhythm*, by Marie-Bernard Giertz, appeared as a booklet in 1857, having originally been published in the journal *L'Univers*.

206. *Joseph* is the best-known opera of Étienne-Nicolas Méhul (1763–1817); it was first performed in 1807.

207. *Joseph*, Act I Scene 2 No. 2.

Daniel-François-Esprit Auber (1782–1871) was a prolific and successful French opera composer, and Director of the Paris Conservatoire from 1842 until his death. His best known works include *La Muette de Portici* and *Fra Diavolo*.

208. This is part of a dialogue between the Music Master and the Dancing Master in Act I Scene 2 of Molière's *Le Bourgeois Gentilhomme*.

209. Based on Boileau, *Lutrin* I 186 (where it describes the spirit of the Church).

210. Amalia Ferraris (1828–1904) was an Italian dancer who performed in Italy, Vienna and London before being engaged by the Paris Opéra.

Le Cheval de bronze is an opera by Auber, to a libretto by Scribe, first performed at the Opéra-Comique in March 1835; later arranged as an opera-ballet and played at the Opéra in September 1857 (both reviewed by Berlioz).

211. 'Herz's' was a recital hall belonging to the Austrian-born composer and piano-maker Henri Herz (1803–88). The first two performances of Berlioz's *The Childhood of Christ* took place there in December 1854.

212. An adaptation of Molière's *Le Misanthrope*, Act I Scene 2.

213. 'Amphitryon' is used with the meaning of a generous host, especially one of doubtful identity, after the husband of Alcmene in Greek mythology. Zeus disguised himself as Amphitryon and gave a lavish banquet to seduce Alcmene, by whom he fathered Hercules.

214. 'Eat, but listen' is an an adaptation of the response of Themistocles (a politician rather than a philosopher) to Eurybiades, Spartan admiral of the Greek fleet before the battle of Salamis, who threatened to strike him with his staff during an argument about whether the fleet should withdraw or fight: "Strike, but listen" (Plutarch, *Themistocles* XI 4).

215. 'Who is the audacious man that in this gloomy place . . .'—Gluck, *Orpheus and Eurydice*, Act II Scene 1.

216. On alexandrines, see above, note 158.

217. The opera *Le Pré aux Clercs* by Ferdinand Hérold (1791–1833) was performed at the Opéra-Comique in 1832.

218. 'It is done, Heaven itself has received their vows, its supreme power has united two lovers'—*Le Pré aux Clercs*, No. 11.

219. J. A. Ducondut, *Essai de rythmique française* (Paris: M. Lévy frères, 1856).

220. The patron saints of cobblers were Saint Crispin and Saint Crispinian.

221. Charles Potier (1775–1838) was a comic actor.

222. The opera *La Vestale* ('The Vestal Virgin') was written in 1807 by Gaspare Spontini (1774–1851) was an Italian composer who settled in Paris in 1803. He and Berlioz enjoyed a relationship of mutual admiration and slightly wary friendship, with an element of father and son about it; a biographical sketch of Spontini appears in the Thirteenth Evening of *Evenings with the Orchestra*. *Der Freischütz* by Carl Maria von Weber (1786–1826) appeared in 1821. Both works were regarded by Berlioz as among the great operatic masterpieces.

223. Alphonse Royer, Director of the Opéra in 1858, thought that the words of the Marseillaise went just as well with the tune of *La Grâce de Dieu* ('The Grace of God'), a tearful romance by Louisa Puget. This was used by Gustave Lemoine and Adolphe d'Ennery (later Dennery) as the basis for a five-act theatre piece, including songs, which was first performed at the Gaieté theatre in 1841 (see also note 282).

'Un jour, maître corbeau': 'One day, Master Crow . . .'

224. 'Come, children of the fatherland, the day of glory has arrived. The bloody standard of tyranny is raised against us! Do you hear the fierce shouts of those soldiers in the fields, coming to slaughter our children and our comrades? To arms, citizens, form up your battalions; let their impure blood drench the furrows of our land.'

225. The air comes from Act IV of *La Juive* ('The Jewess') by Fromental Halévy (1799–1862), with a libretto by Scribe, first performed at the Opéra on 23 February 1835. The words of the air itself were written by the tenor Adolphe Nourrit (1802–39), who inspired this scene.

'Rachel, when our gracious guardian Lord entrusted your cradle to my trembling hands, I dedicated my entire life to your happiness, and now I am the one who delivers you to the executioner!'

226. On Marcello's psalm setting, see note 24.

227. 'The heavens declare the glory of God; and the firmament sheweth his handywork . . .' (Psalm 19).

> 'Ah! What delight to drink outside
> And stuff and gorge and guzzle!
> Ah! What delight to drink outside
> Beneath the shady branches wide,
> And go on the razzle-dazzle! . . .'

228. Georges Cabanis (1757–1808) was a doctor, philosopher and friend of Stendhal.

229. These are the words of the three witches at the beginning of Shakespeare's *Macbeth*, Act I Scene 1.

230. The long closure was caused by a change of administration imposed by the government during 1854.

The opera *La Favorite*, by Gaetano Donizetti (1797–1848), was first performed at the Opéra on 2 December 1840 and revived for its reopening in August 1854. Berlioz delayed his review in protest at the new administration's withdrawal of free entry for journalists.

231. On Mme. Stoltz, see page 46 and note 62. (Léonor is the principal soprano role in *La Favorite*.)

232. Armand Limnander (de Nieuwenhove) (1814–92) was a Belgian composer, based in Paris since 1845. His opera *The Master Singer* was first performed at the Opéra in October 1853. (Wagner's *Die Meistersinger* was first performed in 1868.) *La Reine de Chypre*, by Halévy, was first performed at the Opéra in December 1841.

233. The reference is to *Fables* IX 2 (The Two Pigeons).

234. 'It's too good for people like these.'

235. Jacques Bénigne Bossuet (1627–1704) was a French churchman and preacher, famous as an orator.

236. A quotation from Racine, *Les Plaideurs* ('The Litigants'), Act I Scene 4.

237. On Mme. Sontag, see page 22 and note 28. She died in Mexico of cholera in June 1854.

238. Adapted from La Fontaine, *Fables* II 16 (The Crow Wishing to Imitate the Eagle). The eaglet is Mme. Stoltz, the nightingale Mme. Sontag.

239. Berlioz saw a performance of *The Marriage of Figaro* in London during his visit there from May to July 1851. The aria he refers to is 'Deh vieni' in Act IV.

240. Berlioz's own *Romeo and Juliet*, first performed in 1839, was not an opera but a 'dramatic symphony'. The opera of the same name by Charles-François Gounod (1818–93) did not appear until 1867. It is clear from chapter 35 of Berlioz's *Memoirs* and from his *feuilleton* of 13 September 1859 (reprinted in *A travers chants*), that the 1830 opera *I Capuleti ed i Montecchi* by the Italian composer Vincenzo Bellini (1801–35) fell far short of meeting the criterion of 'a truly Shakespearean opera'."

241. Shakespeare, *Romeo and Juliet*, Act II Scene 2 (somewhat inexactly rendered in French by Berlioz).

242. Shakespeare, *The Merchant of Venice*, Act V Scene 1. Berlioz himself adapted this passage for the glorious love duet 'Nuit d'ivresse et d'extase infinie!' (Night of rapture and infinite ecstasy) between Dido and Aeneas in Act IV of his opera *The Trojans*.

243. 'Accursed hunger for gold'—Virgil, *Aeneid* III 57.

244. Berlioz described his vision of an ideal musical city (with an opera house, of course) in Euphonia, the Twenty-Fifth Evening of *Evenings with the Orchestra*.

245. Tonelli was a member of a small troupe of Italian singers called 'Les Bouffons', who first appeared at the Opéra in Pergolesi's *La Serva Padrona* in 1752.

246. Della Maria (1769–1800) was a French composer of Italian origin.

247. Giovanni Battista Rubini (1794–1854) was the leading tenor of his day— the aria is 'Il mio tesoro', sung by Don Ottavio in Act II.

248. Act II Scene 7.

249. Berlioz describes the journey from Castellamare in chapter 41 of his *Memoirs*.

250. 'Know you the land where the orange-trees bloom?'—Mignon's famous song in Goethe, *Wilhelm Meister's Apprenticeship* III 1 (see also above, page 70 and note 104).

251. Susa and St.-Jean-de-Maurienne are both places in the northernmost part of the then kingdom of Italy, where it borders France in the Alps.

252. La Fontaine, *Fables* IX 4.

253. 'A few are seen keeping afloat', Virgil, *Aeneid* I 118.

254. Henri Brod (1799–1839) played the oboe both for the Conservatoire and

the Opéra orchestras. Luigi Cherubini (1760–1842), distinguished Italian composer and Director of the Paris Conservatoire for 20 years from 1822, was one of Berlioz's personal bugbears (although Berlioz admired much of his music).

255. Édouard Monnais (1798–1868) was a lawyer who dedicated himself to literature and the arts. He was royal superintendent (Commissaire) of the Opéra from 1839 to 1847, and government superintendent of theatres from 1852. He wrote for the *Gazette musicale* (under the name of Paul Smith), as well as for various other publications.

256. These letters originally appeared in the *Revue et Gazette musicale* in 1848. The visits to which they relate took place in June 1845 (Marseilles), July 1845 (Lyons) and June 1846 (Lille).

257. *Les Prétendus* is a comic opera by Jean-Baptiste Moyne, called Lemoine (1757–96), first performed at the Opéra in June 1789. The quotation cited by Berlioz is spoken by a countryman rather than a financier, in Scene 6.

258. Mab (possibly based on the Welsh word for baby, 'maban') was a female fairy believed to be the bringer of dreams. Shakespeare's Mercutio gives an extended description of her in *Romeo and Juliet*, Act I Scene 4, leading Berlioz to include the two Queen Mab scherzos (one vocal, one orchestral) in his dramatic symphony based on the play.

259. Jenny Lind, the 'Swedish nightingale' (1820–87) was the singing superstar of the age. Berlioz heard her in Berlin, and again in London in 1848, and was a considerable admirer of both her musical and dramatic talents (see also page 165).

Johann Baptist Pischek (1814–73) was a Bohemian baritone highly praised by Berlioz in his *Memoirs*.

260. Gustavus Vaughan Brooke (1818–66) and William Charles Macready (1793–1873) were two leading English actors. Berlioz saw Macready in 1847, and the actor gave a dinner for him; he missed Brooke's *Othello* on that occasion, but saw him as *Hamlet* on his next London visit in May 1848, and thought him superior to both Macready and Kemble.

261. The Association of Artist-Musicians was founded and directed by Berlioz's friend Baron Taylor. Three large-scale Festivals on behalf of the organisation took place in September and October 1848 in the gardens of the Élysée National. Later that October, Berlioz conducted a concert given by the Association in the Palace of Versailles.

Philippe Musard (1792–1859) was a director of a popular dance and concert orchestra.

The Mabille garden was a dance-hall in the Avenue Montaigne, founded by the dancer Mabille in 1840.

262. Berlioz is referring to two articles, in November and December 1834.

263. Maurice Schlesinger (1797–1871) published most of Berlioz's works which appeared up to 1846; he founded (in 1834) and directed the *Gazette musicale* (later *Revue et Gazette musicale*). The 'Opéra masked ball' at which the introduction took place was in January 1835. (See also note 122 on Schlesinger's sucessor, Gemmy Brandus.)

264. Étienne Arnal (1794–1872) was a well-known comic actor. Adolphe Adam (1803–56) was the composer of *Giselle* (and of *The Postilion of Longjumeau*, see page 127 and note 203) and also produced adaptations of other composers such as Grétry.

265. On Monsieur Véron, see note 98.

266. This is a reference to Jullien (see note 106), who had gone bankrupt not long after engaging Berlioz to conduct his Grand English Opera at the Theatre Royal, Drury Lane for the 1847–48 season.

267. These concerts took place between January and April 1845.

268. The 'Phocaean city' is Massilia, the Greek city that later became Marseilles; it was founded about 600 BC by colonists from the Ionian city of Phocaea in Asia Minor.

Hippolyte Lecourt was a lawyer friend of Berlioz and a keen amateur musician. Berlioz dedicated his ballad setting of Victor Hugo's *Sara la Baigneuse* for three choirs and orchestra to Lecourt (Op. 11, published in 1851).

269. Berlioz did give two concerts in Marseilles, on 19 and 25 June 1845.

270. Louis Alizard (1814–50) was a singer at the Opéra whose bass voice Berlioz much admired and who had sung the role of Friar Laurence in his *Romeo and Juliet* in 1839.

271. On Méry, see note 127.

272. Phaeton (or Phaethon) was the son of Helios, the Greek sun-god, who came to grief driving his father's chariot.

273. The elder Dumas (1802–70) visited Marseilles almost every year from 1834, and in 1844 sent his twenty-year-old son (1824–95) there for an extended stay.

274. Jean Reboul (1796–1864) was a baker who also wrote poetry; he made a name for himself with *The Angel and the Child* in 1828, as well as a volume of poems in 1836.

275. The Dauphin was the eldest son of the King of France—i.e., the Crown Prince. Berlioz is of course making a pun on 'dolphin'.

276. Elisa Félix, known as Rachel (1820–58), was a leading tragedienne of the day.

277. On the 'pit', see note 23.

278. The 'ode-symphony' *Le Désert*, the best-known work of Félicien David (1810–76), was first performed at the Paris Conservatoire in 1844 and the following April, under the composer's own direction, in Marseilles.

279. The *Hymn to France* was written by Berlioz for the Festival of Industry in August 1844 to words by his friend Auguste Barbier, and performed again with about 1,000 executants in January 1845 (see chapter 53 of the *Memoirs*).

The *Pilgrims' March* is the second movement of Berlioz's *Harold in Italy* symphony, written in 1834.

The *Fifth of May*, also known as *Song on the Death of Napoleon*, was written in 1835.

The '*adagio* of the symphony' is the *Scene in the Fields*, the middle (third) movement of Berlioz's *Symphonie fantastique*.

280. On 'suffering artist', see note 31.

281. Symphony no. 40 (KV. 550).

282. Mlle. Rose Chéri refers to Rose-Marie Cizos (1824–67), a singer who had been discovered in Périgueux in 1841 singing the role of Marie in *La Grâce de Dieu* (see page 141 and note 223); she enjoyed a great success in the vaudeville *Geneviève* in 1846.

283. Berlioz's meaning is not clear here; possibly the 'six columns' might refer to columns of text in a journal or newspaper, although it seems more likely that they relate to commonly used stage sets with six columns.

284. On Jenny Lind, see page 157 and note 259.

285. Juggernaut (or Jagannath, 'lord of the world') is a title of Vishnu, chief of the Hindu gods, represented by an idol in a temple at Puri which was dragged each year in an immense 'car' to another temple. Fanatical pilgrims were believed to throw themselves under the wheels of the car so as to go straight to paradise.

286. Charles-Edmond Duponchel (1795–1863) was another of Berlioz's bugbears; Director of the Opéra from 1835 to 1840, then Administrator under Pillet from 1840 to 1843, and Director again (together with Roqueplan) from 1847 to 1849. Jenny Lind refused all offers from Pillet and Duponchel to sing at the Opéra.

287. Poultier was a tenor, formerly a cooper, born 1815 in Rouen; he made his Opéra debut in 1841.

Maria-Dolores-Benedicta Josephina Nau, born 1818 in New York, made her Opéra debut in 1836. She sang Annette (Ännchen) in the 1841 production of Weber's *Der Freischütz*, with recitatives provided by Berlioz.

288. Berlioz was born at La-Côte-St.-André, 64 kilometres from Lyons in the Département of the Isère, on 11 December 1803.

289. Georges-François Hainl (1807–73), cellist, conductor and composer, and director of the Lyons theatre orchestra from 1840. He later became musical director of both the Paris Opéra and Conservatoire orchestras, and Maître de Chapelle of the imperial court.

290. *Non licet omnibus* ("Not everyone is permitted") is possibly based on Horace, *Epistles* XVII 36, 'Non cuivis homini contingit adire Corinthum ("Not everyone is lucky enough to get to Corinth").

291. In Chapter 4 of his *Memoirs* Berlioz describes Dorant as 'an Alsatian from Colmar, who could play pretty well every instrument and excelled at clarinet, cello, violin and guitar'. He gave Berlioz (and his elder sister Nanci) guitar lessons between 1819 and 1821.

292. Barielle was a singer at the Lyons Grand Theatre. He had a fine bass voice, but almost dried up when singing the part of the Ishmaelite Householder in Berlioz's *The Childhood of Christ* in Brussels in March 1855—Berlioz had to rescue him by audibly singing his part from the podium.

293. 'What really matters' refers to the financial takings.

294. A reference to La Fontaine, *Fables* II 9 (The Lion and the Gnat).

295. Eugène de Pradel (1787–1857) was a well-known improviser who was imprisoned in 1821 for the political content of some of his songs. He published *Les Étincelles, ou Recueil de chants patriotiques et guerriers, chansons de table et d'amour* ('Sparks, or a collection of songs of patriotism, war, eating and love') in 1822, including *L'Enfer, chanson diabolique* ('Hell, a song of the devil'). The couplet quoted by Berlioz is the tenth.

296. Sardanapalus is the Greek name of Assurbanipal, a seventh-century BC king of Assyria. The name is applied to any luxurious, extravagant and self-willed tyrant, as in Byron's poetic drama of the same name (1821). Delacroix's painting, *Sardanapalus*, of 1827, was inspired by Byron's drama.

297. There were in fact two concerts, on Sunday 20 and Thursday 24 July 1845.

298. See Matthew 4:8 and Luke 4:5 (although neither makes any mention of a booth!).

299. Frédérick Lemaître (1800–1876) was an actor famous for his creation of

the brigand-hero Robert Macaire in the 1823 melodrama *L'Auberge des Adrets*. He visited London four times and was a favourite with Queen Victoria.

300. This was Napoleon's remark when he met Goethe at Erfurt on 2 October 1808.

301. Marc-Antoine Désaugiers (1772–1827) was a well-known composer of songs and vaudevilles, as was his younger colleague Pierre-Jean de Béranger (1780–1857).

302. A reference to Boileau, *L'Art poétique* II 94, 'A sonnet without fault is worth as much as a long poem'.

303. Pantagruel, the last of the giants, is the principal character in the satire *The History of Gargantua and Pantagruel* by François Rabelais (c1494–1553). Pantagruelism refers to coarse and boisterous buffoonery and humour, especially with a serious purpose.

304. Luke 17:2.

305. The two performances in Lille of the *Lacrymosa* took place on 25 and 26 June 1838, with 500–600 musicians and an audience of 5,000. Chapter 47 of the *Memoirs* tells of Habeneck writing to Berlioz about the success enjoyed by the piece—his letter was published in the *Gazette musicale* of 1 July 1838.

François-Antoine Habeneck (1781–1849) was a violinist, conductor and composer. As chief conductor of the Conservatoire concerts, he led performances of Beethoven's symphonies in 1839; he was also conductor of the Opéra, holding both posts for the best part of two decades. He conducted the first performance of Berlioz's *Requiem* in the Invalides in December 1837, when, according to the *Memoirs*, he courted disaster by taking a pinch of snuff at a crucial juncture.

306. In June 1846.

307. An accident involving a train from Paris to Arras had recently occurred when Berlioz was writing this letter.

308. Jules Janin (1804–74) was a leading critic and author and Berlioz's colleague on the *Journal des Débats*. His verses for Berlioz's *Chant des chemins de fer* ('Railway Cantata') were exceedingly banal.

The cantata, for solo tenor and large chorus, is included as no. 29 of Berlioz's collection of *33 Mélodies*, published in 1863.

309. A reference, not to Boileau (as recognised by Berlioz below), but to Molière, *Le Misanthrope*, Act I Scene 2.

310. This maxim actually comes from a verse by François-Joseph-Marie Fayolle (1774–1852) in his *Discourse on Writing and Writers*.

311. '*Ululate venti . . . Ingemuit alta domus*': 'Cry, winds! . . . The tall house groaned.'

312. Ossian or Oisin, son of Fingal, was a legendary Gaelic bard and warrior hero of the third century. The purported translations of poems by Ossian published by the Scottish writer James Macpherson between 1760 and 1763 were essentially inventions of Macpherson himself.

313. René, Vicomte de Chateaubriand (1768–1848), French writer and statesman, author of *Atala* and *René*, both of which formed part of his most famous work, *Le Génie du Christianisme* ('The Genius of Christianity'), published in 1802.

314. 'Crying like this she filled the whole house with her groaning'—Virgil, *Aeneid* II 679.

315. Jacques Charles Odry (1781–1853) was a celebrated comic actor of the Gaieté and Variétés theatres.

316. A 'half-moon', also known as a demi-lune (French for 'half-moon') or ravelin, is a detached outwork of fortifications, shaped like a half-moon.

317. The *Apotheosis* is the last movement, for double orchestra and chorus, of Berlioz's *Funeral and Triumphal Symphony*, written in 1840 to commemorate the tenth anniversary of the 1830 Revolution (see also page 14 and note 18).

The 'princes' were the Duc de Montpensier and his brother, the Duc de Nemours, sons of Louis-Philippe, the 'Citizen King' of France from 1830 to 1848.

318. Linstocks were the staffs which held the lighted matches used to fire cannon.

319. The issue of the *Charivari* of 20 June 1846 included an article on 'Pyrotechnic music'.

320. Berlioz had previously used an expression similar to this as an epigraph for chapter 34 of his *Memoirs*.

321. 'Day of wrath, that day when the standard of the Cross will be unfurled and the universe dissolved into ashes'—from the mediaeval hymn written probably by Thomas of Celano (c1190–1260) and used in the Roman Catholic mass for the dead. The source of the text of the second line is obscure: the verse normally reads 'Dies irae, dies illa, / Solvet saeclum in favilla, / Teste David cum Sibylla.'

Sources

The information in this section is based on the notes in the Gründ edition of *Les Grotesques de la musique,* edited by Professor Léon Guichard and first published in Paris in 1969 as part of a centenary edition of Berlioz's literary works. The Gründ edition also includes details of significant variances between the original versions of some of the pieces and those that appear in *Les Grotesques de la musique.*

Unless otherwise specified, the *feuilletons* which were used as sources appeared originally in the *Journal des Débats.* A number of them were later reprinted in the *Revue et Gazette musicale.*

Page(s)

1–6   *Prologue:* This was reproduced in the *Revue et Gazette musicale* of 20 February 1859.

4–5   From 'It's true, of course, . . .' to '. . . to hang himself': Based on *feuilleton* of 20 September 1853.

11   *The right to play a symphony in the wrong key:* Based on *feuilleton* of 7 October 1846.

16–18   *A programme of grotesque music:*
From 'In the days when the Odéon . . .' to '. . . start pelting us with coins': Freely based on *feuilleton* of 6 April 1853.

25–34   *Musical instruments at the Universal Exhibition:* From *feuilleton* of 9 January 1856.

34–35   *A rival to Érard:* This was reproduced in the *Revue et Gazette musicale* of 27 February 1859.

37–39   *Diplomatic correspondence:* From *feuilleton* of 19 October 1855.

40–41   *Prudence and sagacity of a provincial—Alexandre's melodium:* Reproduced in the *Revue et Gazette musicale* of 27 February 1859.

41–42   *The tromba marina—The saxophone—Experts in instrumentation:* Based on *feuilleton* of 13 January 1852, and reproduced in the *Revue et Gazette musicale* of 27 February 1859.

42–44   *Jaguarita—Female savages:* From *feuilleton* of 19 May 1855, a review of *Jaguarita l'Indienne.*

44–46   *The Astucio family—Marriages of convenience—Great news—More news:* All four pieces taken from the *feuilleton* of 8 June 1855.

47–50   *Barley sugar—Heavy music:* From *feuilleton* of 19 December 1856 on the Folies-Nouvelles Theatre.

50–54   *Ordinary music lovers and serious music:* From the start of *feuilleton* of 25 November 1854.

54–65 *Lamentations of Jeremiah:*

54 *From 'How wretched are critics!' to '. . . with both feet':* From the start of *feuilleton* of 6 September 1854.

54–56 *From 'There's a gloom-laden lithograph . . .' to 'Let's not wait to be told a second time "Come on, men look lively!"':* From the start of *feuilleton* of 10 June 1854.

58 *From 'More articles! More operas!' to '. . . (at least those of them who have minds)!':* From the start of *feuilleton* of 5 January 1854.

59–60 *From 'To think that quite probably on this day . . .' to '. . . don't even condescend to visit':* Insertion from the start of *feuilleton* of 22 July 1852.

60–63 *From 'Even the hardest of hearts . . .' to '. . . fresh air, harmony and light':* Resumption of *feuilleton* of 6 September 1854.

63-64 *From 'There are many tales . . .' to 'To what utter oblivion you consign them':* *Feuilleton* of 6 September 1854 continues (after an omitted passage).

65 *From 'The Germans use the term "recensors" . . .' to '. . . a simple bumpkin once again':* From the start of *feuilleton* of 5 October 1854.

66 *A model critic:* Start of *feuilleton* of 6 January 1858.

66–68 *Dramatic emphasis:*
From 'The Opéra-Comique, let's face it . . .' to '. . . three times a week' and from 'Here is a story . . .' to 'How about that?': Extracts from *feuilleton* of 10 June 1854.

68–69 *Success of a Miserere:* From *feuilleton* of 3 May 1856.

69–75 *The season—The bugbears' club:* From *feuilleton* of 26 July 1853.

73–75 *From 'It's not enough . . .' to '. . . are going to make a lot of money':* Extract from *feuilleton* of 20 July 1858.

75–78 *Minor irritations of major concerts:* Mostly (apart from the first two sentences and the final line) from *feuilleton* of 24 September 1857.

79 *20 francs per ticket:* From *feuilleton* of 29 March 1856.

79–80 *War on flats:* This was reproduced in the *Revue et Gazette musicale* of 27 February 1859.

81–93 *Plombières and Baden—First letter:* This first appeared in the *Journal des Débats* of 4 September 1856.

93-103 *Second letter:* First published in the *Journal des Débats* of 9 September 1856.

104–5 *Aural aberrations and delusions:* End of *feuilleton* of 23 April 1858.

109–12 *The débutante—The Director of the Opéra's despotism:* Feuilleton of 17 February 1858 (with some modifications).

110-11 *From '. . . the débutante has been led to believe . . .' to '. . . to feel 100,000 terrors':* Insertion from *feuilleton* of 20 January 1854.

112–14 *The song of cockerels—The cockerels of song:*
From 'Vocal trills . . .' to 'One blushes for them': Extract from *feuilleton* of 8 November 1858.

114–16 *Sparrows:* From the start of *feuilleton* of 17 November 1857 (with the last two lines added).

116–17 **Music for laughs:** From the start of *feuilleton* of 5 February 1858.

117–18 **National fatuities:** Extract from *feuilleton* of 16 May 1858.

118–20 **Ingratitude shows an independent spirit:** From the start of *feuilleton* of 19 June 1858 (with a paragraph omitted near the end).

120–25 **The futility of glory:**
From 'Some works, indeed . . .' to '. . . there'd never be anyone dead!' (at end): Extract from *feuilleton* of 3 July 1857.

125–26 **Madame Lebrun:** Extract from *feuilleton* of 24 October 1857.

127 **Time spares nothing:** Extract from *feuilleton* of 10 November 1852 (with the final line added).

129 **The rhythm of pride:** Another extract from *feuilleton* of 24 October 1857.

129–30 **A remark of Monsieur Auber:** Quoted at the end of *feuilleton* of 26 April 1857.

130–32 **Music and dance:** From the start of *feuilleton* of 26 April 1857.

132 **Dancer poets:** From *feuilleton* of 30 September 1857.

132 **Another remark of Monsieur Auber:** Again from *feuilleton* of 24 October 1857.

132–34 **Concerts:** Extract from *feuilleton* of 26 April 1857.

134–35 **Nelson's bravery:** From the start of *feuilleton* of 4 September 1853.

135–40 **Grotesque prejudices:** From *feuilleton* of 22 January 1858, with a different introduction and some modifications (including the addition of the final paragraph).

140–43 **Non-believers in musical expressiveness:** Reproduced in the *Revue et Gazette musicale* of 27 February 1859.

143–50 **Mme. Stoltz and Mme. Sontag—Making millions:** Feuilleton of 5 October 1854 (with some omissions).

150–51 **The rough and the smooth:** Extracts from *feuilleton* of 6 April 1853.

151–52 **Dilettanti of the fashion world—The poet and the cook:** From the start of *feuilleton* of 24 March 1858 (the indifference to music of the fashionable public is also covered in the *feuilleton* of 6–7 May 1853).

152–53 **Orange groves—The acorn and the pumpkin:**
From 'A certain author . . .' to '. . . passed on from father to son!': Extract from *feuilleton* of 4 July 1854, with modifications.

153–54 **"Duckings":** Start of *feuilleton* of 15 September 1858.

157–63 **Travels in France—Academic Correspondence:** These letters appeared in the *Revue et Gazette musicale* during 1848. This first one was published on 10 September 1848, dated Paris, 14 July of the same year.

164–75 **Second letter:** This second letter appeared on 15 October 1848, dated Paris, July 1848.

172–75 From '. . . *I'm beginning to tire of dishing out adulation . . .*' to '*. . . one of the Brains en passant*': From article in the *Revue et Gazette musicale* on 11 March 1849.

175–77 **A day later:**

176–77 From '*I suspect you think . . .*' to '*. . . great difficulty in emulating them*': From article in the *Revue et Gazette musicale* on 25 March 1849.

177 From '*Now, since I . . .*' to '*. . . unwavering affection*': Resumption of the end of the letter as it appeared in the *Revue et Gazette musicale* on 15 October 1848.

177–88 **Third letter:** This third letter appeared in the *Revue et Gazette Musicale* on 19 November 1848, dated 10 November 1848, with a lengthy preamble which Berlioz omitted here (but without the note about the spelling of 'orang-utan').

Selected Bibliography

This short bibliography lists Berlioz's own writings (original editions, plus the most accessible or up-to-date editions in English and French) and a limited number of other significant volumes in English on Berlioz.

'Essential reading' in English would start with Berlioz's own wonderful *Memoirs* (preferably in the version by David Cairns). Next would come his *Evenings with the Orchestra* (translated by Jacques Barzun), and perhaps one of the collections of his letters (such as that edited by Hugh Macdonald).

These could be complemented by one or more of the several excellent modern biographies: notably David Cairns's brilliant two-volume study, as well as others listed below by Bloom, Holoman and Macdonald. Pioneering earlier works include those by Barzun, Newman, Turner and Wotton. Michael Rose's recent *Berlioz Remembered* provides fascinating insights into how Berlioz was viewed by his contemporaries.

Those wishing to delve deeper into Berlioz's life and works will find more extensive bibliographies in several of the works cited, including the lives by Barzun, Bloom, Cairns and Holoman. The 'Berlioz bibliographies' section at the end contains a number of bibliographic volumes dedicated to Berlioz, for those with a specialist level of interest.

Berlioz's own writings

In English:

The Art of Music, and Other Essays. Translated and edited by Elizabeth Csicsery-Ronay (Indiana University Press, Bloomington 1994). A current English translation of *A travers chants*.

Evenings with the Orchestra. Translated and edited by Jacques Barzun (Alfred A. Knopf, New York 1969; also in paperback from the University of Chicago Press, 1999). The definitive English version of *Les Soirées de l'orchestre*.

Memoirs of Hector Berlioz from 1803 to 1865 Comprising His Travels in Germany, Italy, Russia and England. Translated by Rachel (Scott Russell) Holmes and Eleanor Holmes; annotated, and the translation revised, by Ernest Newman (Dover Publications, New York 1966; paperback edition).

The Memoirs of Hector Berlioz, Member of the French Institute, Including His Travels in Italy, Germany, Russia & England, 1803–1865. Translated and edited by David Cairns (Gollancz, London 1969; also published in paperback by Panther, London 1970). The definitive English version of the *Mémoires*.

Letters:

Hector Berlioz: A Selection from His Letters. Selected, edited & translated by Humphrey Searle (Gollancz, London 1966; reprinted in paperback by Vienna House, New York 1973).

New Letters of Berlioz. With Introduction, Notes and English Translation by
    Jacques Barzun. 2nd edition. (Greenwood Press, Westport, Conn. 1974). A
    bilingual selection of letters.
Selected Letters of Berlioz. Edited by Hugh Macdonald, translated by Roger
    Nichols (Faber & Faber, London and Boston 1995). An excellent selection of
    Berlioz's letters translated into English.
Berlioz's Orchestration Treatise: A Translation and Commentary Hugh Macdonald
    (Cambridge University Press, 2002). A scholarly, well-designed, modern English
    version, superseding the previous translation by Mary Cowden Clarke (J. Alfred
    Novello, London 1856).

In French:

A travers chants: Études musicales, adorations, boutades et critiques.
    – Original edition (Michel Lévy frères, Paris 1862).
    – Edited by Léon Guichard (Gründ, Paris 1971).
Feuilletons, articles, criticism, etc:
    Beethoven. Foreword by J. G. Prod'homme (Buchet/Chastel, Paris 1970; reis-
    sued 1979). A collection compiled from *feuilletons*, etc., in the *Journal des
    Débats, Revue et Gazette musicale de Paris* and *Le Rénovateur.*
    Cauchemars et passions. Edited by Gerard Condé (J.-C. Lattès, Paris 1981).
    Selections from Berlioz's *feuilletons* and other critical writings.
    La Critique musicale d'Hector Berlioz, 1823–1863. Volumes 1–3. General Edi-
    tors: Robert Cohen and Yves Gérard (Buchet/Chastel, Paris 1996–2001). The
    first three volumes (up to 1838) of Berlioz's complete critical output. Volume
    4, covering the three years to 1841, is scheduled for production in 2003.
    Les Musiciens et la musique. Volumes 1 and 2 (Calmann-Lévy, Paris [1903]). A
    selection of Berlioz's *feuilletons* from the *Journal des Débats*, published dur-
    ing the centenary year of his birth.
    Souvenirs de Voyages. Edited by J.-G. Prod'homme (Éditions Jules Tallandier,
    Paris 1932). A collection of letters and articles about Berlioz's travels in Italy,
    Germany, Russia, Prussia and Bohemia, some also appearing in other vol-
    umes such as *Les Musiciens et la musique.*
Grand Traité d'instrumentation et d'orchestration modernes.
    – Original edition (Schonenberger, Paris 1843).
    – *Le Chef d'orchestre: Théorie de son art* (Actes Sud, Arles 1988). This chapter
    on the art of the conductor was added to the *Traité*'s second edition in 1855,
    together with a section on new instruments.
    – *De l'Instrumentation.* Edited by Joël-Marie Fauquet (Le Castor Astral, Bor-
    deaux 1994). A reprint of Berlioz's original articles in *La Revue et Gazette
    musicale de Paris*, November 1841 to July 1842.
Les Grotesques de la musique.
    – Original edition (A. Bourdilliat et Cie., Paris 1859).
    – Edited with an introduction and notes by Léon Guichard (Gründ, Paris 1969).
Letters:
    Correspondance générale. Volumes 1–8. General Editor: Pierre Citron
    (Flammarion, Paris 1972–2003). A complete edition of Berlioz's letters. The

final volume (Volume 8), containing additional letters from the whole period 1824–68 which were missing from earlier volumes, as well as a number of supplements, errata and a general index covering all eight volumes, was published early in 2003.

Mémoires de Hector Berlioz, Membre de l'Institut de France, comprenant ses voyages en Italie, en Allemagne, en Russie et en Angleterre, 1803–1865.
– Original edition (Michel Lévy frères, Paris 1870).
– Edited by Pierre Citron (Flammarion, Paris 1991).
Les Soirées de l'orchestre.
– Original edition (Michel Lévy Frères, Paris 1853).
– Edited with an introduction and notes by Léon Guichard (Gründ, Paris 1968).
Voyage musical en Allemagne et en Italie: Études sur Beethoven, Gluck et Weber, Mélanges et Nouvelles. Volumes 1 and 2 (Jules Labitte, Paris 1844).

Publications in English on Berlioz, his life and his music

Barzun, Jacques. *Berlioz and the Romantic Century.* Volumes 1 and 2 (Little, Brown & Co., Boston 1950; new edition from Columbia University Press, New York/London 1969).
———. *Berlioz and His Century: An Introduction to the Age of Romanticism* (World Publishing, Cleveland/New York 1966).
Berlioz Society Bulletin. The Society is based in the UK, but with an international membership. Its Bulletin is published about three times a year. Further information is on the Society's website: *www.hberlioz.com/BerliozSociety.html.*
Bloom, Peter (editor). *Berlioz Studies* (Cambridge University Press, 1992).
——— (editor). *The Cambridge Companion to Berlioz* (Cambridge University Press, 2000; hardback and paperback versions).
———. *The Life of Berlioz* (Cambridge University Press, 1998).
Cairns, David. *Berlioz:*
Volume 1: *The Making of an Artist, 1803–1832* (André Deutsch, London 1989; 2nd edition: Allen Lane, London 1999).
Volume 2: *Servitude and Greatness, 1832–1869* (Allen Lane, 1999).
Both volumes have also been published in paperback (Penguin Books, London 1999). This is an outstanding modern biography of Berlioz.
Crabbe, John. *Hector Berlioz: Rational Romantic* (Kahn & Averill, London 1980).
Dickinson, A. E. F. *The Music of Berlioz* (Faber & Faber, London 1972).
Ganz, A. W. *Berlioz in London* (Quality Press, London 1950; reprinted by Da Capo Press, New York 1981).
Holoman, D. Kern. *Berlioz* (Faber & Faber, London 1989).
Macdonald, Hugh. *Berlioz Orchestral Music* (BBC Music Guides; BBC, London 1969)
———. 'Hector Berlioz'. In *The New Grove: Early Romantic Masters 2* (Macmillan, London 1985).
———. *The Master Musicians: Berlioz* (J. M. Dent & Sons, London 1982).
Newman, Ernest. *Berlioz, Romantic and Classic.* Selected and edited by Peter Heyworth (Gollancz, London 1972).

Primmer, Brian. *The Berlioz Style* (Oxford University Press, London 1973).
Rose, Michael. *Berlioz Remembered* (Faber & Faber, London 2001).
Rushton, Julian. *The Music of Berlioz* (Oxford University Press, 2001).
———. *The Musical Language of Berlioz* (Cambridge University Press, 1983).
Turner, W. J. *Berlioz: The Man and His Work* (J. M. Dent & Sons, London 1934; new edition 1939).
Wotton, Tom S. *Hector Berlioz* (Oxford University Press, London 1935; reprinted by Johnson Reprint, New York/London 1969).

Berlioz Bibliographies

Holoman, D. Kern. *Catalogue of the Works of Hector Berlioz*. Volume 25 of the *New Berlioz Edition* (Bärenreiter, Kassel 1987).
Hopkinson, Cecil and Richard Macnutt. *A Bibliography of the Musical and Literary Works of Hector Berlioz, 1803–1869, with Histories of the French Music Publishers Concerned* (Edinburgh Bibliographical Society, 1951; 2nd edition, edited by Richard Macnutt: Richard Macnutt Limited, Tunbridge Wells 1980).
Langford, Jeffrey and Jane Denker Graves. *Hector Berlioz: A Guide to Research* (Garland Publishing, New York/London 1989).
Wright, Michael. *A Berlioz Bibliography: Critical Writing on Hector Berlioz from 1825 to 1986* (Saint Michael's Abbey Press, Farnborough [1988]).

Index

Musical and literary works, including those of Berlioz himself, are shown in italics and listed under the names of their composers or authors, with cross-referencing in cases where the name of the author might not be obvious from the text. Buildings, locations, theatres, institutions, sights, etc are generally listed under the names of the cities or towns where they are located: notably London and Paris, as well as (for example) Lille, Lyons, Marseilles and Plombières.

Names of countries and continents are not indexed, except for a few which appear only rarely (e.g., Ireland and Mexico). Unless otherwise indicated, places are (mostly) in France. Similarly, the nationality of individuals listed can be assumed to be French when not specified. Fictional characters are listed separately from the works in which they appear. References to Berlioz himself in the Notes are too numerous to be usefully indexed.

References to musical instruments (except when they are mere passing mentions) are given under 'instruments'. There is also an entry for 'birds', in view of the many references to different birds in the text. Other 'generic' entries include 'conservatoires', 'exhibitions', 'festivals' and 'revolutions'. All biblical references are listed under 'Bible'.

The Musical Madhouse

The Musical Madhouse is the first complete translation into English of Hector Berlioz's *Les Grotesques de la musique*. It is the funniest of all his works, and consists of a number of short anecdotes, witticisms, open letters and comments on the absurdities of concert life. Alastair Bruce's fluid translation brings to life this important composer and *bon vivant*. He does a wonderful job of conveying all the puns, jokes and invective of Berlioz's prose as well as the nuances of his stories. He even imitates a Tahitian accent in the translation, as Berlioz does in the original. The notes will give the reader insight into the innuendos and in-jokes that fill the pages. This translation will take its place among other translations of Berlioz's prose writings, bringing to the reader more lively examples of a still misunderstood composer caught up in the musical life of mid-nineteenth-century Paris.

Alastair Bruce is a London-based management consultant and passionate Berlioz fan. He developed a talent for translation at school and discovered classical music in 1966, and Berlioz in 1967. From 1977 to 1985 he was Honorary Treasurer of the UK-based Berlioz Society, and he continues to write regular concert reviews and other articles for the *Berlioz Society Bulletin*. He and his wife, Libby, have no regrets about naming their son Hector.

Lightning Source UK Ltd.
Milton Keynes UK
UKOW031433070312

188507UK00001B/5/P